SS
THE BLOOD-SOAKED SOIL

SS THE BLOOD-SOAKED SOIL
THE BATTLES OF THE WAFFEN-SS

Gordon Williamson

BROWN BOOKS

First published in Great Britain in 1995 by
Brown Books, 255-257 Liverpool Road,
London N1 1LX

Copyright © Brown Packaging Limited 1995

ISBN 1-897884-14-1

Printed and bound in Italy

PHOTOGRAPHIC CREDITS

Archive of Modern Conflict: 6/7, 10.
Leszek Erenfeicht: 11, 15, 16, 18, 21, 22, 28/9, 32, 35, 36/7, 42/3, 44, 46, 48, 50/1, 53, 55, 56, 58, 66, 69, 70, 72/3, 75, 80, 82/3, 84, 87, 91, 92, 96/7, 99, 100, 102, 103, 104/5, 107, 108, 111, 121, 123, 125, 126/7, 129, 132/3, 134, 137, 140, 148, 151, 152, 154, 157, 159, 166, 178, 180, 183, 187.
Hulton Deutsch Collection: 173, 181. 185.
Hubert J. Kuberki: 2/3, 138, 143, 144.
Private Collection: 76 (both), 77, 93, 145, 175.
TRH Pictures: 8/9, 25, 27, 33, 39, 61, 64, 88/9, 114, 115, 117, 118/9, 120. 122, 160, 162/3, 169, 170.

ARTWORK CREDITS
Colin Woodman: All maps

Previous pages: Waffen-SS infantry hitch a ride on a panzer during the invasion of Russia in 1941. Himmler's legions fought some of their most savage battles on the Eastern Front, a campaign the Waffen-SS conducted with particular ruthlessness.

CONTENTS

Birth to First Blood 1925-40

In almost every campaign in which the German armed forces fought during World War II, the armed SS made a significant contribution. The armed SS, officially titled the Waffen-SS from spring 1940, was one of the four main components making up the German Wehrmacht, or Armed Forces, with the Army (Heer), Air Force (Luftwaffe), and Navy (Kriegsmarine). Initially viewed with distrust, it later proved itself to be a fearsome fighting machine.

In their baptism of fire in Poland, the SS had a somewhat mixed reception from senior Army personnel, suspicious of what they considered 'political soldiers' fighting alongside 'real' troops. By the later stages of the war, however, the top fighting divisions of the Waffen-SS had gained such a reputation for dependability and steadfastness in the worst possible situations that they were sometimes the only troops who could be relied upon to fight on while those around them retreated. Waffen-SS units often formed the rearguard to protect the withdrawal of their Army colleagues.

Later in the war Waffen-SS units were known as the 'Führer's Fire Brigade', being rushed from crisis point to crisis point as the German armies struggled to hold back the overwhelming weight of numbers on the Allied side. Waffen-SS units found themselves not only hurried from one sector of a front to another, but often all the way across Europe as situations on other fronts worsened.

'I suppose it is inevitable that military men desire to see their creations in action, so we were not averse to having the SS troops enter the Polish conflict.' ('Sepp' Dietrich). SS in Poland.

The mere arrival of one of the premier Waffen-SS divisions was often enough to boost the morale of other troops in the area and help to stiffen resistance to the enemy. The Allies, too, would usually proceed with more caution knowing they were up against soldiers of the Waffen-SS.

That Waffen-SS formations often fought with almost unbelievable determination is not disputed, and is confirmed by the number of Waffen-SS soldiers who were among those awarded Germany's highest decorations for bravery. There was another side to the Waffen-SS, though: a total disregard for human life, partly stemming from their belief in themselves as elite troops who put a low value on their own lives, and also because they were the military standard bearers of National Socialism, an ideology that preached Germanic racial superiority. The result was atrocities both on and off the battlefield.

The Waffen-SS can trace its origins back to 1923, when a special guard element was formed within the Nazi Party with the specific task of protecting Adolf Hitler personally. Political gatherings during these stormy times, 10 years before Hitler came to power, would often degenerate into violence as the Nazis fought their political opponents and tried to break up their meetings. This guard element was selected from reliable men of the Sturmabteilung (SA) – Storm Troops – an existing Party body, and was known as the Stabswache or Staff Guard.

The Stosstrupp *Adolf Hitler* was comprised of Party members whose loyalty was foremost to Hitler

Infighting and intrigue within the Party was rife and the Stabswache was rather short lived, being replaced later that same year with a new section known as the Stosstrupp *Adolf Hitler*, or Adolf Hitler Shocktroop, comprised of Party members whose loyalty was first and foremost to Hitler himself. This new unit included such men as Josef 'Sepp' Dietrich and Rudolf Hess. The Stosstrupp *Adolf Hitler* served as Hitler's personal bodyguard until his arrest and imprisonment following the abortive Munich Beer Hall Putsch in November 1923.

Hitler had been impressed by the performance of his bodyguard during the Putsch, several of them having immediately placed themselves in front of Hitler to shield him when the shooting began. When he was released from Landsberg Prison he appointed his trusted chauffeur, Julius Schreck, to form a permanent bodyguard element of eight hand-picked men whose loyalty to their Führer was unquestionable. This 'praetorian guard' was to be known as the Schutzstaffel (SS) or Protection Squad, reportedly at the suggestion of Hermann Göring. From this small beginning, SS units began to be formed in every district, though to retain their élite status, only 10 men and one officer were permitted to join each unit.

Hitler came to trust his SS guards absolutely, while at the same time the SA was increasingly falling out of favour. The SA was becoming far too powerful for Hitler's liking (it numbered three million in 1933), and its loyalty was suspect. The SS was permitted to grow in both size and influence and, soon after Hitler came to power as chancellor in 1933, a new personal guard was formed, the SS having outgrown its original purpose. This new unit, the SS-Stabswache became, a few months later, the *Leibstandarte SS Adolf Hitler*, based at the Lichterfelde Barracks in Berlin. Soon, other fully armed company-strength SS units known as Politische Bereitschaften (Political Readiness) units were being formed, their purpose to support the National Socialist regime in times of unrest.

The SS, and in particular the *Leibstandarte*, proved its loyalty to Hitler when, in June 1934, it helped to assert Hitler's power over the SA, led up until then by

Above: Hitler and, to his left, Ernst Röhm at a Nazi rally in 1931. Röhm's SA brownshirts kept order at Party meetings and fought leftists on the street. However, they were unruly and not totally loyal to Hitler, whereas the SS was both loyal and disciplined.

Ernst Röhm, a move which was intended as much to appease the military establishment who were worried at the explosive expansion in size of the SA, as it was to put down any real danger of a putsch against Hitler. The SS carried out many of the murders undertaken on the so-called 'Night of the Long Knives', the emasculation of the SA, during which the SS executed around 1000 brownshirts and their leaders, including Röhm himself.

The SS was soon to be rewarded for its loyalty. In September 1934 the SS-Verfügungstruppe (SS-VT) was formed. This was to be composed of three regimental-sized formations, organised on military lines. The SS-VT was formally announced to the German Parliament in March 1935, at the same time that Adolf Hitler announced the re-introduction of conscription. The SS-VT was commanded by Heinrich Himmler in his position as Reichsführer-SS, but Hitler made it clear that it was to be at his personal disposal. In times of war it would be available to the Commander-in-Chief of the Armed Forces. In case of internal revolt, it would come under Hitler's direct orders via Heinrich Himmler as Reichsführer-SS.

The three regiments of the SS-VT were the *Leibstandarte*, SS-Standarte *Deutschland* based in Munich and SS-Standarte *Germania* based in Hamburg. In addition, support units in the form of a signals battalion, the SS-Nachrichtensturmbann, and an engineer unit, the SS-Pioniersturmbann, were formed, as well as two SS officer training schools: SS-Junkerschule Tölz and SS-Junkerschule Braunschweig.

There was no shortage of applicants for service in this new branch of the SS. The SS already had a very high profile in Germany. Each time the newsreel films showed the visit of some important dignitary to the Reich, for example, or

Right: SS recruits clean their weapons after a day at the ranges. The training at the various SS schools put the emphasis on physical fitness and aggressive battlefield tactics, allied to comradeship between all ranks and indoctrination that stressed SS superiority in all things and the faith of National Socialism. The result was highly trained and motivated soldiers who believed themselves to be better than anyone.

Hitler himself at some ceremonial function, there would inevitably be seen in the background, a phalanx of tall, strong SS troops in their black parade uniforms. No one could have failed to realise that these young men were the élite of the Third Reich, and it is no surprise that when recruitment for the SS-VT began the SS was overwhelmed with applicants. At the time of its formation, the SS-VT consisted of around 2600 men in the *Leibstandarte* with a further 5000 or so enrolled in the *Deutschland* and *Germania* Regiments.

Following the absorption of Austria into the Reich in the Anschluss in 1938, a new resource was available to the recruitment teams of the SS and a new SS-VT Regiment, entitled Der Führer, was established in Vienna.

It was always the intention that the soldiers of the SS-VT would be trained to the highest possible standards, and to that end, two highly regarded former Army officers were recruited. Both were ultimately to become among the finest of the field commanders of the Waffen-SS: Paul Hausser and Felix Steiner. Both were in full agreement that the fighting doctrine of the SS-VT would centre around aggression and mobility on the battlefield. Both had seen the carnage of World War I and abhorred the prospect of static trench warfare. They wanted the SS-VT to be trained like the Shock Troops introduced by the German Army in the later stages of World War I. The SS-VT was to be light infantry, the emphasis being on speed, aggression and adaptability. SS-VT units were intended to be fully motorised at a time when most infantry units of the German and other armies still relied on movement by foot and on horse-drawn transport. Hausser was appointed to command the training inspectorate of the SS-VT.

MOTIVATION OF SS RECRUITS

What motivated young German men to volunteer for service in the armed SS? Most of the recruits were very young, recruitment in the early days of the SS-VT being restricted to those between the ages of 17 and a half and 22. They had seen the National Socialist regime seemingly pick Germany up from the gutter and restore the pride and self respect of the German people. It is hardly surprising, then, that they supported the ideals of the regime, believed in their Führer and failed to see the darker side of Nazism.

What motivated these men most of all was the desire to serve their country in what was clearly perceived to be a very selective, élite formation. Military service had always enjoyed a high status in German society and it had always been deemed highly honourable and respectable to pursue a career in the military. How much greater then would the rewards be, for one who had carried out his military service in the nation's most select, élite formation? The young recruit would emerge not only having fulfilled his duty to his Fatherland but would enjoy the enhanced social standing which came with being a soldier of the SS.

Recruitment into the SS-VT was on the basis of a four-year service contract for other ranks, 12 years for NCOs and 25 years for officers. Selection criteria imposed were among the toughest in existence at that time. Applicants had to be tall, in perfect physical health, have no criminal record and be racially 'pure'. It is said that so many volunteers came forward that the SS was able to be so selec-

It was always the intention that the soldiers of the SS-VT would be trained to the highest standards

tive that in some cases even having a single tooth filling could be a sufficient imperfection for the candidate to be rejected. The *Leibstandarte* recruited only the tallest men, and attracted some real giants, many over two metres (6 feet 6 inches) tall. Those who were selected immediately felt themselves part of an élite merely for having passed the selection procedures. In one intake of over 500 potential recruits, only 28 were found to be of sufficiently high standard.

From the beginning the SS-VT had no intention of being constrained by outdated ideas on military training. Every SS man had first to serve as an SS-Anwärter (candidate), and all had to complete the same extremely rigorous and physically challenging training programme whether they had elected for a career as a common soldier or aspired to officer status. Those who were chosen as potential officers, (the SS preferred the term Führer or leader to Offizier, as was shown in the SS rank terminology), first had to serve two years in the ranks before proceeding to officer training school. Officers of vision and foresight were put in charge of the training of the future officers of the SS-VT and Waffen-SS. In particular this training emphasised the importance of comradeship and respect between all ranks.

WAFFEN-SS TRAINING

The recruits' day began around 0600 with a full hour of strenuous physical training. Then would follow concentrated classroom work where they would be taught all aspects of weapon handling, infantry tactics etc. The recruits would then be taken out into the field to put their theoretical teachings into practice in battle training of a degree of realism never seen before. The emphasis was always on speed, aggression and ferocity in the attack. The SS-VT were to be shock-troops, light infantry carrying only the minimum of kit to allow them greater flexibility of movement.

Considerable importance was placed on fitness training and sporting activities, with contact sports such as boxing being encouraged. Regular endurance marches were carried out to ensure that once trained, the SS-VT soldier was kept at a peak of physical fitness. Recruits were worked hard, even when not actually carrying out military duties, and for them, like the recruits in all armies of the world, there was the interminable round of barrack room fatigues, scrubbing floors, cleaning and polishing kit. Facilities, however, were of a very high standard, with first-class accommodation, good food and mess rooms and sports equipment of every conceivable type.

Much has been said about SS training standards, and they were indeed tough. Recruits carried out much of their combat training under live fire. The soldier was trained to keep his head down by the simple expedient of having machine guns on a fixed traverse firing at a level just a few centimetres above his heads. Those who kept calm and kept low were perfectly safe. Those whose nerve broke and who stood and ran were liable to be killed or injured.

It has also been reported that SS troops were trained in the art of digging foxholes fast, by allocating them a certain time to do so, then driving tanks across the training grounds at them. If the foxhole had not been dug properly, or not

Those whose nerve broke and who stood and ran were liable to be killed or wounded

dug deep enough, the chances of injury were great. This form of training was, of course, dangerous, and fatalities were not unknown, but troops trained under these methods learned fast and the lessons learned on the training grounds saved many lives when they went into combat for the first time.

There is an oft repeated, apocryphal story about SS recruits being trained to have nerves of steel by having to balance a hand grenade on the top of their helmets and stand stock still while it exploded. If they kept their nerve, the blast from the exploding grenade would be deflected away by the helmet, leaving the recruit with nothing worse than a ringing in his ears. If, however, he shook from fear and the grenade fell and landed beside him, the resultant explosion would certainly maim or kill him.

The author asked many former Waffen-SS soldiers if they had ever experienced this particular training 'lesson'. None had ever been asked to perform this trick, and none knew of any other soldier who had. It seemed as if the story was one of those legends which grow up where everyone has heard of such things but no one knows anyone who actually did it. However, one former Waffen-SS soldier, an SS-Standartenoberjunker who served in the *Westland* Regiment of the *Wiking* Division, did recall performing such a stunt, but only after having a few drinks, to show off to his younger comrades!

It has been suggested that, since a large percentage of SS recruits were from rural areas rather than from cities, they were more likely to feel at home when their unit was in the field. In addition, in the SS-VT academic standards were

Above: Horse-drawn SS artillery moves into Poland in early September 1939. Though the *Leibstandarte* was fully motorised by the time the war with Poland broke out, many SS units still relied on horses for transport. In fact, the German Army as a whole depended on horses for over 80 per cent of its motive power. The only army in the world that was fully motorised in 1939 was the British.

not held to be so important as they seemed to be in the other armed services. The SS-VT had realised that academic qualifications did not necessarily make a good infantry soldier or officer. That said, games such as chess were encouraged as they promoted logical thought and the making of tactical decisions.

The SS-VT was also one of the earliest exponents of camouflaged combat clothing. Virtually every form of dress – trousers, tunics, headgear, coveralls, helmet covers, even face veils – was produced in a camouflaged pattern. Organisation of SS units, too, often differed from their Army equivalent, with a greater proportion of automatic weapons found in the SS infantry section than its Army equivalent. The greater firepower this gave to SS-VT units no doubt contributed to some degree to their aggression in the attack.

Like all German citizens, the young recruits to the SS-VT were subject to a constant flow of indoctrination from the Propaganda Ministry of Dr Josef Göbbels. Not that the typical recruit needed much persuasion to support Hitler and the Nazi Party – most had joined because they agreed with the aims of the Nazis. The aftermath of World War I, the myth of the 'stab in the back' by socialists and Jews and the success of the Bolsheviks in the USSR had combined to intensify already existing nationalist sentiments and the anti-semitism that lay near the surface of many European nations. These feelings were codified by Nazi racial theories about Jews and Slavs, justified by Nazi political warnings from the East, and given a quasi-religious positive aspect by the concept of *lebensraum* and a new crusade against barbarism in the East.

IDEOLOGICAL INDOCTRINATION

Young SS recruits, disposed to sympathise with these ideas anyway, were encouraged to regard Jews and Slavs as *Untermensch* (sub-humans); and also taught that they should be sufficiently hard to show no pity towards these enemies of Germany – for showing pity would lead to defeat. Such beliefs were later to result in many atrocities, both on and off the battlefield.

One particular aspect of their training, which contributed in no small measure to the phenomenal esprit de corps engendered in SS-VT and Waffen-SS units, was the quite deliberately fostered spirit of comradeship between all ranks. Officers were expected to show their men respect. No SS officer was to ask his men to do anything that he would not willingly do himself, and during the war SS officer combat casualties were high, due principally to their tendency to 'lead from the front'.

In the months before the outbreak of war, these young men honed their military skills to a peak of perfection, impressing many previously sceptical Army commanders who were invited to inspect the SS troops. The Anschluss with Austria in March 1938 and the take-over of the Sudetenland district of Czechoslovakia in October gave the SS-VT the opportunity to put its training into practice in full-scale mobilisation exercises and perfect its organisational structures. When war broke out in September 1939, the SS-VT was as highly trained and motivated. All that was lacking was combat experience, something that the SS would find in abundance in the next five and a half years.

No SS officer was to ask his men to do anything that he would not willingly do himself

Both Hitler and Himmler were keen to allow the SS its baptism of fire in the Polish campaign, much to the discomfiture of the Army, which still regarded the SS with considerable suspicion and was by no means impressed with the military potential of Himmler's élite. Himmler and his SS-VT commanders had hoped that the SS-VT would be used as a single formation during the attack on Poland, but to Himmler's irritation, in an attempt to appease the Army somewhat, Hitler decided to split the SS force and allocate it piecemeal among Army units to which it would be subordinated.

Deutschland, the SS-Nachrichtensturmbann and the SS-Aufklärungsabteilung (Reconnaissance Detachment) were allocated to Panzer Division *Kempf* under the command of Major General Werner Kempf as part of I Corps in General Fedor von Bock's Army Group North. The *Leibstandarte*, and the SS-Pionier-sturmbann were allocated to Tenth Army under General Walther von Reichenau. *Germania* was retained in reserve in East Prussia as part of Fourteenth Army, and *Der Führer* took no part in the Polish campaign.

Mention should also be made of SS-Heimwehr *Danzig*, an SS home defence regiment located in the free city of Danzig, and affiliated to the SS-Totenkopf-verbände. Although the SS-Totenkopfverbände did not play any part in the Polish campaign, SS-Heimwehr *Danzig* was used to help secure the port of Danzig and its environs. It was later to be absorbed into the *Totenkopf* Division.

The German plan for the invasion of Poland, codenamed *Fall Weiss*, or 'Case White', involved two army groups comprising five armies totalling some one and a half million soldiers. The main push was to involve Third Army and Tenth Army, which together would form the arms of a massive pincer movement with

Left: SS-Standartenführer Felix Steiner, commander of the *Deutschland* motorised infantry regiment, surveys the front during the first few days of the Polish campaign. Steiner was one of the most gifted Waffen-SS commanders, and a major influence on training and tactics. Among his innovative ideas was that all men, irrespective of rank, should be trained to take over from their immediate superior if the latter was killed.

Above: *Leibstandarte* personnel engage Polish forces on the outskirts of Pabianice. The SS soldiers encountered fierce Polish opposition here, as one SS trooper noted: 'Through the trodden-down vegetation they stormed; across the bodies of their fallen comrades. They did not come forward with their heads bowed like men in heavy rain, but they came with their heads held high like as if they were swimmers breasting the waves.'

its target the Polish capital, Warsaw. Third Army would form the upper arm of the pincer, driving down from its launch point in East Prussia, while Tenth Army would drive eastwards, then turn north to approach Warsaw from the southwest of the city. Panzer Division *Kempf* was part of Third Army in the north and would launch its attack from Niedenburg in East Prussia, with its initial target the tough Polish defensive positions at Mlava to the northwest of Warsaw. The attack on Poland began at 0445 on 1 September 1939.

Deutschland, led by Felix Steiner, struck south towards Mlava and initially made good progress despite difficult conditions and fuel shortages that meant the SS-VT units could not make full use of their motorised capabilities. The Polish terrain through which the Germans marched was dusty and baked by a searingly hot sun by day and as often as not lashed by rain at night.

Deutschland's first important engagement was at the approaches to Mlava, where Polish resistance began to stiffen quite considerably. The Polish positions were strongly built and defended by determined troops. The momentum of the German advance began to falter, and so Kempf decided to prepare a formal attack with artillery and air support.

Deutschland, supported by tanks from 7 Panzer Regiment, was ordered to make a two-pronged thrust against the Polish hill defences after a heavy and prolonged softening-up barrage by German artillery. In the event, the artillery barrage was much less effective than had been hoped for, and the Polish bunker system was not severely damaged.

No sooner had the tanks began their attack than they began to run into well prepared anti-tank obstacles. The tank attack faltered almost immediately and the panzers began to take heavy casualties as Polish artillery zeroed in on them. The German tanks, mostly light Panzer I and Panzer II models, were not sufficiently powerful to smash through the Polish defences and the Polish artillery was able to wreak havoc among them. Some 39 tanks were either destroyed, damaged or broke down. Clearly the attack could not proceed, and so the remaining panzers were pulled back. To make matters worse, promised dive-bombing attacks by the Luftwaffe's Stukas failed to materialise.

The *Deutschland* infantry were now more or less alone and despite their determination to drive out the Poles, the attack could not succeed, though SS troops got to within around 100 metres of the enemy bunkers before being pulled back.

THE DRIVE TO WARSAW

On the next day word was received that German forces had broken the Polish defences at Chorzele and an entire Polish corps was in full retreat. Panzer Division *Kempf* was rushed eastwards to Chorzele to help exploit this success and pursue the fleeing Poles. In this new advance SS battle groups, commanded by Felix Steiner and Matthais Kleinheisterkamp, were supported by a battle group from 7 Panzer Regiment. The Poles were driven swiftly back all the way to the River Narew, where they formed new defence lines at the old Czarist Russian forts at Rozan. A network of four forts was located there and they were defended vigorously by the Poles. While the German attackers inflicted many casualties, their own losses were considerable and the weakened infantry battalions from *Deutschland* were simply not strong enough to winkle the remaining Poles out of their positions. Around 20 German tanks had been rendered unserviceable through mechanical breakdown and 11 had been lost to enemy gunfire. The appearance of Polish cavalry decided the matter and the Germans were forced to withdraw. The Polish success was short lived, however, as German forces had crossed the Narew farther to the south and the Poles were forced to evacuate Rozan to avoid encirclement.

Deutschland continued to pursue the retreating Poles towards the River Bug, capturing Czervin and Nadbory, but was once again temporarily put on the defensive by a strong Polish counterattack launched from Lomza to the north. These attacks were beaten off with the help of 7 Panzer Regiment.

By 10 September Panzer Division *Kempf* had crossed the River Bug. Here the division was ordered to drive south in an attempt to prevent Polish units withdrawing into Warsaw and thus strengthening the defences around the capital. Panzer Division *Kempf*'s route took it ever farther south, capturing Kaloszym, Siedlce and Zelechow before turning eastwards towards Najiejowice. Closely following the German columns came the SS death squads, tasked by Heydrich, head of the SS's security service (the SD), to search out and annihilate all 'undesirables' (Jews, communists and intelligentsia). Kleinheisterkamp and his battle

> **SS troops got to within 100 metres of the enemy bunkers before being pulled back**

group reached the Vistula on 16 September, closing the ring around Warsaw. The Polish capital was now completely encircled. It had been a successful but costly advance, the German forces being constantly harried by determined Polish units, desperate to prevent the fall of their capital city.

Deutschland then found itself moved to the northwest of Warsaw, where it took part in the attack on the Polish forts at Modlin and Zacrozym. Modlin was a powerful fortress containing around 35,000 troops who could be expected to put up a fanatical defence. Patrols sent in to reconnoitre the Polish positions suffered heavy losses. Several days of concentrated dive-bombing attacks by the Luftwaffe's Stukas, however, seriously weakened the defenders' positions. On 29 September SS troops began a final assault on the battered Polish defences. After a concentrated artillery barrage they stormed Zacrozym and captured the fort within 90 minutes. Several thousand Polish prisoners were taken. At 1450 on 29 September, General Zehak, commander of the Polish forces at Modlin, signed the capitulation order for the Polish forces in the fortress there. General Kempf, in recognition of the part played by the SS troops in the successes of his Division said: 'If the infantry is Queen of the Battle, then you from the *Deutschland* Regiment were Empress of the motorised infantry'.

In a secret report to Army High Command, Kempf was asked to comment on the performance of the SS troops under his command. In view of the rather antagonistic attitude of some senior Army officers to the armed SS, even after it had undergone its baptism of fire, Kempf's comments are illuminating. *Deutschland* was described as 'in all respects, a fully capable Infantry Regiment', and SS-

Right: Polish prisoners are escorted from the post office in Danzig after their valiant but hopeless attempts to hold the building during the German assault on the city. Their escorts are men of the SS-Heimwehr *Danzig*, a Totenkopf home defence force, which took the building by storm.

Standartenführer Steiner was said to have commanded it 'with great circumspec-tion'. The SS Artillery Regiment produced 'outstanding results' and displayed 'great combat spirit'. The SS Reconnaissance Detachment, led 'by its extraordi-narily fresh and adventurous commander', made 'exemplary achievements'. Every man in the battalion was said to be 'trained to an exceptional level'. The SS Signals Unit came in for special praise. Kempf reported that its achievements were 'at an exemplary level I have never before experienced'.

Meanwhile, SS Regiment *Germania* had been tasked with protecting the flank of XXII Army Corps in its drive towards Chelm, as part of Tenth Army attack-ing from Silesia. In the event, the regiment was fragmented, with sub-units being allocated to various Army units. The 2nd Battalion was attached to VIII Army Corps, the Armoured Reconnaissance Platoon was attached to the 5th Panzer Division, and 2 and 3 Companies were held in reserve.

GERMANIA'S CAMPAIGN

In fact, the elements of *Germania* guarding the flanks of XXII Army Corps were far too weak and thinly spread for the amount of area they were obliged to cover. Nevertheless, 15 Company, tasked with blocking the Przemysl-Lemberg road, surprised a Polish column of approximately battalion size. Despite being vastly outnumbered, the SS infantrymen took over 500 prisoners. On the evening of the same day, however, a powerful Polish unit comprised of cadets and officers from the Polish War Academy at Kraców who were attempting to fight their way through to Lemberg, ran into the small SS unit and inflicted heavy casual-ties on the Germans, who were forced to withdraw to the north to link up with 1 Company. Despite their perilous position, the SS troops were ordered to hold their positions and succeeded, preventing any Polish troops escaping from Przemysl, which was under attack from the 7th Infantry Division.

The 2nd Battalion of the Regiment, attached to the 8th Infantry Division of VIII Army Corps, advanced towards the line Brzoza-Stadnice-Linica. Its initial task was to capture the vital bridge over the River San at Kreszov. This meant a punishing march of around 80km (130 miles) over just two days to keep to the timetable of the attack. En route the battalion met up with elements of the 5th Panzer Division and, thus reinforced, pushed its way forward, reaching the west bank of the San opposite Kreszov on the afternoon of 12 September. Just as the Germans were preparing to cross, however, the bridge was blown.

During the night of 12/13 September, one platoon each from 3 Company and 5 Company crossed the river, only to find the Poles had withdrawn under cover of darkness. A third company, 6 Company, set off in pursuit of the fleeing Poles, sometimes coming so close that they were in danger of being hit by the Stuka dive-bombers harrying the retreat. By the time the 8th Infantry Division arrived, the eastern banks of the San had been secured.

In the central sector, the *Leibstandarte* was attached to the Tenth Army under General Walther von Reichenau, together with elements of the SS-Pionier-sturmbann. As a fully motorised regiment, the *Leibstandarte* was particularly suited to its task of protecting the exposed flanks of the Wehrmacht units that were

In the central sector, the *Leibstandarte* was attached to Tenth Army under General von Reichenau

racing ahead, in particular the 17th Infantry Division, as the latter drove towards the area west of the Polish capital.

The *Leibstandarte* next found itself transferred to support the 4th Panzer Division in an advance towards Lodz. At first it swept aside everything in its path but, the farther it moved into Poland, the stiffer the opposition became, and the regiment often became bogged down in vicious street fighting in built-up areas of the larger towns. In Pabianice in particular, the SS men found themselves surrounded by determined Polish units and it took the intervention of Army troops to relieve the beleaguered *Leibstandarte*.

As the pincer movement being executed by Fourth Army and Tenth Army began inexorably to close in on Warsaw, vast numbers of Polish troops were cut off to the west of the capital. The natural assumption of the Germans was that these Polish units would attempt to withdraw eastwards. In fact they struck south on 10 September, straight into the exposed flanks of Eighth Army, to which the *Leibstandarte* was now attached. For two days the Poles battered at Eighth Army's flanks, but then their attacks began to run out of steam and they had to turn east in an attempt to reach Warsaw. Finally the *Leibstandarte* was moved westward and took part in the encirclement of Polish forces on the River Bzura.

THE POLISH CAMPAIGN IN RETROSPECT

Recriminations between the Army and the SS-VT began almost immediately the campaign in Poland had been successfully concluded. Worse, the Army was disgusted with regard to SS atrocities, especially those committed by the Death's Head units. Jews and other so-called 'insurgents' had been systematically killed, and their property looted and destroyed, to the horror of Army commanders on the ground. As Himmler himself stated to officers of the *Leibstandarte* some months later: 'we had to drag away thousands, tens of thousands, hundreds of thousands – to shoot thousands of leading Poles.' More Poles had been rounded up and were on their way to concentration camps, where most would die.

It is clear from the opinions expressed by General Kempf that by no means all Army commanders were prejudiced against the SS. What was more important to the SS-VT was that both Himmler and Hitler were particularly well pleased by the performance of their élite troops. Himmler subsequently persuaded Hitler that the effectiveness of the SS would have been greatly improved if its units had been allowed to operate as a single SS division instead of being distributed among Army formations. Hitler agreed that in the forthcoming campaign in the West, the SS-VT regiments (with the exception of the *Leibstandarte*, which would remain an independent formation) and their support battalions – pioneers, signals, artillery and so on – would be grouped together as a single division, the *SS-Verfügungsdivision*. Hitler also authorised the formation of two new SS divisions, the *Totenkopf* Division and the *Polizei* Division.

The Army strenuously opposed the growth of the armed SS and Hitler was not yet willing to antagonise his military leadership to too great a degree. He accordingly ordered that, although the SS units were to operate as divisions, rather than being split up, they would still come under overall Army command

The SS-VT insisted that its troops had been given particularly difficult and dangerous tasks

in the field. The Army also objected to the expansion of the SS on the grounds that the personnel required for the armed SS were being taken from the Army's allocation of the manpower pool. To the Army, every recruit taken into the armed SS was one less real soldier. Himmler was forced to accept that he would have to find the manpower for his new divisions from his own sources. The Army would certainly not tolerate him 'poaching' their men. It should also be noted that, in the course of these reforms, the name Waffen-SS (armed SS) became officially recognised.

A word of explanation may be required here in relation to the *Totenkopf* Division. The Totenkopf units were not initially part of the SS-Verfügungstruppe. They had first been raised to provide guard elements at the concentration camps in which those perceived as being enemies of the state were kept. A Totenkopf unit was co-located with each camp, all under the overall charge of Theodor Eicke. A brutal man who was determined to wipe out all those he considered enemies of National Socialism, Eicke had great ambitions for his command. Initially his units were used as a dumping ground for men considered to be of

Above: SS soldiers checking the papers of civilians in eastern Poland. Even before the campaign in Poland had ended, the SS began to implement its racial policies. For example, the Totenkopf regiment *Brandenburg* arrested and shot 800 civilians at Bydgoszcz in an 'intelligentsia action'.

Right: A field kitchen of the *Polizei* Division in France, May 1940. Essentially composed of policemen, the divison performed poorly in France. In Paul Hausser's words the new division was 'unselected by our process and totally without military experience or training.'

> **Eicke's *Totenkopf* Division encountered great mistrust, both from the Army and the SS-VT**

low quality by the SS administration. Eicke was determined to turn this motley crew into a disciplined force and he was quick to weed out those who did not meet his standards. Gradually, the Totenkopf troops improved somewhat and Eicke was infuriated that his Totenkopfverbände was not considered the equal of the SS-VT.

Service in the SS-VT was counted as fulfilling a man's obligation for military service, but this was not the case for Totenkopf personnel. All Totenkopf men were still obliged to carry out their two years of military service, either with the SS-VT or with the other armed forces. Eicke feared that his best men would be poached from him during their national service.

In 1939 authority for the formation of the *Totenkopf* Division was given. Eicke selected the best of his personnel and these were initially reinforced by police reservists to bring the division up to strength. Despite now being formally constituted as a military formation, Eicke's *Totenkopf* Division still encountered great mistrust, not just from the regular military establishment but from much of the SS-VT too. The feelings appeared to be mutual and Eicke often expressed great contempt for his SS-VT counterparts. As many obstacles as possible seemed to be put in Eicke's way and he literally had to beg, steal or borrow transport and equipment for his division. By 1940 it was considered ready for action and was allowed to join the attack on France and the Low Countries, but, much to Eicke's disgust, his troops were to be held in reserve at first and did not take part in the initial assault.

The other new division available to the armed SS was the *Polizei* Division. This unit was formed from former members of the Ordnungspolizei (the ordinary German police force which had officially been part of the SS since 1936). They would not be regarded as true Waffen-SS soldiers until 1942, when they were finally permitted to wear the SS runes on their collar patches. Until then police rank insignia was worn, but with the SS version of the eagle and swastika national emblem on the left sleeve rather than the police version. The *Polizei* Division was not considered to have the same élite status as the *Leibstandarte* or the *Verfügungsdivision* and it was not allocated the same degree of motorisation, relying to a great extent on horse-drawn transport. Ultimately, however, it did become a fully fledged panzergrenadier division.

For *Fall Gelb*, or 'Case Yellow', the invasion of France and the Low Countries, the Germans had amassed a force of 139 divisions, three of which were SS, plus one SS regiment, the *Leibstandarte*. The force was divided between three Army Groups: Army Groups A, B and C.

One part of Army Group B was tasked to overrun and occupy Holland as a base from which to launch attacks on northern Belgium. The remainder of Army Group B, together with Army Group A, was to invade southern Belgium and Luxembourg and drive west to the coast before turning south into France. Army Group C was held in reserve opposite the Maginot Line defences and to take no active part in the opening moves of the campaign.

As far as the SS units were concerned, the *Leibstandarte* and *Der Führer* Regiment from the *Verfügungsdivision* were part of the first attack wave of Eighteenth Army in Army Group B, tasked with seizing road and rail bridges over the Dutch border. The remainder of the *Verfügungsdivision* was part of a second wave which was also to force crossings over the Dutch border but further to the south. Both the *Totenkopf* and *Polizei* Divisions were held in reserve.

OPENING MOVES IN THE WEST

At 0530 on 10 May 1940, the *Leibstandarte* stormed across the Dutch border and by midday had covered 100km (62 miles), capturing Zarolle and, more importantly, securing a crossing over the River Yssel. The Dutch had succeeded in blowing two major bridges, but an assault group under the command of SS-Obersturmführer Hugo Kraas succeeded in forcing a crossing, allowing the regiment to continue its rapid advance. The *Leibstandarte* then turned south, to link up with elements of the *Verfügungsdivision* on the drive towards Rotterdam. For his achievements, Kraas became the first Waffen-SS officer on the Western Front to be awarded the Iron Cross First Class.

Der Führer, meantime, had crossed the Yssel near Arnhem. In this sector the Dutch had been able to destroy all the suitable bridges but the 2nd Battalion forced a crossing, establishing a bridgehead on the west bank. SS pioneers soon erected temporary bridges, allowing the 3rd Battalion to stream across and storm into Arnhem, which fell to the Germans around midday. This was a disaster for the Dutch, who had counted on the natural defence line offered by the River Yssel helping them hold the Germans for at least three days. In the event, the Germans smashed their way through in just four hours. By the next day *Der Führer* had also burst through the next line of Dutch defences, the Grebbe Line.

SS pioneers erected temporary bridges, allowing the 3rd Battalion to stream across

Pleased with the performance of *Der Führer* Regiment, X Corps now gave it a lead role in the dash across Holland as the pell-mell advance continued. *Der Führer* finished its drive at Zandvoort on the coast. Here and there Dutch troops had put up a spirited defence but were soon swept aside by the unstoppable momentum of the SS attacks.

On 12 May, one of the great tragedies of the campaign occurred when the Luftwaffe bombed Rotterdam. Due to a communications breakdown, news that the Dutch were prepared to surrender the city failed to reach the Luftwaffe bombers in time, and Rotterdam was devastated. Later that day General Kurt Student of the Luftwaffe paratroop forces and Army General Dietrich von Choltitz were in the city negotiating the surrender. Considerable numbers of Dutch soldiers were standing around outside the building in which the negotiations were being conducted when the advance elements of the *Leibstandarte* thundered past. The SS soldiers raced into the square and opened fire without hesitation. In the confusion a stray German bullet seriously wounded General Kurt Student. The *Leibstandarte* pressed onwards, heading towards Delft where 4000 Dutch prisoners were taken, and reached the Hague just in time for the Dutch surrender on 14 May 1940.

THE DRIVE TO THE CHANNEL

The bulk of the *Verfügungsdivision*, meanwhile, had been advancing towards the area north of Antwerp, covering the south flank of the Eighteenth Army against potential attacks by Allied units striking north out of France. When these attacks failed to materialise, the division was permitted to move south into Belgium.

German paratroops had by then captured the vital Moerdijk Bridges just south of Rotterdam and the French had sent a relief force to drive them out. Part of the French force ran smack into the lead elements of 9th Panzer Division, to which the *Leibstandarte* was temporarily attached. A ferocious fight developed which resulted in the French being forced to withdraw.

Meanwhile the *Verfügungsdivision* had received fresh orders, this time to attack towards the coast and capture the heavily defended Walcheren and Beveland islands. Although the Dutch had surrendered on 14 May, Allied troops on the islands refused to yield and the islands had to be taken by storm. This was no easy task as they were supported by artillery fire from around Antwerp and also by Royal Navy ships off the coast.

On 16 May, the *Totenkopf* Division finally went into action with General Hoth's XV Panzer Corps as part of Army Group A. Eicke's division had to struggle its way to the front along roads jammed solid with military traffic and civilian refugees. When the division reached Cambrai its flanks were struck by Allied armour. On 21 May a force of around 130 British and French tanks slammed into the SS formation. The Allied tanks may have been slow, cumbersome, and poorly armed, but their armour was very thick, and the SS anti-tank troops were dismayed to find their 3.7cm anti-tank shells simply bounced off the enemy armour, except when fired at alarmingly close range. A number of *Totenkopf* soldiers fled before the attack was beaten off.

> **When the *Totenkopf* Division reached Cambrai its flanks were struck by Allied armour**

Left: *Totenkopf* Division soldiers under fire during their advance west in May 1940. Eicke's men fought well during the campaign (apart from panicking during an Allied armoured attack at Cambrai when their anti-tanks guns proved useless against the enemy's tanks), though they committed numerous atrocities along the way, such as the murder of British soldiers at Le Paradis This incident was subsequently decreed by Himmler to be a 'state secret'.

On 22 May, the 6th and 8th Panzer Divisions and the *Verfügungsdivision*, were ordered to strike towards Calais with all possible speed. In one action during this hectic advance, a 30-man reconnaissance troop surprised a French force of approximately battalion strength. The entire French unit, stunned at the appearance of the SS troops in their midst, immediately surrendered. The *Verfügungsdivision*, however, was also soon to run into trouble from Allied armour, coming under attack from heavily armoured French tanks. Like their *Totenkopf* counterparts, the troops of the *Verfügungsdivision* found their shells simply bouncing off unless the enemy were allowed to come perilously close.

THE BATTLES AROUND DUNKIRK

By 24 May the *Leibstandarte*, attached to the 1st Panzer Division, was in position by the Aa Canal – its launch point for the drive on Dunkirk. The Allies had by then been squeezed into a roughly triangular area between Terneuzen in the north, Valenciennes in the south and Gravelines in the southwest. Along the southern flank of the area ran a line of canals which formed natural defence lines. The *Leibstandarte* found itself opposite Watten, where the British defenders were located on high ground on the opposite bank, giving them a commanding view of the area, including the *Leibstandarte*'s positions. As the Germans were preparing their assault over the canal, news arrived of Hitler's famous 'halt order'. Dietrich, the *Leibstandarte*'s commander, was stunned. His men were now coming under heavy artillery fire, exposed as they were to the British observers. To the relief of his soldiers Dietrich took the extremely risky step of ignoring a Führerbefehl ('leader's command', which came from Hitler himself) and ordered

The *Leibstandarte* stormed over the canal, and in bitter fighting captured the heights

his troops to continue their planned attack. The *Leibstandarte* stormed over the canal and succeeded in capturing the heights. A furious Guderian arrived soon afterwards demanding to know why Dietrich had disobeyed a direct order from Hitler, but once Dietrich had explained, Guderian gave him his full backing.

A reconnaissance patrol from the *Verfügungsdivision* had in fact actually crossed the canal in a nearby sector before the halt order arrived. It had managed to penetrate behind the enemy defence lines for 8km (five miles) before being intercepted. It was clear that this part of the canal was not well defended and the division immediately threw an assault force across and began to form a bridgehead on the opposite bank.

While this was going on, the *Verfügungsdivision* was also ordered to drive the British forces out of the Forêt de Nieppe. British resistance was firm and the Germans seemed set for a long battle, but the surrender of the Belgians left the British with a dangerously exposed flank, forcing them to withdraw, though slowly and at great cost to the Germans.

THE BRITISH STEM THE GERMAN TIDE

On the night of 26/27 May the halt order was lifted. *Totenkopf* crossed the canal, this time at Bethune, and pushed towards Merville, meeting determined resistance from British troops and suffering significant losses. The *Deutschland* Regiment, meanwhile, was also pushing towards Merville along with the Army's 3rd Panzer Division. The SS troops reached the Lys Canal on 27 May, running into fresh British defence lines. SS-Oberführer Felix Steiner ordered an attack across the canal, and the 3rd Battalion surged across after a softening-up barrage by German artillery, and drove out the British defenders. By the afternoon of that same day, two full battalions of SS troops had crossed and set about forming a bridgehead. The success was to be short-lived, however. The area on both flanks was still securely held by the British and the *Totenkopf*, which was supporting, was still some way behind.

Steiner's troops were suddenly hit by a heavy British tank assault. In a post-battle report, Steiner related the tale of a young SS officer who, determined to set a good example to his men, steadfastly stood his ground against the enemy tanks, defending himself with hand grenades until he was crushed. Then one of his men leapt onto the British tank in an attempt to disable it with grenades but was shot and killed by gunfire from another tank. The remaining SS troopers refused to retreat and continued to resist the enemy tanks with little more than rifle fire. Things looked very black, but just in the nick of time an anti-tank company from the *Totenkopf* Division arrived on the scene and managed to drive off the British armour. Artillery fire, however, continued to fall on the German positions, preventing them from giving chase to the retreating British.

To the north, the *Leibstandarte* continued its drive on Dunkirk. On 28 May its commander, 'Sepp' Dietrich, and his adjutant, Max Wünsche, were on a forward recce near Esquebeck when their vehicle was suddenly peppered with gunfire. The two were forced to take cover in a drainage ditch and were pinned down. Leaking fuel was set on fire and the SS officers were in danger of being

> The remaining SS troopers refused to retreat and continued to resist the enemy tanks

burned alive. They crawled into a ditch and covered themselves with mud to help fend off the flames. On realising what had happened to the regimental commander, two companies were sent out to retrieve them but were beaten back. A further attempt by a tank platoon also failed. Eventually a force comprising tanks, armoured cars and a battalion of SS infantry had to work its way around the British and attack from the rear before Dietrich and Wünsche could be rescued (at this time a *Leibstandarte* company murdered British prisoners at Wormhoudt).

On 30 May, the *Leibstandarte* was withdrawn and went into reserve around Cambrai for a brief spell of rest and refitting. It was joined by the *Verfügungsdivision*, while the *Totenkopf* was allocated to coastal security duties south of the Dunkirk perimeter on 31 May.

With the British forces in the north eliminated by early June, all three German army groups now turned south. Army Group B advanced on a line from the coast to the River Aisne. Army Group A from the Aisne to the Franco–German border and Army Group C attacked through the Maginot Line. Around 140 German divisions were pitted against just 65 French formations. The SS units were ready for action again, having been made up to strength by replacements from Germany. On 5 June Army Group B, including Panzer Group *Kleist*, with the *Leibstandarte* and the *Verfügungsdivision* attached, began its drive towards Paris.

Below: *Totenkopf* armour and infantry on the attack in France. Despite the high casualties the division suffered and the criticism from some Army commanders as to its behaviour in the campaign, it had become a seasoned unit.

By 6 June the *Verfügungsdivision* had crossed the River Somme, meeting only minor opposition. As they drew nearer to Paris, however, French resistance stiffened considerably. As the division approached the River Aisne it came under concentrated French fire and, although *Der Führer* Regiment forced a crossing, it was becoming clear that the French would not give ground without a great struggle. So the SS troops were pulled back over the Somme and moved the line of their advance farther east, to meet less determined opposition. On 10 June Paris was declared an open city and the French moved their main defence lines from north of the capital to the south. On 12 June the *Leibstandarte* crossed the Meuse at Château-Thierry, and at this stage the *Totenkopf* was also released from the reserve to participate in the advance.

Panzer Group *Kleist* drove through the Champagne region towards Dijon to prevent any attempted escape of French units to the southwest. As a fully motorised formation the *Leibstandarte* was able to keep up with the spearhead of the advance, while the slower divisions followed behind, carrying out mopping up operations. The *Verfügungsdivision* took some 30,000 French prisoners for the loss of just 33 of its own men.

On 20 June the *Leibstandarte* took Clermont-Ferrand, capturing the airfield there, along with 242 aircraft, eight tanks, 280 French officers and over 4000 men. Only 24 hours later St Etienne and its garrison also surrendered. The *Verfügungsdivision* was still advancing, more slowly than the *Leibstandarte*, protecting the flanks from attacks by French units attempting to escape encirclement. The *Totenkopf* found itself in a furious battle with French colonial troops at Tarare, taking 6000 prisoners.

On 9/10 June, the *Polizei* Division crossed the Aisne River and the Ardennes Canal with Army Group A. The French counterattacked with armour and the fighting see-sawed back and forwards for some time, until the French were eventually overcome by the sheer pressure of the German advance. The *Polizei* Division then advanced through the Argonne region, before being withdrawn and sent into reserve once again on 20 June.

On 25 June, as the French capitulated, the *Verfügungsdivision* and the *Totenkopf* were allocated to coastal security duties near the Spanish border. The *Polizei* Division was allocated to the Army Group A reserve along the River Maas, and the *Leibstandarte* began a trek towards Paris to join in the great victory parade.

Hitler once again expressed delight at the performance of the Waffen-SS. However, there had been the usual crop of atrocities, such as *Totenkopf* soldiers

As a fully motorised formation the *Leibstandarte* was able to keep up with the advance

murdering French Moroccan prisoners it had taken during its advance to the English Channel, plus the murder of British prisoners mentioned above.

There could be no doubt that the Waffen-SS had won its spurs, and six Knights Crosses were awarded to SS personnel: Dietrich for his leadership of the *Leibstandarte*; Georg Keppler for his command of the *Verfügungsdivision*; Felix Steiner for his command of the *Deutschland* Regiment; Fritz Witt for leading the 1st Battalion of the *Deutschland* Regiment; SS-Obersturmführer Fritz Vogt, a platoon leader in the Reconnaissance Battalion of the *Verfügungsdivision*; and SS-Hauptscharführer Ludwig Kepplinger, 11 Company, *Der Führer* Regiment.

Above: Hitler and Himmler study a destroyed French Char B tank during a visit to the *Leibstandarte*. The French campaign had convinced Hitler that the Waffen-SS could perform well in battle.

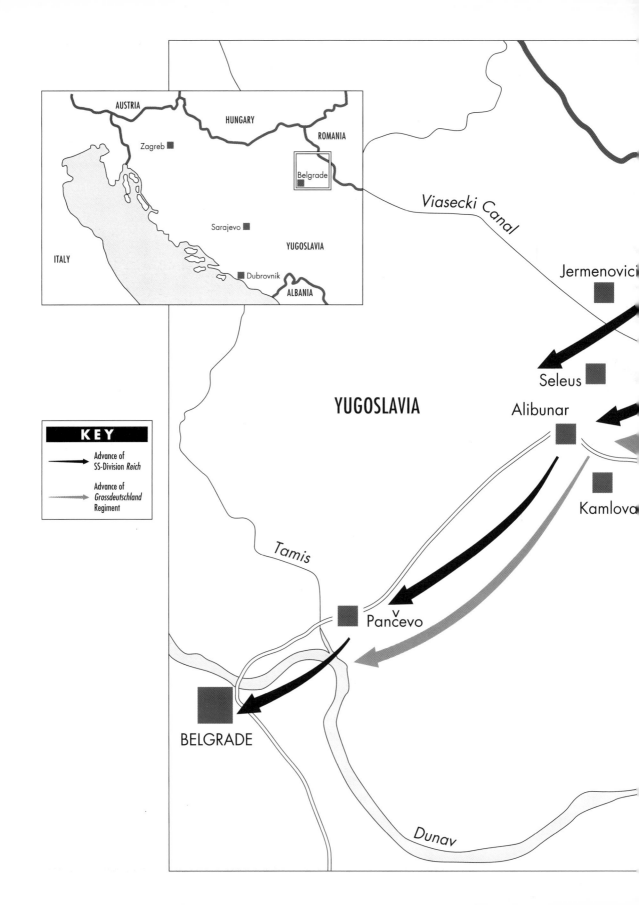

AUSTRIA

HUNGARY

ROMANIA

Zagreb

Belgrade

Sarajevo

ITALY

YUGOSLAVIA

Dubrovnik

ALBANIA

Viasecki Canal

Jermenovic

YUGOSLAVIA

Seleus

Alibunar

KEY

Advance of
SS-Division *Reich*

Advance of
Grossdeutschland
Regiment

Kamlova

Tamis

Pančevo

BELGRADE

Dunav

ROMANIA

Gaiu-
Mic

eliki
Gaj

Margita

Vrsac

Balkan Blitzkrieg

In October 1940, the Italians invaded Greece from Italian-occupied Albania. A month later, however, the Greeks had expelled the Italians from their soil, and by mid–January 1941 occupied a quarter of Albania itself. Hitler had initiated plans for a more effective invasion of Greece in November 1940, as part of his desire to dominate the Balkans. The Axis Tripartite Pact had secured the allegiance of Hungary, Romania and Slovakia in 1940, and Bulgaria and Yugoslavia in 1941. However, the Yugoslavs then overthrew the government that had signed it. Hitler therefore decided to crush both Greece and Yugoslavia militarily. Among the units sent south were two crack Waffen-SS divisions.

The German plan was codenamed Operation 'Marita' and called for 16 divisions to attack south into Greece from bases in southern Romania, drive out the British and Commonwealth troops and force the Greeks to surrender. In February 1941, the *Leibstandarte* Division was transferred from France to Romania in preparation.

A further setback for Hitler's plans occurred in March. After successfully persuading the Yugoslavs to sign a treaty with him, he was outraged when the Yugoslav military revolted and overthrew the government. The young Peter II was proclaimed King and a new anti-German government formed. Infuriated, Hitler ordered that 'Marita' be expanded to include an invasion of Yugoslavia.

Above: SS-Hauptsturmführer Fritz Klingenberg, the man who captured Belgrade single-handedly, recounts his story for German radio listeners. Klingenberg went on to fight with distinction on the Eastern Front, eventually rising to command the 17th SS Panzergrenadier Division *Götz von Berlichingen*. He was killed in action in April 1945.

On 28 March, the *Verfügungsdivision*, renamed SS-Division *Reich* and then *Das Reich*, was ordered to move with all speed from Versoul in France to Temesvar in southern Romania to take part in the invasion of Yugoslavia. Remarkably, the division took just one week to move its entire strength to its new location. During the move, however, there were several incidents of friction between Waffen-SS units and their Army counterparts. On one occasion elements of SS-Infantry Regiment 11 were moving slowly eastwards in a convoy mixed in with Army units. Convoy discipline was poor and an SS officer became enraged at the sight of Army vehicles casually overtaking his group. He halted one Army column, had mines placed under the wheels of the lead vehicle with an armed guard to make sure no one removed them, and warned the Army troops that no further movement would be allowed until the SS units had moved off. In a similar incident, another SS officer became infuriated by an Army column trying to pass his unit. He halted the Army vehicles and shouted that if they drove off again without his permission he would order his men to open fire.

On 6 April 1941 the German attack on Yugoslavia and Greece began. The *Das Reich* Division, part of XLI Panzer Corps under General Georg-Hans

Reinhardt, took part on the drive on the Yugoslav capital, Belgrade. Reinhardt had declared that the first unit to reach the initial objective, the main road leading from Alibunar to Zagreb, would be given movement priority to allow it pole position for the assault on the enemy capital. As the terrain over which *Das Reich* was due to advance was boggy marshland, it seemed that there would be little chance of the SS unit gaining this prize but the divisional commander, SS-Gruppenführer Paul Hausser, was determined that his men would be the first to reach Belgrade.

At 0900 on 11 April, *Das Reich* began its push for the Alibunar/Zagreb road. As expected the heavier vehicles soon began to bog down in the soft terrain, and progress was very slow. The Kradschutzen (Motorcycle Reconnaissance) Battalion, equipped with motorcycles for reconnaissance tasks, was able to drive its vehicles along railways tracks and keep up a swift, if bumpy, pace. In this way, elements of the division were indeed first to reach the road. When the rest of the division arrived, it was to find their initiative seemingly wasted. Corps had ordered that the retreating Yugoslavs were not to be pursued over the Danube and that all units were to halt on the banks of the river.

SS-Hauptsturmführer Fritz Klingenberg and his motorcycle recce troops from 2 Company of the Kradschutzen Battalion were the first to reach the river. Undaunted by the halt order, Klingenberg decided to explore the terrain on the opposite side. Using a captured small boat, he was able to ferry himself, 10 of his

Below: The *Das Reich* Division rolls into Belgrade, and the Waffen-SS notches up another notable victory. The fact that *Das Reich* had beaten its Army counterpart to the city did not improve already poor Army/Waffen-SS relations.

men and their motorcycles to the other bank. The tiny force then set off towards Belgrade. Entering the city, they made their way towards the War Ministry and were setting up machine-gun posts when an employee of the German Embassy approached and asked them to take the embassy staff under their protection.

Klingenberg was taken to the embassy nearby. An audacious plot forming in his mind, Klingenberg had the Military Attache summon the Mayor of Belgrade. Klingenberg introduced himself to the unfortunate official as the commander of a major German assault force waiting at the gates of the city. If the city was not immediately surrendered, a massive air strike would be called down. The monstrous bluff worked perfectly, and at 1845 hours Belgrade was formally surrendered to Klingenberg and his men. During the night, the advance guard of the 11th Panzer Division arrived only to find, to their chagrin, that a handful of Waffen-SS men had secured the surrender of the Yugoslav capital.

On 18 April Yugoslavia formally surrendered, and *Das Reich* was withdrawn, returning to Temesvar in Romania before being moved to Austria for training and some leave for the men of the division. On 14 May, a delighted Hitler decorated Klingenberg with the Knights Cross for his bold victory.

On the southern sector, General Wilhelm List's Twelfth Army, comprising eight infantry divisions, four panzer divisions, plus the élite *Grossdeutschland* Regiment from the Army and the *Leibstandarte* from the SS, was poised to strike into Greece at the opening of the attack on 6 April. The *Leibstandarte* and the 9th Panzer Division struck from Romania, via Bulgaria and through Yugoslavia, taking Skopje in the course of their advance, and in three days were at Monastir on the Greek border, having suffered only five casualties, with none killed.

TAKING THE KLIDI AND KLISSURA PASSES

The way to Greece lay via the Klidi Pass, which was defended by Commonwealth troops. On 10 April the *Leibstandarte* Division opened the assault. The roads which led through the pass had been heavily mined, which precluded a simple armoured attack. The 1st Battalion of the *Leibstandarte* under SS-Obersturmführer Gerd Pleiss was to be used, in effect, as a mountain battalion, scaling the rocky sides of the pass with fire support from the regiment's 8.8cm guns. As the SS infantry worked their way up through the rocks, under cover of heavy fire from the 88s, assault guns were brought in along the road, following behind an engineer group working frantically under enemy fire to clear the road of mines. The defenders were overwhelmed by the momentum of the German attack, and the pass quickly fell, along with 100 Allied prisoners.

By early the following morning, the far end of the pass had been reached. British tanks counterattacked in an attempt to force the Germans back into the pass and contain their advance. Once again, the 8.8cm guns of SS-Obersturmführer Dr Naumann were brought into play and quickly took their toll of the British tanks, which were forced to withdraw.

The *Leibstandarte*'s next objective was Koritza, the headquarters of III Greek Corps. Before this target could be reached, however, there lay ahead a much tougher nut to crack, the heavily defended Klissura Pass, its peaks rising up to

> # The monstrous bluff worked perfectly, and at 1845 hours Belgrade was formally surrendered

Left: Waffen-SS infantry in the mountains of Greece, April 1941. The *Leibstandarte* fought well during the campaign, its men often having to seize enemy mountain strongholds, such as at the Klidi and Klissura Passes, in the face of determined resistance.

The 1st Battalion of the *Leibstandarte* under Gerd Pleiss was to be used

---

1400 metres (4600 feet) on each side of the road. The Greek defenders were well established and supported by their own mountain artillery. The *Leibstandarte*'s route to the pass lay over roads, which were often blocked and stoutly defended by elements of the Greek 21st Infantry Division. Although the Greeks were no match for the Waffen-SS troops and were inevitably overrun, these constant minor clashes delayed progress considerably.

Above: 'Sepp' Dietrich (standing on his staff car) during the *Leibstandarte*'s lightning advance along roads that were often blocked with refugees and Greek prisoners (as here). Dietrich's men forced the surrender of the Greek armies by blocking their line of retreat, and almost caught Commonwealth forces at Corinth.

By the evening of 11 April, as daylight faded, the *Leibstandarte*'s leading elements were approaching the foothills of the pass. The initial advance was rapid and the first ridges were in German hands within 30 minutes. The German vehicles followed the twisting road high into the mountain, meeting no serious obstacles until they were forced to stop at a shallow ravine, because the bridge over it had been blown. As the German column drew to a halt, it came under fierce attack from machine-gun fire and grenades thrown by the Greek defenders in the rocks above. Next mortar shells began to land. The Germans were unable either to advance or retreat. Their vehicles could not turn on the narrow mountain roads.

The onset of night gave the Germans a degree of respite. SS engineers blasted rocks out of the mountain into the ravine and on top of the remains of the bridge. Building on this foundation, the ravine was gradually filled with boulders passed by hand along a human chain. Though not ideal, a narrow section of the ravine was in-filled to a degree that would allow some vehicles to pass.

The German plan was for two groups of SS infantrymen to scale the walls of the pass under cover of the remaining darkness, infiltrate behind the Greek defenders and be ready to attack them at first light. Meanwhile, SS-Sturmbannführer Kurt Meyer would lead a third group, of around 30 men accompanied by a handful of armoured cars, some anti-tank (including 8.8cm) guns in a further advance along the road.

As Meyer approached the crest of the pass he halted his small force and deployed his artillery. With a sheer wall of rock on one side and a sheer drop on the other, the guns were unable to use their trails to anchor them for firing in the normal way. Each time a shell was fired there was a risk that the gun would roll over the edge of the road and plunge down the mountainside. However, they went into action and the artillery fire was the signal for the infantry, who had infiltrated towards the rocky summit to attack.

The Greeks had been tasked with holding the pass to protect the retreat of III Greek Corps from the Albanian front, where it had been fighting the Italians. It was essential that they escaped to join with other Greek, British and Commonwealth troops in the defence of the southern part of the country. The defenders of the Klissura Pass were therefore determined not to be driven from their positions – the Waffen-SS had other ideas.

As Meyer's group continued along the road, a shell landed right in front of him, opening up a huge crater. Machine-gun fire ricocheted off the rocks as Meyer and his men took cover. Meyer yelled at his men to press onwards but, with bullets zipping through the air all around them, they looked at Meyer as if he was crazy. He knew he had to break the stalemate and calmly lifted a grenade. Shouting to his men to ensure they were all watching, he pulled the pin and rolled the grenade behind the rearmost man. The spell was broken and the SS infantrymen dashed forward away from the grenade and into fresh cover, grinning despite themselves at the crazy antics of their commander.

Meyer and his men stormed forward towards the summit, where the concentrated fire of the 88s, machine guns and grenades of the SS troops had finally crushed the last of the fighting spirit of the Greeks, who now began to emerge from their positions with their hands held high. The Klissura Pass was in German hands. Over 1000 prisoners were taken, including one regimental and three battalion commanders.

The Germans had no time to celebrate, however. The *Leibstandarte* forthwith began its descent into the plain and, by that afternoon, had began reconnoitring the approaches to Kastoria, only to be rebuffed by concentrated Greek artillery

> **Over 1000 prisoners were taken, including one regimental and three battalion commanders**

fire. Clearly these positions would not be taken easily by infantry alone. The *Leibstandarte*'s regimental artillery was therefore brought up, along with the 3rd Battalion. A squadron of Stuka dive-bombers was called up in support and an artillery and dive-bomber barrage was launched on the unfortunate Greeks. Before they could recover from this, the SS infantry had stormed into their positions and the Greeks were overcome.

The armoured cars of Meyer's Reconnaissance Detachment now went racing in towards the city of Kastoria and on the way met large columns of retreating Greek troops, who were so startled by the appearance of the SS troops that they quickly surrendered. Those who did not were swiftly put out of action. By late afternoon Kastoria was in German hands. Over 12,000 Greek prisoners were taken. For his storming of the Klissura Pass and subsequent capture of Kastoria, Meyer was decorated with the Knights Cross of the Iron Cross.

MOPPING-UP OPERATIONS

On 19 April, the *Leibstandarte* was ordered to drive southwest towards Joannina and captured the Metsovon Pass, cutting off some 16 Greek divisions to the west of the Pindus range. They all surrendered on 21 April. The surrender was accepted by the *Leibstandarte*'s commander, SS-Gruppenführer 'Sepp' Dietrich, a coup which infuriated Mussolini. Despite the poor performance of the Italian troops in the Greek campaign, Mussolini insisted on his share of the glory. The surrender of the Greeks to Dietrich was turned into a mere preliminary, and further formal surrender ceremonies were organised, in which the Italians were fully to participate.

On 24 April, the *Leibstandarte* began its pursuit of the retreating British and Commonwealth forces, first south towards Mesolongion then eastwards towards Navpaktos on the Gulf of Corinth. The Germans arrived just too late, the British having managed to evacuate their men over the gulf to Patras.

Meyer and his reconnaissance unit were out of radio contact with the regiment. Unable to obtain fresh orders, Meyer decided to sent a patrol across the gulf, using two small commandeered fishing boats. After a nail biting 90-minute wait, the two boats reappeared, bringing with them 40 British prisoners! Meyer immediately began to ferry the rest of his battalion across into Patras using every fishing boat that could be found.

On the following morning Meyer despatched 2 Company of his battalion with orders to strike east and make contact with the units of Paratroop Regiment 2, who were fighting the British at Corinth. No heavy vehicles were up with the advance so the SS troops were forced to commandeer whatever was available. This led to the unusual sight of an anti-tank gun being towed by a civilian saloon car, mortars protruding from a fast sports car, and the engineer platoon setting off in a bus!

After establishing contact with the paratroops, the SS men returned to Patras to begin their march south towards Olympia in pursuit of the fleeing British. All along the road were British vehicles abandoned through lack of fuel, which were gladly appropriated by the SS. The *Leibstandarte* reached as far south as Olympia

For his storming of the Klissura Pass and capture of Kastoria, Meyer was awarded the Knights Cross

before its advance was halted because the collapse of the Greek Army and the evacuation of the British and Commonwealth forces rendered it unnecessary. The regiment then moved to Athens, where it took part in the victory parade in front of Field Marshal List, before returning to barracks for rest and refit.

The high profile part played by the *Leibstandarte* and *Das Reich* Divisions in the whirlwind Balkan campaign served only to enhance the standing of these élite troops in the eyes of their Führer. Meanwhile, Hitler's willingness to expand the Waffen-SS had led to the creation of two new Waffen-SS Divisions: *Wiking* and *Nord* (in fact *Nord* was at this stage only equivalent to a battle group in strength, full divisional status not being reached until September 1941).

Pressure from the Army against further expansion of the Waffen-SS continued unabated, however, and Hitler was still unwilling completely to disregard the wishes of his Wehrmacht commanders. The Army's antagonism to the Waffen-SS was still based on the potential drain it represented on the national manpower pool. Hitler was, however, persuaded by Himmler to permit the recruitment of foreign nationals and ethnic Germans from the conquered territories into the Waffen-SS, as the Army had no prior claim to these men. Providing the potential recruit was of good 'Germanic' bloodstock, Hitler was agreeable. In fact, ethnic Germans from outside the Reich had been trickling into the SS for some time. Just as well, because the Waffen-SS's biggest challenge was about to begin: the invasion of the Soviet Union.

> **Hitler was persuaded to permit the recruitment of foreign nationals into the Waffen-SS**

Left: Two *Leibstandarte* soldiers photographed during the Greek campaign. Despite the German victory in the Balkans, the venture had delayed the all-important invasion of the Soviet Union, which, in Himmler's eyes, was what the Waffen-SS had been preparing for. To the Reichsführer-SS, the campaigns in Yugoslavia and Greece had been unnecessary diversions. The real test of strength would be in Russia, against what he described as the 'eternal enemy of Germany'.

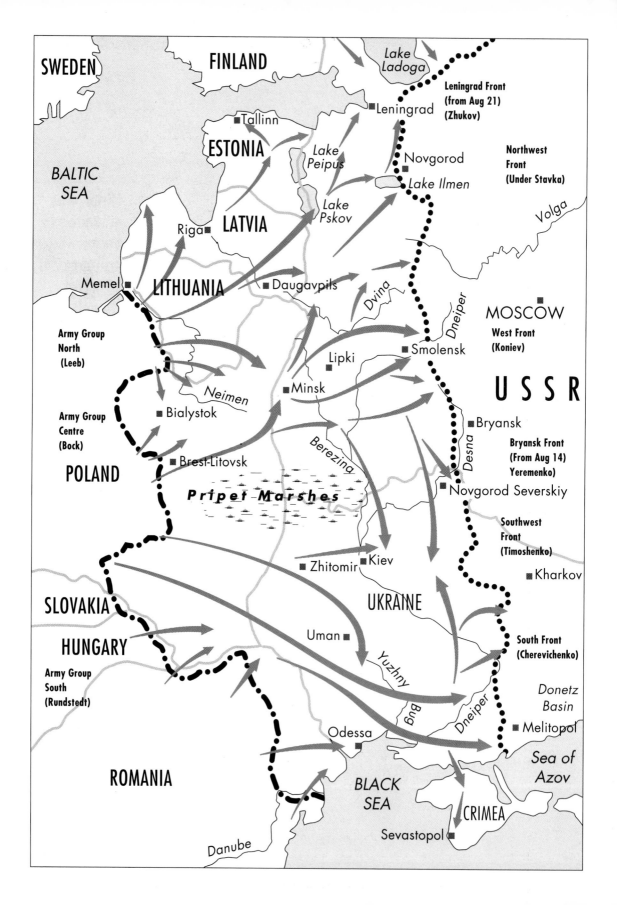

Operation 'Barbarossa'

For the Nazi Party, and the Waffen-SS, the campaign in Russia was to be a crusade, a crusade against those groups Nazism despised: the Slavs, the Bolsheviks and the Jews. Above all, it was to be a clash of ideologies: National Socialism versus Communism, and the *Herrenvolk* (master race) versus the *Untermensch* (sub-humans). For the Waffen-SS, the military and ideological elite of the Third Reich, the war in Russia would bring spectacular victories, but it would also bring a new kind of war, one in which both sides gave and received no quarter.

In all 11 German armies, four of them panzer, and three air fleets, totalling around three million soldiers, were ranged against the Soviet Red Army, which was still reeling from the loss of some of its best soldiers in the Stalinist purges of the late 1930s. Many experienced Russian officers had been executed, such as three of the five marshals and 13 of the 15 army commanders.

The *Leibstandarte,* along with the *Wiking* Division, was allocated to Army Group South, commanded by Field Marshal Gerd von Rundstedt, *Das Reich* was part of Army Group Centre under Field Marshal Fedor von Bock, and *Nord* was committed to the far northern sector of the front as part of the Norway Mountain Corps. The *Polizei* and *Totenkopf* Divisions were part of Army Group North's reserves.

Army Group South's initial task was to drive east and cut off all the Soviet armies west of the Dnieper with a force of some 46 divisions, comprising Sixth

Right: During the final days before the opening of Operation 'Barbarossa', the invasion of Russia, Field Marshal von Rundstedt, commander of Army Group South, visited the *Leibstandarte* Division to examine its combat readiness. The picture shows, from left to right, Rundstedt, SS-Sturmbannführer Kurt Meyer, 'Sepp' Dietrich, commander of the *Leibstandarte,* and SS-Standartenführer Fritz Witt.

Army, Eleventh Army, Seventeenth Army and First Panzer Group. The *Leibstandarte* was allocated to XIV Corps of First Panzer Group. The task of First Panzer Group was to break through the Russian lines south of Kowel, and cut off and contain Red Army units to the southwest until they were destroyed by the infantry. This was to require a rapid advance of over 480km (300 miles) across difficult terrain. Few Russian roads were properly surfaced, and their solid packed dirt could be turned into deep quagmires once rain started to fall.

Opposing Army Group South were approximately 69 infantry, 11 cavalry and 28 armoured divisions of the Red Army, under the command of General Kirponos and later Marshal Budyenni. The Russians based their defences along the lines of the Rivers Pruth, San, Bug and Dnieper, making full use of the natural obstacles.

Operation 'Barbarossa' commenced on 22 June 1941, but the *Leibstandarte* was not in fact committed to battle until 27 June, when it left its assembly area and joined the reserve of the First Panzer Group. It finally went into combat on

1 July when it crossed the River Vistula southwest of the town of Zamosc. By this time, the two arms of First Panzer Group's pincer movement were well extended into Soviet territory and III Panzer Corps, under General von Mackensen, had been cut off near Rovno. The *Leibstandarte*'s first major task of the eastern campaign was to re-establish contact with von Mackensen's Corps.

German forward elements were soon in action against Soviet tanks. At one stage while passing through a heavily wooded area, two Soviet tanks joined a German column, assuming them to be a retreating Soviet unit. Night had fallen when the column came to a brief halt just short of Klevan and the Soviet tank crews realised their error and burst out of the column, tearing off into the dark.

Klevan was swiftly taken and the advance continued. A foretaste of things to come occurred when the lead elements of the *Leibstandarte*'s Reconnaissance Battalion reached a spot just a few kilometres to the east of Klevan. An abandoned German howitzer was discovered alongside an empty, blood-soaked ambulance. A few hundred metres away the corpses of several German soldiers were discovered, their hands bound with barbed wire and their bodies mutilated. The Waffen-SS replied in kind, declaring the Russians 'must be slaughtered ruthlessly'.

The armoured units attached to III Panzer Corps were making such rapid progress that great gaps opened up between the widely dispersed German formations. The Soviets, attacking out of the Pripet Marshes to the north, spotted these gaps and attempted to exploit them. The Soviet intention was to slice through the main German supply highway, the so-called Rollbahn Nord, and cut off the advancing German units from their supplies of food, fuel and ammunition. The *Leibstandarte*'s task was to give flanking cover to the First Panzer Group as it struck towards Zhitomir and Kiev, and the Waffen-SS troops soon found themselves fending off desperate attacks by Soviet forces, often with armoured support.

On 7 July, *Leibstandarte* spearhead units smashed through the Stalin Line defences at Mirupol and drove eastwards toward Zhitomir, encountering stiff Soviet resistance. Heavy rains rendered many roads useless and the Germans were often forced to strike out across country but, by the evening of that day, the bulk of the *Leibstandarte* had caught up with its spearhead elements at Romanovka. One particular incident during this phase illustrates just how far ahead of their parent units the reconnaissance elements could stray.

The incident involved Kurt Meyer and his reconnaissance battalion. Meyer and a small group of his recce troops had outstripped the main body of his battalion and Meyer discovered that he and his men had inadvertently passed through

> **An abandoned howitzer was discovered alongside an empty, blood-soaked ambulance**

Right: During the opening phase of 'Barbarossa', many Russians welcomed the German invaders as liberators. That soon changed when the notorious Einsatz-gruppen followed in the wake of the advancing German armies and began the systematic rounding up and murder of what Nazi ideolo-gists defined as their racial and ideological enemies. In this work they were often assisted by units of the Waffen-SS.

Meyer started walking among the Soviet soldiers, indicating they should lay down their weapons

a gap between two Soviet units. The Germans quickly found themselves surrounded by Soviet infantry. An officer stepped forward and Meyer saluted. The salute was returned and the two men shook hands, Meyer offering the Russian a cigarette, which was gratefully accepted. It became apparent that the Soviets had thought the Germans wished to surrender. Meyer retorted, through his interpreter, that it was the Soviets who should surrender, then started walking among the Soviet soldiers passing out cigarettes and indicating they should lay down their weapons.

Meyer could see that the Soviet officer was far from taken in and quietly told his interpreter to play for time. Meyer expected the arrival of other elements of the battalion any minute. The Soviet officer was becoming irritated as the two argued about exactly who should surrender to who. It looked as if Meyer's bluff had failed when a German armoured car came into sight, only to be hit by a Soviet anti-tank shell. The next armoured car returned the fire and Meyer yelled to his own men to open up. A furious firefight developed. The arrival of German armour shifted the balance in their favour and the Soviets were overcome.

On 8 July, the *Leibstandarte* captured the vital Keednov road junction just west of Zhitomir, in a battle fought principally by Meyer's battalion in which the recce troops stormed across the River Teterev supported by 8.8cm artillery fire.

The Soviets were, on some occasions at least, proving to be much tougher opponents than the Germans had anticipated, and were adept at exploiting the gaps which were constantly forming in the German lines between the fast-moving armoured units in the spearheads and the slower-moving infantry divisions following behind.

Hitler's staff, the High Command of the German armed forces (OKW), however, now felt that the primary objective of Army Group South had been all but achieved and the bulk of the Soviet armies in the southwest destroyed. This was an optimism not shared by the troops at the front, and correctly so, as it turned out when a Soviet counteroffensive began. Once again, the Soviet attack was aimed at cutting the main supply route. Though the Soviet attacks were beaten off, it was by no means an easy task. Hand-to-hand fighting with bayonet, knife and entrenching spade was common. The wooded areas through which much of the fighting raged brought its own nightmares as shell bursts in the trees, showering everyone with lethal splinters of wood. Casualties were heavy on both sides. The battle lines were so fluid that the combatants rarely knew exactly who had the upper hand or who was outmanoeuvring who. However, the *Leibstandarte* did manage successfully to exploit a temporary easing off of enemy pressure to go over to the attack and capture Shepkova on 9 July.

THE UMAN POCKET

On 10 July Hitler unexpectedly altered the whole thrust of the attack in the south, from an advance in the direction of Kiev, to a drive towards Uman, in an attempt to cut off and surround the Soviet armies there. Weeks of savage fighting ensued in this sector. On 31 July, the *Leibstandarte* was allocated to XXXVIII Corps and tasked with a drive on Novo Archangelsk to close this Uman Pocket. The whole weight of the Soviet attempts to break out of the German encirclement were falling in this area. Some of these Soviet attacks involved massed infantry formations with concentrated armour support and were barely beaten back. The SS soldiers made good use of their fearsome multi-barrelled rocket launcher, the Nebelwerfer. These weapons made a low groaning howl as they fired, which would later earn them the nickname 'Moaning Minnies' from British and American troops (the Soviets had a similar weapon system known as the Katyusha, or to the Germans as the 'Stalin Organ').

Ultimately the Soviet breakthrough attempts weakened as the SS lines held firm. When the Soviet forces in the Uman Pocket surrendered, over 100,000 men from the Soviet 6th and 12th Armies went into captivity. The part played

> **The wooded areas through which much of the fighting raged brought its own nightmares**

Right: A *Leibstandarte* motorcycle patrol moves through a destroyed Russian town during the division's advance east. The first few weeks of 'Barbarossa' brought spectacular victories in the face of desperate Russian resistance, yet the Red Army kept on fighting.

Wiking moved off from its launch point on 29 June 1941 and advanced through Soviet-occupied Poland

by the *Leibstandarte* in the Uman Pocket came in for special praise from General Kempf: 'The *Leibstandarte* has played a most glorious part in the encirclement of enemy forces around Uman. Committed at the height of the battle for the seizure of the enemy positions at Archangel, it took the city and the high ground to the south with incomparable dash. In a spirit of devoted brotherhood of arms, the *Leibstandarte* intervened on its own initiative, in the desperate situation which had developed for 16th Infantry Division on their left flank, routing the enemy and destroying many tanks. Today, with the battle of annihilation around Uman concluded, I wish to recognise, and express my special gratitude to the *Leibstandarte* for their exemplary efforts and incomparable bravery.'

On the northern wing of Army Group South, *Wiking* moved off from its launch point on 29 June 1941 and advanced through Soviet-occupied Poland, led by the *Westland* Regiment. Spearhead units reached Lemberg on 30 June and ran into the Soviet 32nd Infantry Division. The Waffen-SS elements were put under considerable pressure by the numerically superior Soviet forces and had to withstand repeated attempts to push them back. The arrival of armour from the division's reconnaissance battalion finally swung the balance in the German favour and the Soviet counterattacks were beaten back. Unfortunately for the *Westland* Regiment, its commander, SS-Standartenführer Hilmar Wackerle, was killed during this action. He was fatally wounded by a single shot fired by a lone Soviet straggler as his command car drove past.

THE *WIKING* DIVISION

Lead elements from *Wiking* were soon in the thick of the fighting again when the Waffen-SS troops forced a crossing of the Slucz at Husyantin, part of the Stalin Line defences, and ran straight into particularly strong Soviet forces, who immediately counterattacked. The fighting raged back and forward for some time and things began to look bleak for the Germans, until the Army's 1st Mountain Division arrived on the scene and relieved the beleaguered force.

On 8 July *Wiking* drove towards Kozmin. A torrential downpour turned the roads into morasses and the division was only able to make slow progress, and that with some difficulty. At Toratscha the divisional HQ was almost overrun, and the *Germania* and *Nordland* Regiments became involved in bitter fighting. The *Westland* Regiment continued its push eastwards on a four-day forced march on foot through heavily wooded terrain to the River Ross. By 23 July, the *Wiking* Division was making its way through masses of abandoned Soviet vehicles and materiel. At this point the division was temporarily placed under the control of III Panzer Corps, while the *Westland* Regiment was diverted south to Talnoze to aid in the closing of the Uman Pocket.

From 7-16 August, elements from *Wiking* served alongside the Luftwaffe's élite *Hermann Göring* Regiment, fighting around Korsun and Schandorovka to secure the northern flank of the First Panzer Group. A battle group from *Westland* was also despatched to Dnepropetrovsk to help contain Soviet attacks.

After the fall of Uman, First Panzer Group renewed its advance, moving in the direction of Bobry. The Soviet defence, consisting in the main of cavalry units, was soon overrun and the town fell on 9 August. The *Leibstandarte* moved on to Zaselye. No sooner had it fallen to the Germans than the Soviets mounted a furious counterattack. For a whole week the *Leibstandarte* held on grimly to its positions while the Russians tried with equal determination to eject them. On 17 August the Soviet attacks finally ceased. Total enemy losses in killed, wounded and taken prisoner were almost 1000 men.

The *Leibstandarte*'s next objective was Cherson, a large city in an industrial area. Here, for the first time in Russia, the Waffen-SS infantry would be forced to take a sizeable city by storm. Cherson was defended by Soviet Naval Infantry who contested every street. Bitter house-to-house fighting ensued with heavy losses on both sides. The Germans were by now becoming accustomed to the degree of fanaticism with which some of the Soviet units defended their

After the fall of Uman, First Panzer Group renewed its advance, moving in the direction of Bobry

Right: Taganrog, a city some 300km inside Soviet territory, falls to the *Leibstandarte* Division, 17 October 1941. The advance continued, though by this time illnesses – dysentery, bronchitis and other lung disorders – and stiff Russian resistance were taking their toll on the division.

homeland. Hand-to-hand combat with Soviet troops equally as determined and fearless as themselves was to cost the Germans dear. After three days of fierce engagements, the city fell to the *Leibstandarte* on 20 August. The division was rewarded with a few precious days of rest and reorganisation in corps reserve, before crossing the Dnieper and striking out across the barren steppe once again.

Meanwhile, to the north, German units had established a small bridgehead over the Dnieper at Dnepropetrovsk, but were coming under heavy Soviet artillery fire. There had been a Soviet artillery school in the area and the entire district had been expertly plotted by the artillery cadets, so the Soviets had little trouble in pinpointing German targets. Crossing the river at the bridgehead, *Nordland* struck north towards Mogila Ostraya while *Westland* and *Germania* strengthened the forces on the western edge of the bridgehead and captured the heights at Kamenka on 6/7 September, taking over 5000 Soviet prisoners.

A surprise Soviet counterattack then developed which once again sought to exploit the gaps between the German units. This saw Soviet forces penetrate German-held territory to a depth of 32km (20 miles). The *Leibstandarte* was hastily brought back over the Dnieper to help eliminate this new Soviet threat. Novya Mayatschka fell to the Germans on 9 September, and within a couple of days the *Leibstandarte* was passing Novo Alexandrovka on its way east.

Hitler then altered his plans once again. Large numbers of Soviet troops had been withdrawing into the well-defended Crimea, access to which was over a narrow neck of land which had been heavily fortified. Rather than simply bypass the Crimea, Hitler decided that this potential threat to the flank of the German advance must be eliminated.

> ## Meanwhile, to the north, German units had a small bridehead over the Dnieper

The *Leibstandarte* first attempted to force its way through the western side of the entrance to the Crimea, the Perekop Isthmus. This was blocked by deep minefields and well constructed fortifications, backed up by heavily armed armoured trains. These defences proved far too strong to be penetrated, and so the division moved to the eastern edge of the Crimean 'neck'. There, under cover of heavy fog, it penetrated the enemy defences in a dawn attack and smashed its way past Balykov to capture high ground at Genichek. From this vantage position, the Waffen-SS troops could see the Soviets making preparations for a counterattack and were able to plan their defences accordingly.

Having secured the entrance to the Crimea, the *Leibstandarte* then struck eastwards on the Russian 'mainland' once again. It continued in the direction of Melitopol, reaching Rodianovka on 18 September, where it dug in. Several counterattacks were launched against the German positions but were successfully rebuffed before the Waffen-SS troops were moved westwards yet again to help deal with another crisis.

While LIV Corps attacked into the Crimea, Soviet units had counterattacked, smashing deep into a sector of the German lines held by Romanian troops, virtually annihilating them. Once again the skills of the Waffen-SS were in demand, and the élite troops of the *Leibstandarte* became the mainstay of the German defence. By 30 September, though, the Soviet attacks had run out of steam. The First Panzer Group could now continue its advance eastwards, heading for Rostov on the River Don.

THE WAFFEN-SS TAKES ROSTOV

The *Leibstandarte* drove aggressively eastwards over almost 400km (250 miles) of inhospitable terrain to reach Taganrog on 11 October. The assault on the city began with a crossing of the River Mius under heavy fire. Fighting raged for six days before Taganrog fell. Three days later Stalino was also taken. On 10 October, *Wiking* was withdrawn from III Panzer Corps and transferred to XIV Panzer Corps, advancing along the Melitopol to Stalino railway line towards Wolnowacha in an attempt to overtake fleeing Soviet units and cut them off. Rain once again slowed progress dramatically, turning roads into seas of mud. The rain continued for more than a fortnight, giving the Russians time to regroup and re-assemble their scattered units. At the beginning of November the *Westland* Regiment was hit for the first time by a barrage from Katyushas. The psychological effect of a salvo of these projectiles landing among unprotected and unprepared infantry units was staggering, and a complete panic among the Waffen-SS troops was only narrowly averted.

The onset of colder weather allowed the muddy roads to firm up once again, and the German units achieved a much better degree of mobility for a few weeks until winter proper set in. By mid-November the bulk of III Panzer Corps had caught up with its spearhead units and the assault on Rostov began. The fall of this essential communications link was greatly aided by the capture on 20 November of a vital bridge over the Don by the *Leibstandarte*'s SS-Hauptsturm-führer Springer, a feat which earned Springer the Knights Cross.

The *Leibstandarte* drove aggressively eastwards over almost 400km of inhospitable terrain

Above: Some of the hundreds of thousands of Russian prisoners taken during Operation 'Barbarossa', many of whom had been taken by the Waffen-SS. As one young SS grenadier wrote: 'No time to disarm them; a quick hands up, a gesture towards the west and we roared on again. Numbers? – who knows how many we took.'

Springer and his group had discovered the rail bridge still intact, although Soviet engineers had set demolition charges and its destruction looked imminent. Springer spotted a locomotive waiting by the bridge which seemed to have a full head of steam in its boiler. He therefore ordered his men to open fire with every weapon available, and the high pressure steam hissed out from countless holes in the locomotive. Under cover of the resulting confusion, Springer and his men stormed the bridge and were able to remove the demolition charges. The Waffen-SS troops then held the bridge against frenzied Soviet attempts to dislodge them, until reinforcements arrived. Rostov fell later the same day, and 10,000 Russian prisoners were taken.

Up to this stage the Germans had experienced the scorching heat and choking dust of the Russian summer, and rains which turned roads into impassable quagmires. Now they were about to face the worst horror of all, the Russian winter. Temperatures began to plummet, catching the Germans totally unprepared. German troops were still wearing the same summer uniforms with which they had begun the campaign in June. No warm winter clothing was available. Oil began to freeze in the sumps of the engines in the Germans vehicles and the

thin lubricant in the mechanisms of their guns also froze. Troops were forced to light small fires under their vehicle engines to thaw them out enough to be started. The Soviets, of course, were perfectly familiar with the problems of winter in their own land and had fur-lined winter clothing aplenty for their troops. Soviet vehicles in the main were also built with Russian weather conditions in mind and would function when German vehicles had been rendered useless by the cold.

The German position in Rostov became untenable, and the *Leibstandarte* was obliged to withdraw from the city and retrace its steps westward into positions along the River Mius. Soon afterwards the overwhelming severity of the weather all but put an end to military operations of any significance throughout this whole sector.

During this first phase of the war on the Eastern Front, the *Leibstandarte* had excelled itself in both offensive and defensive actions, earning the praise and admiration of several senior Army commanders. General von Mackensen was to comment in an unsolicited letter to Reichsführer-SS Heinrich Himmler that, in his opinion, the *Leibstandarte* was 'a real élite unit'.

Farther to the north, before winter finally closed in, the *Wiking* Division had been given a new objective, Schachty, and began its advance on 5 November. An unexpected, though brief, thaw once again turned the roads into swamps. The Waffen-SS troops crossed the River Mius, pushing towards the higher ground towards Perwomaisk-Oktjabrisk in order to reach the road to Astachowo. The conditions became so bad that instead of trucks carrying the troops, it was the troops who were obliged to disembark and push the trucks through the thick mud.

On 7 November the division reached Oktjabrisk, whereupon a battle group was diverted south into the area between the 16th Panzer Division and the 14th Panzer Division, where the German forces had become dangerously overstretched. During this period *Germania* seemed in almost constant combat with Soviet units probing for weak spots in the German positions, while the Waffen-SS troops determinedly attempted to carry their advance forward. *Nordland*, meantime, continued its push northeast towards Alexandrovka.

Soviet resistance was now hardening. The Germans were encountering the Soviet T-34 tanks in increasing numbers. These had come as a nasty shock not only to the anti-tank gunners, but to the German tank crews who, up until then, had swept aside anything in their path. During the opening phase of the campaign the Germans had encountered mostly light, thinly armoured and obsolete vehicles such as the BT-5. The T-34 was an entirely different matter: reliable, fast, well armoured and packing quite a punch with its 76mm gun (later

> **Troops were forced to light fires under their vehicle engines to thaw them out**

up-gunned to 85mm). The 3.7cm anti-tank guns fielded by most German units in 1941 were ineffective against the T-34, unless at extremely close range.

On 23 November, powerful Soviet forces began to counterattack and XIV Panzer Corps was forced onto the defensive. Conditions were worsening as temperatures hit 20 degrees below zero. The SS infantry were without adequate winter clothing and many of them were soon crippled by frostbite. The Soviet 9th and 37th Armies gradually pushed the SS back to defensive positions on the River Tusloff. The curves and loops of the river meant that the line to be defended was long, and the available manpower was nowhere near adequate. It became clear that holding these positions would be almost impossible and the Germans were forced to pull back farther west to positions along the River Mius, where they dug in around Amwrosjewka.

The *Totenkopf* was on the move through central Lithuania, meeting determined resistance

THE DEATH'S HEAD DIVISION

When 'Barbarossa' began, the *Totenkopf* Division was under the control of Field Marshal Wilhelm Ritter von Leeb's Army Group North. This army group comprised General Kuchler's Eighteenth Army, tasked with driving east through Latvia and Estonia, Fourth Panzer Group under General Erich Hoepner in the centre, pushing towards Leningrad, and, on the right, General Busch with the Sixteenth Army giving flank protection.

The *Totenkopf* was part of Hoepner's Fourth Panzer Group, the principal units of which were XXXXI Panzer Corps and LVI Panzer Corps, with the *Totenkopf* and the 269th Infantry Division in reserve. Hoepner is known to have disliked Eicke and his division, and it was his personal decision to keep the *Totenkopf* in reserve, much to Eicke's disgust.

On 22 June Fourth Panzer Group smashed its way through the Soviet border positions, its first objective the key bridges over the River Dvina. Running from Vitebsk to the Gulf of Riga, the river formed an excellent natural obstacle that the Germans would have to overcome. In the event, initial resistance was extremely light and Hoepner's troops were able to cover over 80km (50 miles) in the first day alone. By 26 June Fourth Panzer Group had reached Dvinsk and captured the bridges over the Dvina, almost 320km (200 miles) into Soviet-held territory. The spearhead units, however, had outpaced the slower-moving infantry divisions and were obliged to halt at Dvinsk to allow them to catch up.

A considerable gap had opened between the southern flank of General von Manstein's LVI Panzer Corps and the northern flank of its neighbour, Sixteenth Army. Because of the phenomenal rate of advance the Germans had achieved, considerable numbers of Soviet stragglers were still active behind the German armies. The *Totenkopf* was brought out of reserve and sent into action to clear up the Soviet stragglers while it moved up to Dvinsk to join with the main force of the group. As the division progressed, it found resistance stiffening as bewildered Soviet units got over the initial shock of the German attack and began to reorganise and reform.

On 27 June, the *Totenkopf* Division was on the move through central Lithuania, meeting ever more determined resistance. Its spearhead unit, the divisional

Left: 'Then we, too, pulled back through the burning village, holding off the pursuing Russians with bursts of machine-gun fire and grenades. Our officer was busy organising the evacuation of the wounded, although he had lost a leg and died on the way to the Dressing Station.' (NCO, *Das Reich* Division, Russia, July 1941) *Das Reich* infantry in the battles around Yelna.

It was decided to send one infantry battalion and also the Panzerjäger Battalion to Dvinsk

Reconnaissance Battalion, ran into a sizeable enemy force with tank support and was halted in its tracks. The tanks were eventually beaten off, but fanatical, almost suicidal attacks by Soviet infantry continued, exasperating the *Totenkopf* soldiers as they tried to maintain the pace of their advance.

Although the *Totenkopf* was invariably able to drive off these assaults, progress was being significantly slowed. It was decided, therefore, to send one infantry battalion and also the Panzerjäger (Tank-Hunter) Battalion to Dvinsk with all haste, to help repel the Soviet counterattacks on LVI Panzer Corps there, while the remainder of the division followed behind. On reaching Dvinsk, the *Totenkopf* became part of von Manstein's LVI Panzer Corps. Shortly thereafter XXX-XI Panzer Corps reached Dvinsk, followed by elements of the Sixteenth Army.

On 2 July Fourth Panzer Group resumed its advance. The *Totenkopf* was tasked with protecting Manstein's flank and maintaining contact with the Sixteenth Army, to prevent the opening of dangerous gaps in the German line. The terrain through which the *Totenkopf* now moved was heavily wooded marshland, difficult for a motorised unit to traverse, but ideal for straggling Soviet units to defend. At Dagda, the Soviet 42nd Rifle Division caught the *Totenkopf* in a well prepared ambush, killing or wounding over 100 Waffen-SS troops. As Soviet reinforcements with armoured support arrived, the whole division was brought to a standstill. Frenzied Soviet attacks began to force the division back, and the situation was only relieved on the next day by the appearance of Luftwaffe Stuka dive-bombers, which devastated the enemy tanks and artillery, allowing the *Totenkopf* slowly to regain the initiative. The advance continued and, on 4 July, the *Totenkopf* captured Rosenov.

THE ADVANCE TO LAKE ILMEN

On 6 July, the *Totenkopf* smashed into the Stalin Line. The defensive network in this sector was particularly extensive and the division incurred heavy losses, but by nightfall had forced its way through and established a bridgehead over the Velikaya river. The *Totenkopf* soldiers came under fierce artillery fire, however, and Eicke himself was wounded when his command car hit a mine.

On 12 July the division moved to Porkhov as part of the group reserve. It only gained a few days of welcome rest, though, as on 17 July it was back in action in support of LVI Panzer Corps, which had run into trouble to the north-east of Porkhov. Soviet forces had once again begun to attack the corps' flanks and the *Totenkopf* was sent to fend them off. The division then remained with the corps, relieving the 8th Panzer Division, which went into reserve.

On 21 July the advance began once again, the *Totenkopf* moving through the dark forests and swamps to the west of Lake Ilmen. The Soviets withdrew to new defence lines, known as the Luga Line, which ran along the Rivers Mshaga and Luga. On 8 August the *Totenkopf* began its assault on these obstacles. A highly debilitating period for the division then began. During the day all the efforts of the *Totenkopf* soldiers were needed to force the determined defenders back but, as soon as night fell, the Russians would begin counterattacks under the cover of darkness. Any form of rest was all but impossible. Soviet losses could apparently be made good without delay, but the attrition suffered by the Germans was weakening their strength considerably, as losses took much longer to be made good with fresh replacements. In addition, partisans were already operating in the *Totenkopf*'s rear areas, and had tapped into the field telephone lines. The information they gleaned from intercepted conversations allowed them to determine where the division's weak points were and plan their attacks accordingly. Worst of all, the *Totenkopf* troops had been attacked by their own side, when they were mistakenly strafed by Luftwaffe aircraft.

The Soviet 42nd Rifle Division caught the *Totenkopf* in a well prepared ambush

Left: The murder of a Red Army Commissar captured by the Waffen-SS. To the latter the enemy were sub-human Slavs and Bolsheviks. It was therefore all too easy for Himmler's ideological warriors to participate in atrocities and genocide in the East.

In mid–August the Soviet 34th Army powered into the German flanks, and so the *Totenkopf* and 3rd Motorised Division was formed into a counterattack force. Surreptitiously working their way around to the flank, the two German divisions in turn smashed into the unsuspecting Soviets, causing utter devastation. Many Soviet prisoners were taken, as well as huge numbers of vehicles and massive amounts of equipment. The shattered remnants of the 34th Army were rounded up, the *Totenkopf*'s Military Police Troop alone snatching over 1000 prisoners. Eight Russian divisions had been destroyed. Although this had been an important victory for the Germans, overall losses had been heavy, and the attacking German units were significantly weakened.

The *Totenkopf*'s advance resumed on 22 August as the division crossed the Polist and headed east towards the Lovat and Pola rivers. The push continued almost unhindered for several days, with considerable numbers of POWs being rounded up. This situation was not to last, however. When the *Totenkopf* reached the Lovat, it was to find that the retreating Soviets had dug in and were waiting for them. In addition, the enemy had the advantage of considerable air support, as the Luftwaffe had temporarily switched its efforts to other areas. The *Totenkopf*'s attempts to force a crossing of the river failed, and so powerful were the Soviet counterattacks that the Germans were forced to withdraw and take shelter in the woods near the river, out of sight of marauding Soviet fighters.

On 26 August, the *Totenkopf* was ordered to renew its attack and once again suffered considerable casualties trying to oust the enemy from their well prepared

The enemy had the advantage of considerable air support, as the Luftwaffe had switched to other sectors

Right: Exhausted *Das Reich* infantry move through yet another burning Russian village during the encirclement of Kiev, September 1941. As ever, Soviet resistance was intense. In one incident at Putivi, for example, the pupils of the Kharkov Military Academy were wiped out when they charged across open ground against a divisional strongpoint.

positions. By this stage the division had suffered the highest casualty rate in the corps. On 27 August, the Luftwaffe once again appeared in the skies over the Lovat, and the Soviet fighters and fighter-bombers were swiftly driven off.

The advance continued. The *Totenkopf*'s Reconnaissance Battalion reached the River Pola at Vasilyevschina just as the rains came and the division's vehicles almost immediately began to bog down in the mud. Before the Germans could prepare an attack, though, they themselves were hit by the Soviets and the *Totenkopf* spent two days beating off determined assaults.

On 30 August, orders arrived from LVI Panzer Corps demanding that the division press home its advance and secure a crossing of the Pola. Since Eicke's evacuation after his wound, the division had been commanded by George Keppler, who now appealed to von Manstein that the remnants of the battered *Totenkopf* Division were so exhausted and weakened that they were in no fit state to attack such a well defended line. Von Manstein agreed and postponed the attack for a few days. Unfortunately for the *Totenkopf*, though, there was to be no real rest as the Soviet attacks continued unabated.

The Russians had ensured that the *Totenkopf*'s route was well peppered with mines

On 5 September the weather briefly improved, allowing the *Totenkopf*, supported by the 503 Infantry Regiment, to force its way over the Pola. Before the day was out, however, the rains had resumed, and furious Soviet counterattacks began. From 7 September the weather improved for long enough for the roads to start to dry out and allow the Germans more freedom of movement. The Russians had in the meantime ensured that the *Totenkopf*'s route was well peppered with mines and booby traps, slowing progress again. By 12 September, resistance had stiffened considerably and the ferocity of Soviet counterattacks had forced the *Totenkopf* onto the defensive once more.

In the middle of the month the *Totenkopf* was tasked with clearing Soviet stragglers from the forests north of Demyansk. Eicke returned to resume command on 21 September, in time to hear intelligence predicting a major Soviet push in that area and reporting that fresh enemy units were arriving to bolster Soviet strength. Probing attacks soon began, and at noon on 24 September the offensive began. Soviet infantry, with armoured support, began to batter the German lines. The *Totenkopf* anti-tank gunners managed to knock out nine enemy tanks and the SS artillery fired round after round of high explosive over open sights. By the end of that day the *Totenkopf* troops had just managed to force the Soviets back out of Lushno.

The attacks continued still more powerfully on 26-27 September. The equivalent of three divisions, with 100 tanks in support, was thrown against the *Totenkopf*. Things looked bad once again for Eicke and his men. Eicke himself and all his staff officers and other non-combatant personnel took up weapons and joined their comrades in the trenches. With almost superhuman endeavour, the *Totenkopf* soldiers, weakened as they were, repeatedly threw back an attacking force three times their own strength, and eventually the Soviet attacks petered out.

THE EXPLOITS OF FRITZ CHRISTEN

One episode amply demonstrates the phenomenal determination of the soldiers of the division when faced with such overwhelming odds. On 24 September, just north of Lushno, 2 Battery of the *Totenkopf*'s Tank-Hunter Battalion came under attack from strong armoured forces. Every soldier in the entire battery was killed, with the exception of SS-Sturmmann Fritz Christen. Despite the apparent hopelessness of his position, Christen stayed with his gun, loading, aiming and firing all by himself, knocking out six enemy tanks. When darkness fell, he crept to the other gun positions and retrieved ammunition for his weapon. On the following day he destroyed a further seven tanks. By 27 September, when the *Totenkopf* counterattacked and Christen was relieved, 13 tanks and over 100 soldiers had fallen to his fire. He was immediately recommended for the Knights Cross of the Iron Cross for his conspicuous gallantry. He was flown to the Hitler's HQ at Rastenburg and awarded this decoration by Hitler himself

On 8 October, the *Totenkopf* resumed its march eastwards, pursuing the retreating Russians towards the Waldai Heights. Once again, on 16 October, the division ran into well-constructed defences around Samoskye, 10km (6 miles) deep in places, amid densely wooded terrain. The *Totenkopf* and the 30th Infantry Division launched an offensive on 17 October, only to have it founder almost immediately. Instead both divisions soon found themselves on the defensive as the Soviets launched frenzied attacks.

The *Totenkopf* Division alone had lost almost 9000 men since the start of the campaign, and it soon became clear that it, and most other German divisions, would be unable, in their weakened state, to progress any further, particularly in view of the onset of winter. The Germans, therefore, dug in all along this sector of the front, the rest of the year being spent in fighting partisans in the rear areas and holding off Soviet attacks.

Christen had personally knocked out 13 tanks and killed 100 Russian soldiers

Right: Waffen-SS meal bearers carrying soup brave enemy artillery shells as they bring sustenance to the troops in the forward positions. The rapid advance of the Waffen-SS divisions during 'Barbarossa' often meant the troops went hungry, as the slower-moving ration trucks lagged far behind.

Army Group Centre included the Fourth and Ninth Armies and the Second and Third Panzer Groups

Army Group Centre included the Fourth and Ninth Armies and the Second and Third Panzer Groups. The *Das Reich* Division was allocated to General Heinz Guderian's Second Panzer Group, serving together with the Army's 10th Panzer Division and the élite *Grossdeutschland* Regiment in XLVI Panzer Corps.

Das Reich was not committed in the first few days of the campaign, but went into action on 28 June to force a river crossing between Citva and Dukova, and cover the northern flank of the German advance along the main road from Minsk to Smolensk. By 4 July it had reached the Beresina, and crossed over a temporary bridge constructed by the division's engineers.

The contribution of the engineer units to the rapid progress accomplished by the Waffen-SS in the early phases of the campaign in the east cannot be overstated. Were it not for the efforts of these men, often under heavy fire, in clearing mines and other obstacles, and especially in constructing temporary bridges, the rate of advance the SS units were able to maintain would simply not have been possible. The engineers may not have had the opportunities for glory that their comrades in the infantry or armoured units achieved, but their tasks were no less dangerous and costly in terms of combat attrition. For example, Soviet forces ambushed 2 Company of the Engineer Battalion of the *Das Reich* Division while they were repairing a bridge over the Pruth. The entire company was all but wiped out, with 72 of its soldiers being killed.

On 22 July, *Das Reich* was tasked with pushing along the main Minsk-Moscow road to take the high ground east of the small town of Yelnya on the Desna river, an important road junction. The *Deutschland* and *Der Führer* Regiments, together with armour from the 10th Panzer Division, made the assault. *Deutschland*, with Army tanks on the left and *Der Führer* on the right, made its initial attack without the benefit of artillery support, but by nightfall had secured the first ridge of the heights. *Der Führer* also made good progress and had penetrated the Soviet defensive lines by the end of the day.

THE DRIVE TO KIEV

The Germans continued their push on the following day and, ultimately, the Soviets were forced off the high ground. However, the Germans were considerably weakened, as much as by the climactic conditions as by losses to the enemy. The landscape was baked by a searing hot sun and, being open ground, offered little or no shade. Water supplies were low. Corps realised that these units were in no fit state to continue the advance against a stiffening enemy resistance and allowed the SS troops to go temporarily on the defensive. The decision was fortuitous, as the SS infantrymen found themselves hard pressed to defeat the vicious Soviet counterattacks which soon followed.

The German positions were often penetrated and the Soviets only driven out after fierce hand-to-hand fighting. Several spots changed hands two or three times before the Soviet attackers were driven off. As ammunition began to run low, the SS gunners were ordered only to fire at clearly defined targets. Eventually the attacks died down and it was possible to relieve the Waffen-SS troopers. In the second week of September, *Das Reich* was moved south to take part in the drive to Kiev, in which it was to operate on the right flank of XXIV Panzer Corps, still as part of the Second Panzer Group.

During the advance through Russia in the opening phases of Operation 'Barbarossa', German forces both to the north and to the south of the great Pripet Marshes had made rapid progress. The marshes themselves formed a formidable natural obstacle and, by September, the area around the marshes formed a huge salient into German-held territory. Within the salient were at least five Soviet armies comprising around 50 divisions, which were now to be cut off and destroyed in a massive pincer movement.

The German positions were often penetrated and the Soviets driven out only after fierce fighting

Sixth Army was to swing up and attack the southwest end of the salient and draw the Soviet armies defending that area. Meanwhile, the Seventeenth Army with the First Panzer Group in the south, and the Second Army with the Second Panzer Group in the north, would form the arms of a great pincer which would close to the east of Kiev, trapping the Soviet armies.

During the rapid drive south the vital bridge over the Desna at Makoshim was ordered to be taken by the *Das Reich* Division, with air support from the Luftwaffe's Stukas. On reaching the approaches to the river, the opposite bank of which could be seen to be well defended, *Das Reich* awaited its air support, in vain. The Waffen-SS commanders thus decided to attack without it. Motorcycle troops from the Reconnaissance Battalion made a high-speed dash over the bridge, surprising the defenders and engaging them in close combat. Meanwhile, other units on the bridge frantically began to cut the wires to the demolition charges. The bridge was captured completely intact. As the SS troops set about securing their bridgehead against potential counterattacks, the Luftwaffe belatedly appeared and began to dive-bomb its own side, killing 40 Waffen-SS soldiers in the process.

Das Reich then began pushing south out of the bridgehead over the Desna, towards Priluki and Borsna and the crossings at the River Uday. These were successfully seized by the SS infantry and the ring around Kiev was closed on 15 September. Frantic attempts were made by the entrapped Red Army units to break out of the encirclement, but all were beaten back by the Germans. Over one million Soviet troops were either killed or captured in the Kiev Pocket.

Das Reich's part in Operation 'Typhoon', the attack on Moscow, began on 4 October

OPERATION 'TYPHOON'

Das Reich's part in Operation 'Typhoon', the attack on Moscow, began on 4 October. Accompanied by the 10th Panzer Division, progress was initially good, but when the autumn rains came the roads were quickly reduced to swamps and the division bogged down, only reaching Gzhatsk on 9 October. By mid-October, *Das Reich* was on the march again, driving along the main Moscow highway and meeting fierce resistance. Temperatures had dropped dramatically and the first of countless numbers of frostbite cases were being reported by troops whose protection against the Russian winter climate was wholly inadequate. Crossing the River Moskva, the division seized the town of Mozhaisk on 18 October.

From late October until mid-November, German offensive operations were reduced. Ammunition supplies were running low and weather conditions had worsened, so the Germans concentrated on consolidating their gains. On 18 November, however, XLVI Panzer Corps was ordered to continue its advance with an attack towards Istra. On 26 November, after fierce fighting, *Das Reich*, and the remaining tanks of 10th Panzer Division, finally forced their way into the town, still hoping to push on towards Moscow itself.

With every day that passed, however, weather conditions were becoming more severe. Night-time temperatures fell as low as 50 degrees below zero, with day-time temperatures around 30 degrees below. Mechanical wear and tear on vehicles and the freezing temperatures had rendered all but seven of the tanks of the 10th Panzer Division inoperable. So great had been the loss in manpower that both the *Deutschland* and *Der Führer* Regiments had to disband one battalion each and redistribute the men.

On 4 December 1941, soldiers of the *Das Reich*'s Reconnaissance Battalion actually reached the terminus of the Moscow city tramcar system before the weather closed in and forced a pause in the attack. It was to be the farthest point reached in the attack on Moscow. Two days later, the Soviet winter offensive began. A total of around one and a half million Soviet troops, representing 17 whole armies, was thrown at the exhausted German forces. On 9 December the order to retreat was given and *Das Reich* began to retire westwards.

During the first campaign on the Eastern Front the Waffen-SS had proved that it could fight as well as the German Army. Few in the military hierarchy could now doubt the value of the Waffen-SS man as a combat soldier, though many still harboured grave suspicions and resentment concerning the 'political' nature of Himmler's troops. Accusations were still levelled that the incautious attitudes of many Waffen-SS officers led to excessive casualties in their units. What was beyond doubt, however, was that the Waffen-SS was fast acquiring a reputation for fanatical bravery which few other units could match.

Left: An NCO of the *Das Reich* Division during Operation 'Typhoon'. By the end of 1941 the Germans were fighting two enemies in the East: the Red Army and General Winter. The first winter in Russia came as a shock to the Waffen-SS, as one young *Leibstandarte* soldier wrote: 'It is not possible in words to describe winter on this front. We have to strip the fallen, theirs and ours, for warm clothing. I don't think I will ever be warm again.'

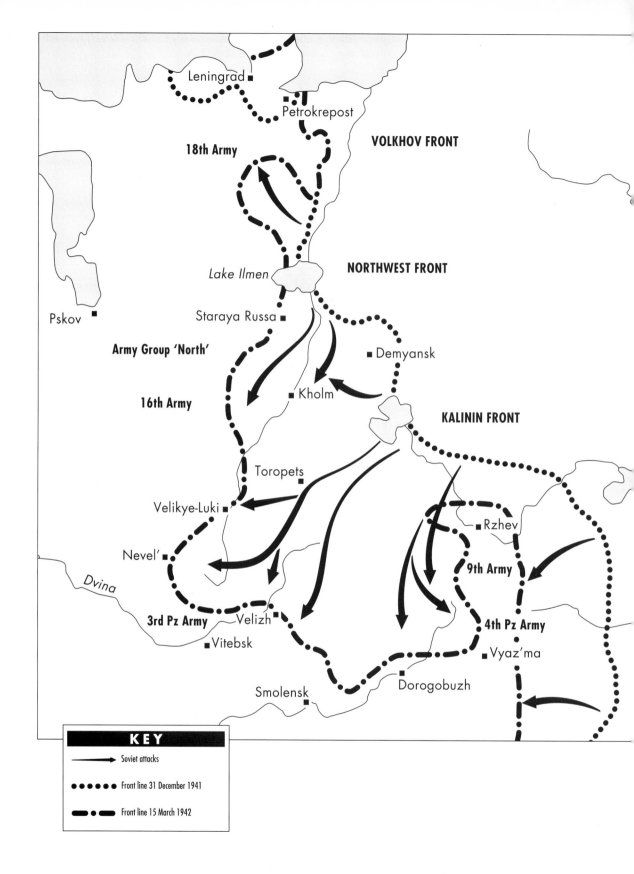

Leningrad

Petrokrepost

VOLKHOV FRONT

18th Army

Lake Ilmen

NORTHWEST FRONT

Staraya Russa

Pskov

Demyansk

Army Group 'North'

Kholm

16th Army

KALININ FRONT

Toropets

Velikye-Luki

Rzhev

Nevel'

9th Army

Dvina

3rd Pz Army Velizh

4th Pz Army

Vitebsk

Vyaz'ma

Smolensk

Dorogobuzh

KEY

→ Soviet attacks

●●●●● Front line 31 December 1941

▬ ▬ ▬ Front line 15 March 1942

Volga

MOSCOW

WEST FRONT

The Demyansk Pocket

By early December 1941, the German armies that had steam-rollered into the Soviet Union in June of that year had run out of momentum. Supply lines were over-stretched, the troops were exhausted and the full horrors of the Russian winter were being visited upon German soldiers who, in the main, were still equipped with little more than the summer weight clothing with which they had begun the campaign. The Red Army, although driven back to the very gates of Moscow itself, had established a reserve to the east of the Soviet capital. Its winter offensive smashed into the German lines, tearing huge gaps in the front. In the north six German divisions, including the *Totenkopf*, were cut off in the Demyansk Pocket.

On 5 December 1941, Marshal Zhukov unleashed the Red Army's fresh, well-equipped divisions against the exhausted soldiers of Army Group Centre, and the German lines began to crack almost immediately. The German front-line generals favoured a withdrawal to Smolensk, forcing the Red Army to fight at the end of a long supply line in deep snow. Hitler would have none of it and bluntly refused to allow any form of withdrawal whatsoever. Every German soldier was to stand firm. Senior officers who sought to disregard Hitler's orders swiftly found themselves cashiered and replaced by those who would obey without question. Hitler's determination never to permit retreats

Right: The first overlord of the concentration camp system and from 1940 commander of the *Totenkopf* Division – SS-Obergruppenführer Theodor Eicke. Despised and ridiculed by the Army and many in the SS, Eicke displayed sound and calm leadership during the battles in the Demyansk Pocket. He shared in the hardships and meagre rations endured by his men, and lived in a dugout like them. The ferocious fighting spirit he had infused into his men meant the Russians were unable to defeat the Waffen-SS division. For his efforts a grateful Führer awarded Eicke the Knights Cross and then the Oakleaves.

would in later years cost the lives of many thousands of German soldiers in pointless attempts to defend so-called 'fortress areas' long after they had ceased to have any real strategic value. However, in this particular case his inflexibility did much to prevent a total rout of the German armies before Moscow. Gradually, the German defences firmed up, the front stabilised and by the end of January, the Soviet offensive in the central sector had exhausted itself.

To the north, Soviet forces were also gathering, with the 11th and 34th Soviet Armies, and the 1st Shock Army forming one attack intent to advance along the southern shore of Lake Ilmen. The 16th Shock Army also advanced, aiming to sweep around the lower edge of Lake Seliger to join the other thrust, encircle and annihilate the German Sixteenth Army, and thus create a vast gap between Army Group North and Army Group Centre, through which the Red Army would flow.

German intelligence in the north had detected the build up of the Soviet forces, as large-scale Soviet troops movements had been spotted by reconnais-

sance flights. Thus forewarned that they, too, were about to come under heavy pressure, German forces in the north were able to organise their defences accordingly, and for most of December the Germans concentrated on firming up their defence lines. In the area between Lake Ilmen and Lake Seliger, and along the River Lovat to the west, lay two German corps, II Corps and X Corps, part of whose strength was the *Totenkopf* Division under the command of SS-Obergruppenführer Theodor Eicke.

During the night of 7/8 January 1942, under the cover of a fierce blizzard, the Red Army launched its attack along the whole of Army Group North's southern flank. The 11th Army, 34th Army and 1st Shock Army smashed their way with full force into the *Totenkopf*'s neighbours, the 30th and 290th Infantry Divisions. Within just 24 hours the 290th Infantry Division had been all but annihilated, and the enemy had pierced the German lines by up to 32km (20 miles) in places.

By 9 January, the 11th Army had advanced as far as Staraya Russa and there turned south into the rear of II Corps. In conjunction with these moves, the 16th Shock Army punched its way west from the shores of Lake Seliger then turned north along the line of the Lovat river, intending to link with 11th Army and 1st Shock Army. If the Soviets succeeded, the German Sixteenth Army would be trapped.

To Eicke's fury, his division was split up, on the orders of Sixteenth Army, with sub-units being despatched to various crisis points. The *Totenkopf*'s Reconnaissance Battalion and Engineer Battalion, together with two battalions of infantry, were despatched to Staraya Russa with orders to hold at all costs. Two further infantry battalions were sent to Demyansk to help strengthen the flanks of the Sixteenth Army.

By 12 January 1942, the situation had become critical and a worried Field Marshal Leeb asked permission to withdraw both his corps over the Lovat to form a new defensive line. Hitler refused outright and ordered his troops to stand firm. An outraged Leeb, certain that this was a death sentence for the Sixteenth Army, asked to be relieved of his post. Hitler agreed and, on 17 January, Leeb was replaced by Colonel-General Küchler.

The German situation, meanwhile, had continued to worsen. The two German corps were being slowly constricted into a pocket around Demyansk. Within three days of Küchler taking command, the Soviet armies had broken through along the Lovat, separating the German units on the west and east banks of the river, though the *Totenkopf* elements at Staraya Russa, together with the Army's 18th Motorised Division, held and inflicted heavy losses on the Soviets.

> **A worried Field Marshal Leeb asked permission to withdraw both his corps over the Lovat**

SS

Right: Precious supplies of ammunition are ferried to *Totenkopf* units at the front. The Luftwaffe did a good job in supplying the men in the pocket, but food was soon in short supply and had to be strictly rationed. Most of the horses either died of malnutrition or were slaughtered for food.

Hitler once again reiterated his order that no withdrawals from Demyansk would be contemplated

On 8 February, the Soviet ring closed firmly around II and X Corps, trapping the 12th, 30th, 32nd, 123rd and 290th Infantry Divisions, plus the remainder of the *Totenkopf* Division. Against the exhausted and badly battered Germans, the Soviets fielded 15 fresh divisions, supported by a number of independent ski battalions and armoured units. With supply lines totally disrupted, the Luftwaffe took on the responsibility for supplying the encircled German units.

Hitler once again reiterated his order that no withdrawals from the Demyansk area would be contemplated. The units were to stand firm and hold their positions until arrangements could be made for a counterattack by German forces on the west bank of the Lovat. Food, ammunition, medicines, weapons and all other needs were to be brought in by air.

Unlike in the later debacle at Stalingrad, Göring's transport squadrons were able, initially at least, to more than match the daily requirements of the encircled units. It had been estimated that a minimum daily supply of just under 200 tonnes would be required, and, at its peak, Göring's supply operations actually reached a total of just under 300 tonnes. This was not to last, however, and the deliveries gradually dropped off until the Luftwaffe struggled to meet even half the required amounts. One thing in the *Totenkopf*'s favour was that the division's supply officers had managed to procure, through SS sources, sufficient warm winter clothing for its troops before the supply lines were cut.

When the Soviet ring around the Demyansk Pocket finally closed, command of the troops within the pocket passed to General Graf Brockdorff-Ahlefeldt, who further infuriated Eicke by splitting the remaining *Totenkopf* units within the pocket into two battle groups, formed with a mixture of the *Totenkopf* and Army personnel. The larger group was commanded by Eicke and was ordered to defend the large network of villages and their interlinking roads in the southwest sector of the pocket. Eicke's principal task was to hold firm in his sector to prevent the corridor which had been driven between German units on the western and eastern banks of the Lovat from being widened by the Soviets. The second battle group was commanded by SS-Oberführer Max Simon, and was sited on the northeastern edge of the pocket, facing the Soviet 34th Army.

Eicke's battle group, fighting in snow well over one metre deep and in temperatures of minus 30 degrees, came under extreme pressure as it tried to hold its line of scattered villages. Soviet aircraft dropped incendiary bombs wherever a building stood, to deny the *Totenkopf* troops any form of shelter. On the ground the Red Army pounded Eicke's men incessantly with artillery, and by late February the Soviet forces had penetrated the German lines in a number of positions. A number of individual villages were cut off, surrounded in their own little pockets. During this period the *Totenkopf* also had to put up with the indignity of being attacked by its own side as Luftwaffe aircraft strafed the Waffen-SS troops while dropping supplies right into the laps of the Soviet attackers, so confused had the situation on the ground become. The *Totenkopf*'s losses were mounting dramatically, but it held its ground.

Eicke now feared for the survival of his battered and fragmented division and appealed directly to Himmler, who was eventually able to procure several hundred replacements ready to be flown into the pocket, only to find that the Luftwaffe insisted that it could not spare space on any of its supply flights to transport them. Even more fresh Soviet divisions were now thrown into the frenzied assault on the German positions in bitter and prolonged fighting, during which no quarter was asked or given by either side.

FRAGMENTATION AND ATTRITION

By late February Eicke's battle group numbered only 1460 officers and men and, by the end of that month, Eicke's sector had been so widely infiltrated by Soviet troops that all contact with neighbouring German units had been lost. Eicke signalled his desperate situation to II Corps, feeling that everything was hopeless and the annihilation of his battle group imminent.

Soviet attacks became even more desperate in this period, as they attempted to crush the Demyansk Pocket before the spring thaw turned the frozen landscape into a muddy quagmire and bogged down their operations. Such conditions would disadvantage the attackers far more than the defenders.

Himmler, meanwhile, had intervened and spoken personally to Hitler about the dire situation facing the *Totenkopf* Division, and Hitler gave orders that the replacements procured by Himmler be flown in as soon as possible. These fresh *Totenkopf* troops finally arrived at Demyansk on 7 March. An improvement in weather conditions also allowed the Luftwaffe to make a substantial drop of essential food, medicines and ammunition to the beleaguered defenders.

By the time the Soviet attacks began to tail off in mid-March, as the spring thaws set in, they had lost well over 20,000 troops in their attempt to crush the Demyansk Pocket. The *Totenkopf* Division, in the same period, had lost around

By late February Eicke's battle group numbered only 1460 officers and men

7000 men. Shortage of manpower was never a problem for the Soviets and their losses would quickly be made good. The same could not be said for the German side, though. For example, the *Totenkopf*'s losses of 7000 were compensated for by only 5000 replacements.

From the beginning of March 1942, a build up of German forces on the west bank of the Lovat had been under way as a relief force assembled under the command of Lieutenant-General Walter von Seydlitz-Kurzbach. A total of five German divisions, the 5th and 8th Light Divisions, and 122nd, 127th and 329th Infantry Divisions, were to punch their way eastwards over the Lovat towards the pocket and, when the time was ripe, a signal would be given for Eicke's battle group to make a corresponding push to the west. The relief of the Demyansk Pocket was codenamed Operation 'Fallreep'.

PARTIAL RELIEF FOR EICKE'S MEN

The offensive began on 21 March, and for the first two days Seydlitz-Kurzbach's troops made good progress, supported by massive air power. Then Soviet resistance began to stiffen and progress slowed as the enemy frantically battled to prevent a link up between the German forces. Seydlitz-Kurzbach was not confident enough to give Eicke his orders to begin his attack westwards until two weeks after the push eastwards began. The delay meant that Eicke's troops would have to move through ground turned into boggy marshland by the spring thaws. Nevertheless, the *Totenkopf* infantry launched themselves at the Soviets with a frenzied determination and the fighting frequently deteriorated into vicious hand-to-hand combat. Due to the horrendous conditions and stiff Soviet resistance, the *Totenkopf* only managed to achieve a rate of advance of around 1.5km (1 mile) per day.

On 20 April, a company from the *Totenkopf*'s Tank-Destroyer Battalion reached the east bank of the Lovat, to be joined by the remainder of the battle group on the following day. On 22 April, after 73 days, the bridgehead over the Lovat was sufficiently secured for Seydlitz-Kurzbach to start moving troops and supplies into what had now become the Demyansk salient.

This was to be far from the end of the *Totenkopf*'s ordeal, however. The troops were now in a dreadful physical condition, and Eicke's hopes that the remnants of his once mighty division would be pulled out of the front for extensive rebuilding and refitting were dashed when Hitler ordered that they remain in the salient to hold open the German corridor which, it was anticipated, would soon come under renewed enemy attack.

Eicke was given command of all SS and Army troops within the western part of the salient. These troops were to be combined into a new 'Corps', but in reality the total strength of this formation was only around half that of a single fully manned division. Eicke made his pessimism concerning the *Totenkopf*'s situation known to Colonel-General Busch, who was very sympathetic, having seen at first hand the shocking state of many of the *Totenkopf* soldiers. Busch interceded personally with Himmler, insisting that Eicke's battered corps could only continue with its allotted tasks if it received an immediate influx of at least

The *Totenkopf* infantry launched themselves at the Soviets with a frenzied determination

Left: Typical conditions in the Demyansk Pocket, February 1942. Fighting in chest-high snow in temperatures of minus 30 degrees Celsius soon became the norm for Eicke's troops. The freezing weather brought not only personal discomfort for the *Totenkopf*. The Russians were able to move across the frozen Lake Ilmen and the usually marshy delta of the River Lovat.

The frequency of Soviet attacks gave the exhausted SS troops no chance of rest

5000 fresh troops. In the event, Reichsführer-SS Himmler was only to send a further 3000 replacements.

By May 1942, the Red Army had once again gone over to the offensive and had begun attacking the corridor, which was only held open with great difficulty. Soviet actions grew in strength and determination through into early summer as the Russian build-up continued. The frequency of Soviet attacks gave the exhausted SS troops no chance for any sort of rest, and constant attrition through these defensive actions weakened Eicke's corps significantly, as well as physically exhausting the commander himself.

In mid-June Eicke was ordered to take a spell of leave, being replaced temporarily by SS-Oberführer Max Simon. At the end of his spell of leave, Eicke was ordered to report to the Führer Headquarters at Rastenburg, where he was decorated personally by Hitler with the Oak Leaves to his Knights Cross. Eicke took this opportunity to have a private chat with Hitler, during which he plainly described the dreadful condition of his remaining soldiers. Hitler expressed his sympathy but refused to allow the *Totenkopf* to be withdrawn from Demyansk just yet. He did promise Eicke that when the division was eventually relieved, it would be fully rebuilt and reformed as a panzergrenadier (armoured infantry) division, complete with its own tank battalion. Eicke was ordered to remain on leave until the division was withdrawn from the front.

By early July, Soviet pressure on the areas defended by the *Totenkopf* was building up yet again. Simon made desperate pleas for the removal of the division before it was destroyed. In his opinion it was only a matter of time

> **By July, Soviet pressure on the areas defended by the *Totenkopf* was building up yet again**

Right: Well-wrapped Waffen-SS soldiers in the Demyansk Pocket. Fortunately for Eicke's men, the SS had managed to procure adequate winter cloth-ing for its encircled troops. This was one reason why they performed so well.

before the *Totenkopf* was annihilated. On reading Simon's reports, Eicke once again pleaded for the removal of his division, but to no avail. Hitler insisted that the remnants must stand firm and could not be released until X Corps had strengthened the salient sufficiently to hold off future enemy attacks. It was estimated that this would take at least a further six to eight weeks.

On 17 July, massive Soviet assaults smashed into the SS units and were only held back by the fanatical determination of the exhausted *Totenkopf* troops, and with considerable losses. On 18 July the Red Army captured Vasilyevschina, wiping out its *Totenkopf* defenders to a man. Simon was instructed to launch an immediate counterattack but flatly refused, and in an amazing display of insubordination to his Army superiors suggested that if the Army wanted the job done they should do it themselves. Presumably the poor condition of the Waffen-SS troops must have been appreciated by the corps command, as there were no repercussions for Simon's refusal to obey the order to assault, and indeed the Army did send in its own troops to carry out the attack. The 8th Light Division replaced the *Totenkopf* for the mission, and failed to oust the Soviets, taking heavy losses in the process.

In atrocious weather conditions, Soviet attempts to crush the salient continued. Fighting raged for several days, the combatants thigh-deep in glutinous mud. Eventually, on 30 July, the Soviet attacks eased off, the Red Army soldiers as exhausted as the SS. By now the *Totenkopf* was literally on its last legs. Simon's exhausted troops were suffering the consequences of long periods of fighting in what amounted to swamp conditions. Pneumonia, dysentery and many other diseases spread like wildfire among the *Totenkopf*'s shattered remains.

WEATHER SAVES THE DIVISION

Eicke was furious at his division being left to languish in these conditions and once again presented himself to his Führer, demanding that either the division be pulled out of the Demyansk salient for a rest and complete refit, or that he be allowed to return to the front and die with his men. Not surprisingly, Hitler refused and ordered Eicke to take long-term convalescent leave.

On 6 August, the Soviet 11th Army and I Guards Corps launched major attacks on both the northern and southern edges of the corridor. The *Totenkopf* suffered debilitating casualties once again. The SS troops were pounded by massed artillery barrages and the Red Army air force bombed and strafed the German troops at will, the Luftwaffe being conspicuous by its absence. By 12 August all the *Totenkopf* non-combatant personnel – cooks, clerks, medics and military police – had been armed and had taken their places in the trenches with their comrades. There were now no reserves left whatsoever.

Just as the Red Army looked set to overrun the *Totenkopf*, the heavens opened and torrential rains began. For two days the weather was so bad that all military operations ceased. The respite this gave allowed the Germans a brief time to regroup, and over the next week or so the desperate *Totenkopf* soldiers summoned up enough strength to keep the enemy at bay. The *Totenkopf* 'Corps' now numbered a mere 7000 or so men, most of them non-combatant troops. Simon,

The SS troops were pounded by massed Red Army artillery barrages

Right: A *Totenkopf* column photographed in the Staraya Russa region. Though the division fought along-side Army units, Eicke believed that the Wehrmacht was not pulling its weight. In a letter he wrote to Hans Juttner, the chief of the SS's main leadership office, he stated: 'The Army will fight at Demyansk to the last drop of SS blood. I believe it is all part of a determined effort by the Army to destroy the Waffen-SS.'

in despair, suggested that the *Totenkopf* be written off as a division, as there was hardly anything left worth saving.

On 25 August, the corridor was once again the target of massive Soviet attacks as the 7th Guards Division, 129th, 130th, 364th and 391st Infantry Divisions and the 30th Rifle Brigade hurled themselves at the Germans. The Red Army units bludgeoned their way into the German positions, splitting the *Totenkopf* into a number of isolated pockets. Simon's command lost over 1000 men in just a few hours but determinedly held its positions, fighting off all Soviet attacks success-fully. Eicke was then allowed to return to his battered division, but had to commute back to Germany each week to oversee preparations for its rebuilding.

The *Totenkopf* was finally withdrawn in October 1942, after German counter-attacks had finally driven the Soviets far enough back for the salient to be consid-ered secure and troop movements in and out of the salient to be made out of the range of Soviet artillery. Only 6400 *Totenkopf* soldiers remained alive.

Hitler authorised the institution of a special campaign decoration in com-memoration of the defensive battles around Demyansk in 1942. It took the form

of a metal shield, topped by an eagle and swastika over a field bearing crossed swords and an aircraft over the date 1942, with the legend *Demyansk* above. The shield itself was attached to a piece of backing cloth, which was then sewn on to the upper left sleeve of the recipient's uniform. Many photographs of *Totenkopf* soldiers show them proudly wearing this evidence of their participation one of the most costly battles in the division's history.

It is also worth noting that several *Totenkopf* soldiers were decorated with the coveted Knights Cross of the Iron Cross for gallantry during the battles at Demyansk. Study of some of the actions for which these decorations were awarded illustrates just how ferocious the fighting during these hectic months could be.

Wilfried Richter was born in Pforzheim on 9 May 1916 and joined the SS in 1937. During the Demyansk battles, he commanded a small combat group located at Kalitkino, on the banks of the Robja river. Furious Red Army artillery barrages had reduced the village itself, and most of the immediate vicinity, to a wasteland of rubble and shell craters, and the Waffen-SS occupants were all but exhausted by their defence of the area against attacks by Soviet infantry. On 5 April a particularly powerful Soviet attack hit Kalitkino, threatening to overrun it. Normally, the defenders would have been forewarned of an impending attack by a 'softening-up' barrage from the enemy artillery. As day broke on this particular morning, however, the Soviets, supported by around 16 T-34 tanks, struck without warning. Quickly overrunning the anti-tank defences on the northern edge of the village, they established a toehold, but only after losing six of their tanks. Then the *Totenkopf* troops immediately counterattacked, using Teller mines against the Soviet tanks and destroyed five more in this fashion.

Richter decided to call down German artillery fire on his own positions

The Soviet infantry force was still substantial and the situation looked bad for the greatly-outnumbered Waffen-SS troops. Richter decided to call down German artillery fire on his own positions. As his men took shelter in their well constructed bunkers, the enemy were caught in the open, suffering horrendous losses. As soon as the barrage was over, Richter and his men stormed out and engaged the Russians in ferocious hand-to-hand combat. The battle raged until all the Soviet troops had been killed or had fled. For his personal gallantry and the leadership qualities he had shown during this action, SS-Obersturmführer Richter was decorated with the Knights Cross of the Iron Cross on 21 April 1942, and was promoted to SS-Hauptsturmführer. Richter ended his career as a battalion commander in the 38th SS Panzergrenadier Division *Nibelungen* and survived the war.

Erwin Meierdress was born in December 1916 and originally joined the élite *Leibstandarte SS Adolf Hitler*. After completing his officer training course at the SS-Junkerschule Braunschweig, he was posted to the *Totenkopf* Division.

In early 1942, Meierdress was in command of a small battle group of around 120 men located near Bjakowo in the Demyansk Pocket. The desperate defence put up by Meierdress and his men succeeded in keeping the enemy at bay, but only at the cost of many casualties. Although relatively few of his men were actually killed, three-quarters of them were wounded. His group consisted of a mixture of *Totenkopf* troops, Army personnel from a construction battalion, Army artillery observers and some members of an SS-Polizei battalion.

One radio message received at corps HQ from Meierdress reported attacks from the west, north and northeast, but that the enemy had suffered heavy losses, with 200 Soviet troops killed. A few hours later, a second message arrived: 'Bjakowo once more attacked from the east. 150 enemy dead. Own losses, one dead and seven wounded.' The one-sided fight continued, with the numerically superior Soviets unable to winkle the small group of SS defenders from their positions and suffering heavy losses.

Ultimately Meierdress himself was severely wounded and was flown out in a Fieseler Storch reconnaissance plane. On 13 March 1942 he was decorated with the Knights Cross of the Iron Cross. His battle group finally emerged from the battle with 85 survivors, of whom 56 had been wounded. Meierdress recovered from his wounds and went on to command the 1st Battalion of the *Totenkopf*'s Panzer Regiment with great success, winning the Oak Leaves to his Knights Cross on 12 October 1943. He was killed on 4 January 1945 in Hungary.

SS-STURMBANNFÜHRER KARL ULLRICH

One of the most prominent figures of the *Totenkopf* Division, and another of its Knights Cross' recipients for actions around Demyansk, was Karl Ullrich, then an SS-Sturmbannführer and commander of the division's engineer battalion. Ullrich and his men were located with the 18th Motorised Infantry Division near Staraya Russa, defending a strongpoint at the bridge crossing over the Lovat between Korowitschina and Kobylkina. Against Ullrich's battle group were ranged three Soviet Guards regiments, two ski battalions and up to 30 T-34 tanks. Soviet artillery barrages and attacks by fighter-bombers had left virtually every building in the area a burned-out ruin. With no decent shelter available, Ullrich's men were left huddling together for warmth in their trenches in blizzard conditions and in temperatures reaching 45 degrees below zero. Almost every man had suffered frostbite to some degree.

Remarkably, in view of the condition of his men and the overwhelming Soviet superiority in numbers, Ullrich's battle group repulsed attack after attack. At night, the enemy would attempt to infiltrate the German lines under the cover of darkness, dressed in white snow suits to camouflage themselves against the frozen winter landscape.

During these actions Ullrich was always to be found in the thick of the fighting alongside his men. His signals personnel had kept the parent corps appraised

Ullrich's men were left huddling together for warmth in their trenches in blizzard conditions

of developments, only to receive the reply, 'Führerbefehl! [a direct order from Hitler himself] Kobylkina must be held.' Along with one such message came the news that Ullrich had been awarded the Knights Cross in recognition of his group's superhuman efforts in the face of overwhelming odds. On hearing the news, Ullrich simply replied: 'I'd rather have a fresh regiment.'

Eventually, Ullrich was given the authority to fight his way east to link up with Eicke's main battle group in the southwest of the Demyansk Pocket. Ullrich went on to reach the rank of SS–Oberführer and later served as the commander of SS–Panzergrenadier Regiment 6 *Theodor Eicke*.

At Wassiljeschtschina in the northern part of the Demyansk Pocket, SS–Sturmbannführer Franz Kleffner and the men of the Kradschutzen (Motorcycle Reconnaissance) Battalion of the *Totenkopf* Division were coming under overwhelming Soviet pressure and held their sector with great difficulty and considerable losses. Against the battered Kradschutzen Battalion were thrown two and a half battalions of fresh Soviet assault troops. After five hours of furious combat, some 300 Soviet troops lay dead in front of the German trenches. Two days later, two Soviet battalions attacked once again, and this time were driven off with the loss of 150 of their men. Such tenacity in the defence achieved some remarkable results, but there was also a price to pay.

Above: *Totenkopf* **soldiers attacking Red Army positions in the west of the pocket. Hitler had promised Eicke that, if the position south of Lake Ilmen was stable, 'the division could be transferred to France in August [1942].' However, the division remained at the front until October, when its shattered remnants were at last relieved.**

The *Totenkopf* troops were cold, exhausted, lice-ridden and suffering from frostbite, but had driven off Soviet units greatly superior in numbers. When the Soviet dead were eventually cleared from the battlefield, it was discovered that the majority had been killed by head wounds, testimony to the marksmanship of the *Totenkopf* riflemen. For his leadership during these important battles, Kleffner was awarded the Knights Cross on 19 February 1942.

It was not only officers from the division who were decorated with this coveted award. At Kobylkina, for example, SS-Oberscharführer Ernst Staudle was serving as a forward observer for the *Totenkopf's* Artillery Regiment when a heavy Soviet mortar barrage forewarned the Germans of a likely infantry attack.

When the Soviet infantry started pouring out of the cover of nearby woods towards the German positions, Staudle had his radio operator call down artillery fire from his battery and, after a few seconds, the shells came whooshing overhead. Still the enemy came on towards the German trenches and Staudle sent in new fire orders. Soon the Soviet troops were too near to allow the use of artillery against them. Staudle then leapt up and ran to an anti-aircraft machine gun and sent a deadly hail of bullets whizzing towards the charging enemy. His position was dangerously exposed, and soon the Soviets began to respond to his fire. Enemy machine-gun bullets began zipping past Staudle and his loader. Suddenly his loader fell, only to be replaced immediately by another *Totenkopf* soldier. Despite Staudle's efforts the Russians continued to move nearer and were soon too close for the gun to be brought to bear.

Staudle called to his loader and the others troops around him to run for cover into the nearest houses. As soon as they made it, Staudle called up the artillery once again and brought down a barrage of fire on top of his own position. Caught in the open, while the *Totenkopf* troops sheltered in the ruined houses, the Russians suffered dreadful casualties as the artillery shells began to land. Soviet troops began to rush into the ruins seeking shelter, only to find them already occupied. Bitter hand-to-hand fighting broke out, in which both Staudle and his radio operator were wounded. The attack was driven off and, while in hospital, Staudle learned that he had been decorated with the Knights Cross for his part in the action.

Dr Eduard 'Eddi' Deisenhofer was born in Upper Bavaria on 27 June 1909 and joined the SS in 1934, being accepted as a volunteer in the élite *Leibstandarte*. Recognised as a potential officer, he attended the SS-Junkerschule at Bad Tölz and was commissioned into the *Deutschland* Regiment, before eventually transferring to the *Totenkopf* Division.

During the defence of the Demyansk Pocket, Deisenhofer commanded the 1st Battalion, SS *Totenkopf* Infantry Regiment 1, which was based around the strongpoint at Nish-Ssossnowka. In one period of just 17 days, Deisenhofer's men threw back 23 Soviet assaults. So spirited was the *Totenkopf* defence that not only were Deisenhofer and his group able to repulse Soviet attacks but also carried out limited counterattacks. Well over 1000 dead Soviet troops lay in front of 1st Battalion's positions.

When the time came for Eicke's *Totenkopf* troops to take the lead role in smashing their way from the west of the pocket to link up with Seydlitz-Kurzbach's relief force, Deisenhofer and his men once again played a significant part in the action. Deisenhofer, as ever at the front of his battalion, led his troops into the attack, storming the Soviet-held village of Nowosselje. The village was held by a battalion-strength Soviet unit, on paper an even match

for Deisenhofer's battalion, but in fact much stronger, since the Waffen-SS troops had suffered heavy casualties, for whom few replacements had been received. In addition, the *Totenkopf* troops were exhausted, frostbitten, filthy and hungry, whereas the Soviets were reasonably fresh. Nevertheless, after fierce hand-to-hand fighting, Deisenhofer and his men were victorious and drove the Soviets out of this key village. Soon afterwards a Soviet counterattack, supported by tanks, was launched against the southwest edge of the village. Once again Deisenhofer personally led his men, being wounded in the process. He refused to be taken out of the line for treatment, and stayed with his unit until the area was secured. For his exploits Eduard Deisenhofer he received the Knights Cross.

The other *Totenkopf* soldiers who received the Knights Cross of the Iron Cross for their part in the Demyansk battles were SS-Hauptsturmführer Georg 'Schorsch' Bochmann for gallantry and leadership of Battle Group *Bochmann*; SS-Oberscharführer Ludwig Kochle, for personal gallantry in the face of the enemy; SS-Sturmbannführer Otto Baum, for his exemplary performance as commander of the 3rd Battalion, SS *Totenkopf* Infantry Regiment 3; and SS-Hauptsturmführer Max Seela, for his gallantry and successful leadership of 3 Company of the *Totenkopf* Division's Engineer Battalion.

A total of around 96,000 German soldiers had been cut off in the Demyansk Pocket, and the fact that the pocket held and the survivors were eventually relieved was due in no small measure to the tenacity of the men of the *Totenkopf* Division. Mention should also be made of the Luftwaffe's transport flyers who managed to bring in over 64,000 tonnes of supplies into the pocket, and at the same time evacuate over 35,000 wounded German soldiers. Over 250 Luftwaffe transport aircraft were shot down by Soviet aircraft or by ground fire. The Luftwaffe, too, had made its sacrifices.

Some of the men who received the Knights Cross for their exploits in the Demyansk Pocket:
Opposite, above: SS-Sturmbannführer Karl Ullrich, the commander of the *Totenkop*'s engineer battalion.
Opposite, below: SS-Obersturmführer Erwin Meierdress, a picture taken while he was recovering in hospital.
Above: SS-Obersturmführer Wilfried Richter, who ended up as a battalion commander in the 38th SS Panzergrenadier Division and who survived the war.

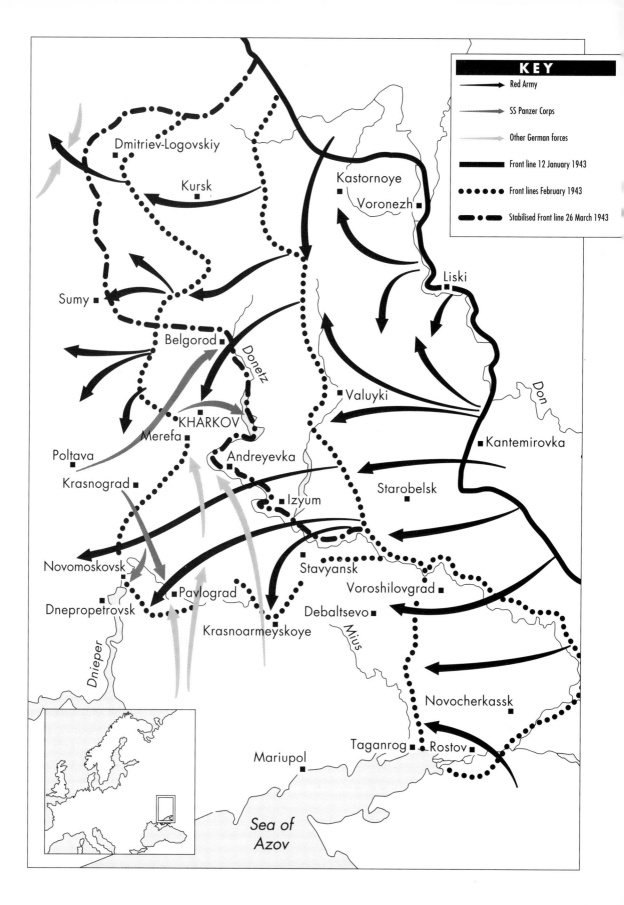

KEY

Red Army
SS Panzer Corps
Other German forces
Front line 12 January 1943
Front lines February 1943
Stabilised Front line 26 March 1943

Dmitriev-Logovskiy

Kursk

Kastornoye

Voronezh

Liski

Sumy

Belgorod

Donetz

Valuyki

Kantemirovka

Poltava

Merefa

KHARKOV

Andreyevka

Starobelsk

Don

Krasnograd

Izyum

Novomoskovsk

Stavyansk

Voroshilovgrad

Dnepropetrovsk

Pavlograd

Debaltsevo

Mius

Krasnoarmeyskoye

Novocherkassk

Dnieper

Taganrog

Rostov

Mariupol

Sea of
Azov

The Battles for Kharkov

The Soviet winter offensive of 1942 struck the Germans in the southern sector of the Eastern Front like a hammer blow, destroying a number of Romanian, Hungarian and Italian divisions, as well as the remnants of the German Sixth Army at Stalingrad. The battered Axis divisions were driven back towards the Dnieper, and at the same time the Soviet 3rd Guards Tank Army smashed its way towards the southwest. All seemed lost, as the newly formed I SS Panzer Corps took the field in the depths of the Russian winter.

During the second week in January 1943, Hitler ordered the newly formed I SS Panzer Corps moved to the Eastern Front with all possible speed. The *Leibstandarte*, *Das Reich* and *Totenkopf* Divisions, which formed the corps, had all been fully rebuilt and reformed as panzergrenadier divisions and were now stronger than they had ever been. The corps was an immensely powerful force and Hitler pinned his hoped-for stabilisation of the southern sector of the Eastern Front on it. The SS divisions were given top priority for transport by road and rail to the front, the first unit to arrive being the *Der Führer* Regiment from the *Das Reich* Division. The corps was to be formed up in a concentration area near the city of Kharkov and would be under the command of SS-Obergruppenführer Paul 'Papa' Hausser, initially holding an area between Volokomovka on the River Oskol and Kupiansk on the River Donetz.

The *Leibstandarte* was put into the line at Chegavayev, holding a sector over 12km (70 miles) long. The élite grenadiers of Hitler's Guard division held the

Right: A German artillery spotter on the Eastern Front in January 1943. By this time the Germans had lost hundreds of square kilometres of territory to the Red Army, and the whole of the southern front was in danger of collapsing. The arrival of I SS Panzer Corps helped stabilise the front.

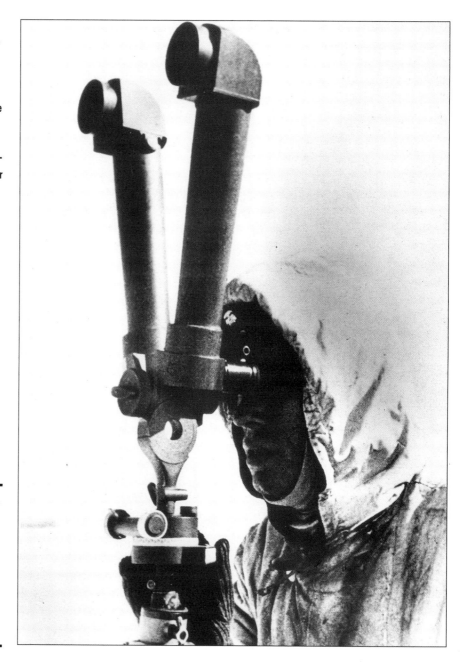

Throughout the first weeks of February the *Leibstandarte* repulsed numerous Soviet attacks

line firm while a host of retreating Italian, Hungarian and fragmented German units streamed westwards past them. Throughout the first week of February the *Leibstandarte* repulsed numerous Soviet attacks, inflicting serious losses on the enemy, who were somewhat shocked at running into strong SS units.

The Soviets then developed their push on Kharkov with a huge pincer movement, the southern arm of which punched its way through the area between the territory held firmly by the *Leibstandarte* and that held by the Army's 320th Infantry Division, while the northern arm battered its way through the Army units holding the area to the northeast of Belgorod on the River Donetz. It quickly became clear that sooner or later, Kharkov would become endangered by the Soviet advance and a decision would have to be made as to whether to defend the city and risk the destruction of the SS panzer corps, or to evacuate, reform and prepare a counterattack.

On 9 February the *Das Reich* Division began withdrawing slowly westwards, during blizzard conditions, in waist-deep snow, with many of its vehicles floundering in deep drifts. The SS grenadiers were subjected to frequent ambushes by Soviet troops using the blizzard as cover for their movements. On reaching the Donetz, where it was intended that the division would form a new defensive line, the Germans found that the Soviets had beaten them to it and *Das Reich* was forced to pull back farther west, to the area east of Kharkov itself.

THE RUSSIANS TIGHTEN THEIR GRIP

Meanwhile, the Soviets had forced a breach between the *Leibstandarte* and the 320th Infantry Division, and were pushing rapidly westwards. The Soviet flanks were weak, however, and a strong counterattack was mounted by the Waffen-SS, intending to slice through the salient created by the Soviet advance and link up with the 320th Infantry Division to the south. A battle group under the command of SS-Obergruppenführer 'Sepp' Dietrich was formed to make this three-pronged attack. On the right flank would be the Reconnaissance Battalion of the *Leibstandarte* led by Kurt Meyer, in the centre the *Der Führer* Regiment and the Panzer Regiment from the *Leibstandarte*, and on the left, 1st SS-Panzergrenadier Regiment from the *Leibstandarte*.

The *Leibstandarte*'s Reconnaissance Battalion succeeded in capturing Merefa, approaching the village under the cover of a blizzard. The snowdrifts covering the landscape meant off-road movement was almost impossible. Using the lead armoured personnel carriers like snow-ploughs, the battalion entered Merefa and ejected the Soviet occupants after fierce fighting. The *Der Führer* Regiment, meanwhile, had captured Borki, driving into the Soviet salient for almost 50km (30 miles) and effectively cutting off the Soviet spearhead units from VII Guards Cavalry Corps. The SS counter-strike soon lost contact with its own parent corps, however, and a battle for supremacy developed within the Soviet salient, while in the north the Germans were being pushed back towards Kharkov.

To the south, growing Soviet pressure had forced the Germans out of Zmiyov to the southwest of Merefa. Kharkov was in imminent danger of being surrounded. The German defences now no longer formed a continuous line, but rather scattered strongpoints, each in danger of being encircled by the enemy.

At Rogan, the troopers of the *Leibstandarte* held firm despite powerful Soviet attempts to oust them. The fighting was prolonged and bitter, with each side losing and retaking ground. For example, *Leibstandarte* Division lost the airfield at Rogan, then regained it during a counterattack. Needless to say, the losses suffered by both sides were high.

On 9 February the *Das Reich* Division began withdrawing slowly westwards, in blizzard conditions

One incident during these hectic and confused days brought the Knights Cross of the Iron Cross to a young officer who was to become one of the *Leibstandarte*'s best known and most highly decorated soldiers: SS-Sturmbannführer Joachim Peiper.

The battered 320th Infantry Division had been struggling westwards to reach German-held territory before it could be overtaken by the Soviet pursuers. The division, however, was burdened with over 1500 seriously wounded soldiers and was unable to make much speed. The divisional commander was unwilling to abandon his wounded, and so the division was by-passed by the fast-moving Soviet units and eventually surrounded.

The task of leading a relief column behind enemy lines to rescue the infantrymen fell to Peiper's 3rd Battalion, SS Panzergrenadier Regiment 2. This battalion was fully motorised and was equipped with armoured half-track personnel carriers rather than 'soft-skinned' trucks. Peiper's force crossed the Donetz south of Zmiyov and pushed eastwards for over 40km (25 miles) into Soviet held-territory, fending off all enemy attempts to halt it. Once contact was made with the 320th Infantry Division, the medics from Peiper's relief force toiled through the night to help treat the worst of the wounded. When morning dawned, the Waffen-SS troops formed an armoured shield around the divisional perimeter and escorted the battered Army units on their trek westwards towards the Donetz and relative safety.

On reaching the river at Udy, Peiper had hoped to cross at a small bridge which he thought was still in German hands. On arriving he discovered that the bridge had been attacked and destroyed by the Soviets, who had killed most of the German defenders, as well as many of the wounded. Peiper's men fell upon the Soviet troops with a fury and a vicious battle ensued. Peiper's men gave no quarter, and the bridge was retaken.

The Waffen-SS men then had to make the best repairs they could to the bridge, and a makeshift crossing was eventually prepared which would support the retreating infantry but would never be able to withstand the weight of Peiper's armoured vehicles. Peiper was thus forced to turn into Soviet-held territory again, travelling along the banks of the Donetz for several kilometres until he could find a suitable crossing place for his vehicles. Eventually, the relief force reached German-held territory safely, and without the loss of one of the invaluable armoured vehicles. 'Sepp' Dietrich recommended Peiper for the award of the Knights Cross on 7 March 1943, and a delighted Hitler approved the award just two days later.

At the bridge the Soviets had killed most of the defenders, as well as many of the wounded

On 13 February Alexeyevka was captured by the *Leibstandarte*, but the Germans themselves were quickly surrounded there. This was now the most easterly point around Kharkov still in German hands and the Soviets were determined to eliminate it. Although all Soviet attacks were beaten off for some time, this was only achieved with considerable losses. During these actions, SS-Obersturmführer Rudolf von Ribbentrop, son of the German Foreign Minister Joachim von Ribbentrop, was shot through the lung by a Soviet sniper. He resolutely refused to be evacuated for medical treatment, wishing to be shown no favouritism either as an officer or as the son of a high-ranking dignitary, stating that he would not accept evacuation unless all wounded NCOs and rankers were evacuated first, knowing of course that this was all but impossible. This sort of solidarity with his men made von Ribbentrop a popular and respected officer. (Rudolf von Ribbentrop was decorated for conspicuous gallantry in July 1943,

Above: The Kharkov battles of 1943 witnessed the arrival of the German Goliath, a remote-controlled demolition vehicle that carried a 100kg charge and was controlled by a cable up to 2000 metres in length. Unfortunately, it was vulnerable to small-arms fire.

Right: A Waffen-SS soldier asleep in his trench. This is one of a series of photographs taken by an SS war correspondent named Gottschmann, who was killed while covering the retaking of Kharkov. His camera was found several weeks after his death with the film still in it, hence the rather poor quality of the picture.

Hausser immediately shortened his defence lines, which were far too widely spread to be effective

during the Battle of Kursk). Meanwhile, an armoured relief force under the command of SS-Sturmbannführer Max Wünsche was battling its way past strong resistance in an attempt to relieve their beleaguered comrades.

In Kharkov, SS-Obergruppenführer Hausser had received orders from Hitler that the city be held at all costs. Hausser immediately shortened his defence lines, which were far too widely spread to be effective, but knew that any such moves would only be of limited value. Hausser was well aware that Kharkov was doomed, and gave orders for all military installations to be destroyed to avoid capture by the enemy when the city fell. The southern and eastern defences of the city itself were coming under severe pressure from enemy attacks, and the end would not be far away. Hausser was a realist and would not willingly see his panzer corps sacrificed in a pointless defence of a city he already knew was lost.

Meanwhile Kurt Meyer, or 'Panzermeyer' as he had become known, was still launching counterattacks against the Soviet units ranged against him, storming and capturing Bereka at considerable cost to the enemy. Alexeyevka itself was in danger of being overrun, however, and Meyer was forced to pull his troops back to defend it. The return of his force was sufficient to drive off the enemy troops who had penetrated into the town.

Meyer was well aware that the enemy was preparing a major assault, which was likely to succeed in crushing his small force, or at least finally driving it from Alexeyevka. His troops had suffered many casualties and were tired, hungry and low on ammunition. He therefore decided that his best bet lay in launching a pre-emptive strike against the Soviet units forming up to the east. This move caused panic among the Soviet troops. An attack from the beleaguered garrison of Alexeyevka was the last thing they expected and they fled in disarray. Meyer's battered battalion, however, was too weak to exploit its success. Nevertheless, as his troops pulled back into the town Wünsche's relief force finally appeared. Thus reinforced, Meyer and his troops were able to break out from Alexeyevka and rejoin the corps.

By the evening of 14 February, Soviet forces had penetrated into the suburbs of Kharkov and within 24 hours had also infiltrated the SS corps' rear areas. Elements of *Das Reich*, however, inflicted heavy losses on the enemy during a counterattack to the northwest of Kharkov, and this unexpected advance temporarily halted the Soviet push.

HAUSSER ABANDONS KHARKOV

Around noon on 15 February, Hausser once again requested permission for his corps to withdraw from the city to regroup. No reply had been received by 1250 hours so he took a unilateral decision to break out. At 1300 he advised army group headquarters of his intentions. At 1630 fresh orders arrived insisting that Kharkov must be held at all costs. Hausser bluntly replied that it was too late: 'It is already settled, Kharkov is being evacuated.' He would not countenance the destruction of his corps in a pointless attempt to save Kharkov.

Hausser's troops left the city in the nick of time. The corridor linking the city to German-held territory farther west was now only 1.5km (1 mile) wide at best. Hitler was beside himself with rage when he discovered that his orders had been disobeyed and flew personally to the headquarters of Army Group South at Zaporozhye to demand an explanation from Field Marshal von Manstein. His fury was caused as much by the realisation that Hausser's decision had been the correct one as by the fact that his order had been disobeyed.

The Soviets were overjoyed at their success in ousting the Fascist invaders from this strategically important city, but their own offensive was now rapidly

The Soviets were overjoyed at their success in ousting the Fascist invaders from this important city

running out of steam. The tenacious defence put up by the Germans had cost the lives of many thousands of their men, and those who survived were exhausted. Hitler insisted that the SS panzer corps be used to launch an immediate counterattack to regain Kharkov. The *Totenkopf* Division's arrival was imminent and the Führer maintained that, thus reinforced, the SS panzer corps should have no trouble in throwing the Soviets out. Von Manstein, however, wished to use I SS Panzer Corps as the upper arm of a huge pincer movement intent on encircling and destroying the Soviet armies as they approached the Dnieper. The lower arm of the pincer would be formed by the Army's Fourth Panzer Army under General Hermann Hoth.

MANSTEIN'S MASTER STROKE

Hitler continued to demand the immediate recapture of Kharkov as the first priority. Despite arguing his case with great vigour, von Manstein could see that it was unlikely that he would be able to sway Hitler from his views. He was just about to accept the inevitable when news arrived which changed things dramatically in his favour: the *Totenkopf* Division was completely bogged down by an unexpected thaw and could not arrive in time for Hitler's plan.

Eicke's *Totenkopf* Division had been making good progress when he decided that they would be able to move even faster if he pulled the division off the main roads and moved across country, the frozen, rock-hard soil providing good going for his heavy vehicles. This proved to be correct at first and the division moved rapidly towards its destination when, unexpectedly, temperatures rose and the frozen ground began to thaw. Within a short space of time, Eicke and his men found themselves floundering, their vehicles axle-deep in mud.

Hitler now reluctantly approved von Manstein's alternative and the German counterattack began almost immediately, with XLVIII Panzer Corps moving from its positions east of Dnepropetrovsk to seize bridgeheads over the Samara, ready to strike northwards into the areas to the rear of the Soviet 6th Army. Taken completely by surprise by this unexpected German push, the Soviets retreated northwards in near panic. German morale soared, with the troops pleased to be on the attack once again. The *Totenkopf* and *Das Reich* Divisions also began to advance. Their thrust, towards the southeast from their locations around Poltava, was delivered in atrocious conditions, the snow-covered landscape being shrouded in damp clinging fog, but they, too, smashed into the rear of the Soviet 6th Army.

During the opening moves of the counterattack, *Das Reich* had the task of striking to the west and southwest of the area around Krasnograd before pressing on to seize Peretschepino, which was swiftly overrun. On 20 February, the division received a personal message from Hitler detailing their tasks, thus boosting their morale even further. *Das Reich* struck out towards Pavlograd on 22 February, supported by Luftwaffe ground-attack Stukas. The fully motorised Waffen-SS troops, equipped with the latest weaponry, found themselves doing battle with Soviet cavalry units, equipped not with armoured vehicles but mounted on horseback and carrying sabres. While these formidable characters

Within a short space of time Eicke and his men were floundering, their vehicles in axle-deep mud

Left: Two Waffen-SS soldiers, one of them a signaller, photographed during I SS Panzer Corps's offensive in February 1943. The operation began in appalling weather — fog, snow and intense cold — but Hausser's troops began well and kept up a cracking pace.

So rapid were the German advances that a number of 'friendly fire' incidents occurred

may well have struck terror into the hearts of defenceless infantry, they were no match for the Waffen-SS troops and were swept aside with heavy losses as the German advance continued. Pavlograd fell to the SS on 24 February. Indeed, so rapid were the German advances that a number of 'friendly fire' incidents occurred when German troops attacked their own side. In one such incident,

Right: The *Totenkopf* Division rolls into Kharkov, March 1943. This was one of the division's greatest triumphs, but not for its commander. Theodor Eicke had been killed only a few days earlier.

elements of the *Das Reich* Division came under fire from the tanks of the *Totenkopf*'s Panzer Regiment.

Having then linked up, *Das Reich* and the *Totenkopf* swung to the northeast and ran parallel to the Soviet lines of retreat, hammering into the flanks of the fleeing enemy. Many of the Soviet units began to run out of fuel, and the Waffen-SS troops encountered long columns of abandoned trucks, tanks and other vehicles, in full working order, which the Soviets had simply left behind. Unfortunately for them, the Germans had despatched SS *Totenkopf* Panzergrenadier Regiment 1, under SS-Obersturmbannführer Otto Baum, together with elements from the *Das Reich* Division, to race ahead and cut off their escape. What followed over the next few days was little more than a slaughter as the powerful SS units wreaked havoc among the demoralised enemy. The Luftwaffe, too, played its part. Everywhere enemy troops were spotted, the Luftwaffe's dive-bombers would join the panzers to take their toll.

Two entire Soviet armies were destroyed, and over 600 enemy tanks were either knocked out or captured, most of them the latest T-34 models. So many were taken that the *Das Reich* Division was able to add a full tank detachment of recovered T-34s to its panzer regiment. Over 400 artillery pieces and 600 anti-tank guns were also captured. The tally of prisoners was not quite so impressive. Though the Germans succeeded in surrounding and putting out of action the two Soviet armies, the ring they formed around the hapless Soviets was not without gaps, so great was the area involved. Although they had to abandon their heavy equipment, many Soviet troops were able to make good their escape on foot. Around 9000 were taken prisoner and 23,000 killed.

These battles were not without Germans losses, too. For example, the *Totenkopf* Division lost its commander, SS-Obergruppenführer Theodor Eicke. On 26 February the divisional HQ temporarily lost contact with its panzer regiment. Unable to raise the regiment by radio and beginning to feel some concern, Eicke decided to investigate personally and called up one of the division's scout aircraft. After some searching, he spotted elements of the regiment in a small village and ordered his pilot to land nearby. Eicke had not seen that the adjacent village was still occupied by Soviet troops and, as his aircraft came in to land between the two villages, it was met by a hail of enemy fire and crashed, bursting into flames. Immediate attempts by the panzer regiment to rescue Eicke were beaten. On the next morning an assault group was formed, with armoured support, and the charred remains of Eicke, his adjutant and the pilot were then recovered.

On the next morning an assault group was formed, and Eicke's remains were recovered

Eicke's death came as a great shock to his men. Throughout his career he had many enemies, his abrasive manner endearing him to few of his SS colleagues or Army counterparts. A brutal man, he had nevertheless been popular with his troops by sharing the privations of the common soldier, living in the same cold, damp, filthy trenches and eating the same meagre rations. SS *Totenkopf* Infantry Regiment 3, later to be redesignated SS Panzergrenadier Regiment 6, was named *Theodor Eicke* in his memory, and given the distinction of wearing a cuffband bearing his the former divisional commander's name.

Despite the battering its units were taking, STAVKA, the Soviet High Command, moved further troops into the sector, sending an armoured corps into the area south of Kharkov to block any German moves towards the city. In fact, these fresh Soviet troops walked straight into a German trap. The Red Army units facing the *Totenkopf* and *Das Reich* to their south, suddenly found that Hausser had moved the *Leibstandarte* into their rear, blocking any retreat. The

Totenkopf and *Das Reich* began to push the enemy inexorably northwards against defensive positions rapidly established by the *Leibstandarte*. The *Leibstandarte* infantry had considerable armoured support, including the division's new heavy battalion equipped with formidable Tiger tanks. The Soviets were totally crushed and the last major obstacle before the gates of Kharkov was removed.

I SS Panzer Corps and Fourth Panzer Army now linked up for the assault on Kharkov itself. The *Leibstandarte* moved off from Staroverovka on 4 March and forced a bridgehead over the Mscha at Valki. On the division's right flank was *Das Reich* and to the left, the *Totenkopf*. The latter, meanwhile, had captured Stary Mertschyk and pushed on to reach Olshany, which fell on 9 March while, by the evening of the same day, the *Leibstandarte* had taken Peretdinaga and Polevaya, while *Das Reich* found itself struggling through atrocious terrain, making slower progress. Despite this, advance units from *Das Reich* reached the outskirts of Kharkov on 9 March.

I SS PANZER CORPS RETAKES KHARKOV

Hausser had originally planned to have Kharkov taken by a three-pronged attack. The *Leibstandarte* was to have hit the city from the north and the *Totenkopf* from the northwest, while *Das Reich* swung around the north of the city and attacked down its eastern side towards Smiyev. This latter move was now scrapped, and *Das Reich* was instead ordered to attack Kharkov from the west.

When *Das Reich* first reached the outskirts of the city the defence was not very determined, but soon resistance stiffened dramatically. A battle group from the *Deutschland* Regiment, for example, met fanatical opposition and its advance only continued with great difficulty. To the north, SS-Standartenführer Fritz Witt, with SS Panzergrenadier Regiment 1, battered his way into Kharkov along the main Belgorod-Kharkov highway. On Witt's right was SS Panzergrenadier Regiment 2 under SS-Standartenführer Theodor 'Teddi' Wisch. On the left flank, 'Panzermeyer' decided to take his reconnaissance battalion off the road and through the woods north of the city to cut the road from Kharkov to Liptsy.

While his comrades made good progress in their advance into Kharkov, Meyer soon found himself wondering, as his armoured vehicles toiled through the great forest, if his had been a good move after all. Then, spotting sled tracks, he decided to try following them. Almost immediately he began to experience further problems negotiating the narrow track. Once he was committed to it the track soon became too narrow for vehicles to be turned round, and the column was forced to stop on more than one occasion to manhandle vehicles which were in danger of getting stuck. Meyer left his subordinates to cope with all this and set off to catch up with the lead elements, commanded by SS-Obersturm-führer Gerd Bremer. Eventually the track led Meyer into a large clearing, where Bremer and his men had taken cover.

On the main road at the foot of the sloped clearing, were thousands of Red Army soldiers, along with artillery and tanks. Meyer and Bremer had command of just over 20 soldiers and a handful of light vehicles. Clearly, the Germans would have to keep their heads down and wait for the remainder of their force

When *Das Reich* first reached the outskirts of the city the defence was not very determined

Left: Waffen-SS infantry in recaptured Kharkov. This victory further enhanced the reputation of the SS in Hitler's eyes, and convinced him, wrongly, that the Waffen-SS could retrieve any situation on the Eastern Front. While they were busy congratulating themselves, the Führer and his henchmen seemed to forget that the Eastern Front was 470,000 men below establishment.

to catch up. Messages were sent back to warn the oncoming column of what lay ahead. Suddenly, the Germans heard the sound of approaching aircraft, identifiable to the experienced soldiers as Stuka dive-bombers.

The Soviet column was ripped apart by German bombs and cannon fire. Meyer saw his opportunity and immediately ordered his tiny group into the attack, just as the first of the German tanks began to appear. To the panicked Soviets, it seemed as though they had walked straight into an ambush, and many began to raise their hands in surrender while others, unsuccessfully, tried to flee.

Leaving a few men to guard the hundreds of prisoners, Meyer's column set off at full speed towards Kharkov, seeking to maximise the element of surprise. The northern outskirts of the city were reached without incident, the rapid progress of the Germans being maintained until the column came to a halt at a disused brickworks on the edge of the city.

Meyer's column set off at full speed towards Kharkov, seeking to maximise the element of surprise

Right: 'How pleased we all are with our success... We have thrown them back and Kharkov is German once again. We have shown the Ivans that we can withstand their terrible winter. It can hold no fear for us again.' (*Totenkopf* trooper after Kharkov).

By dawn the next day the entire force was once again regrouped and ready to resume the advance

Meyer and his men returned to the site of the earlier engagement, to find masses of Soviet prisoners guarded by just a few grenadiers. The enemy troops seemed happy to be out of the fighting. Over the next few hours the remainder of Meyer's battalion arrived, and by dawn the next day the entire force was once again regrouped and ready to resume its advance towards Kharkov.

This time the enemy tanks near to the brickworks were no match for the Germans and were all driven off or destroyed. By now shortage of fuel was becoming a major problem for Meyer. Further progress was impossible and, on 11 March, he ordered his group to dig in, choosing, of all places, a graveyard. Unknown to Meyer, his force was sited alongside the main escape route from the city, and over the next few hours the Waffen-SS grenadiers threw back countless Soviet attempts to overrun them.

Soon afterwards a fuel truck managed to make its way through to Meyer's group, bringing with it reports that the road to the north of the city had been cut. Meyer's escape route, should this become needed, was gone. There was also the good news that Fritz Witt's regiment had penetrated into the centre of the city and seized Red Square. Meyer's only course of action was to press onwards into Kharkov, but this was met by ever more fanatical opposition as Soviet units caught in the city fought to battle their way out to the north. At the same time as Meyer and his force were battling to hold back Soviet units intent on escaping capture, the *Das Reich* Division was forcing its way into the west of the city, reaching the main railway station in the centre of Kharkov on 12 March in the face of heavy opposition. Meyer and his reconnaissance group to the north of the city were relieved by SS-Sturmbannführer Peiper and his panzergrenadier battalion. Joining forces, they battled their way through to the east and southeastern sectors, flushing out the remaining Soviet defenders. Once Kharkov had been secured, Peiper and his battalion raced to the north, attacking Belgorod, which fell to him on 18 March 1943, and establishing contact with the Army's élite *Grossdeutschland* Division.

The *Totenkopf*, meanwhile, had swung around the north of the city, its panzers eliminating the Soviet units which had cut the Kharkov-Belgorod road, before swinging to the southeast and capturing the Donetz crossings at Tshuguyev. For the next few days the *Totenkopf* was obliged to fend off Russian units fleeing from Kharkov, and counterattacks from fresh Soviet formations to the east. In these actions the Soviet 25th Guards Rifle Division was annihilated.

The battle for Kharkov had been a great victory for the Waffen-SS, and its standing in Hitler's eyes rose even further. The victory was not without its costs, though, over 11,500 Waffen-SS troops being killed in action. Many of these casualties were in the city itself, which only fell after three days of intense close-quarter combat.

From the battles in and around Kharkov, the *Leibstandarte* emerged with 13 Knights Crosses to its credit, *Das Reich* 10 and the *Totenkopf* six. Many of those who were so honoured would go on to become some of the best known of all Waffen-SS soldiers, their future careers marked by further awards for gallantry and leadership. Men such as SS-Standartenführer Albert Frey, SS-Standartenführer Max Hansen, SS-Brigadeführer Hugo-Kraas, SS-Obersturmbannführer Max Wünsche, and SS-Obersturmbannführer Rudi Sandig of the *Leibstandarte*. From *Das Reich*, Heinz Harmel would go on to reach the rank of SS-Brigadeführer and command the élite *Frundsberg* Panzer Division, and add the coveted Oak Leaves and Swords to the Knights Cross won at Kharkov in the winter of 1943.

If the victory at Kharkov had served to reinforce the reputation of the Waffen-SS for steadfastness in defence and fearless gallantry in the attack, it also had the effect of convincing Hitler that in certain circumstances, the Waffen-SS were the only troops capable of carrying out the most dangerous and difficult of missions. Thus, in the two years of war to come, the Waffen-SS would increasingly be depended on to procure their Führer the victories he desired. The weary SS grenadiers would soon be preparing for one of the greatest battles in history, and one which would certainly be the turning point of World War II: Kursk.

Below: One of the many Waffen-SS soldiers who won the Knights Cross for their efforts at Kharkov, SS-Hauptsturmführer Heinz Macher, *Das Reich* Division.

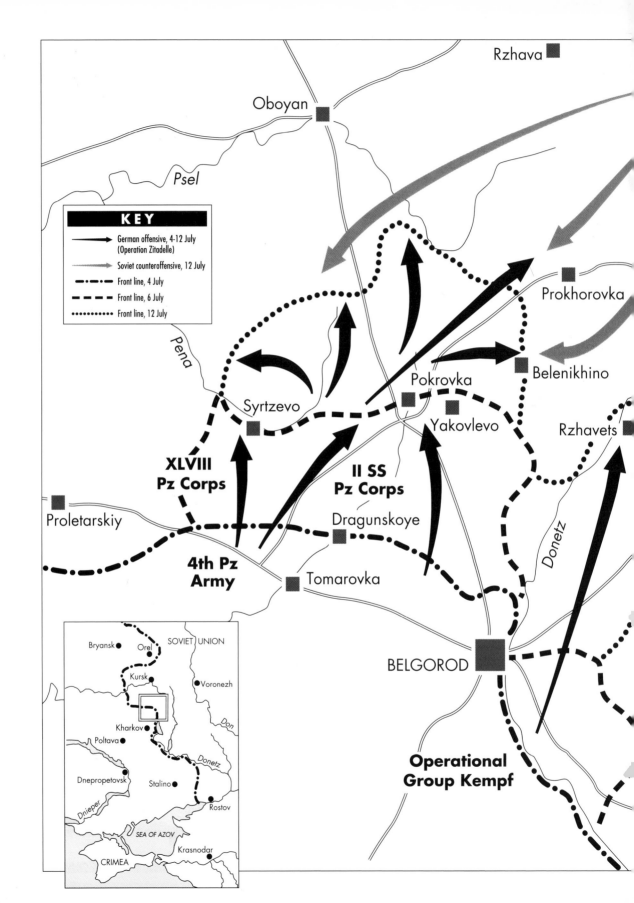

Rzhava

Oboyan

Psel

KEY

→ German offensive, 4–12 July
(Operation Zitadelle)

→ Soviet counteroffensive, 12 July

·–·–· Front line, 4 July

– – – Front line, 6 July

·········· Front line, 12 July

Pena

Prokhorovka

Pokrovka

Belenikhino

Syrtzevo

Yakovlevo

Rzhavets

**XLVIII
Pz Corps**

**II SS
Pz Corps**

Donetz

**4th Pz
Army**

Dragunskoye

Proletarskiy

Tomarovka

BELGOROD

**Operational
Group Kempf**

Bryansk ●   Orel ●   SOVIET UNION

Kursk ●   Voronezh ●

Don

Kharkov ●

Poltava ●   *Donetz*

Dnepropetrovsk ●   Stalino ●

Dnieper   Rostov ●

SEA OF AZOV

CRIMEA   Krasnodar ●

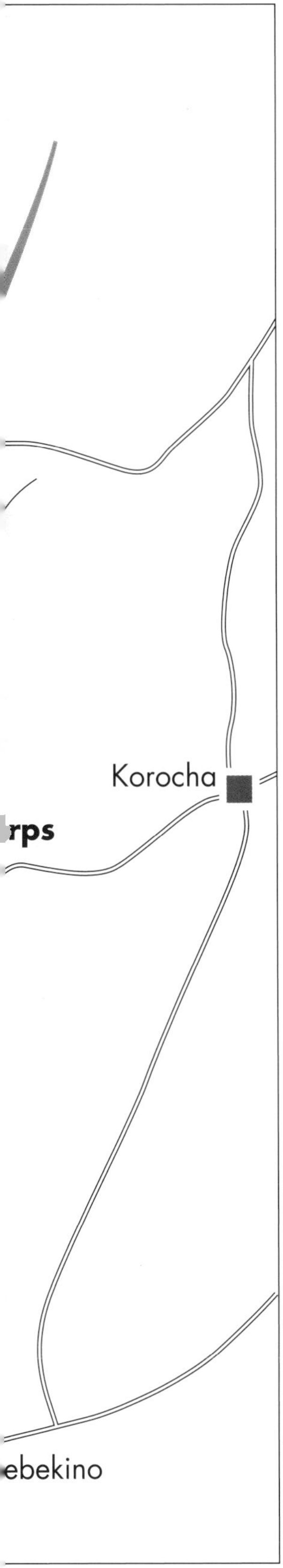

Korocha

rps

ebekino

The Battle of Kursk

By July 1943, the Eastern Front was dominated by a huge Soviet-occupied salient around the city of Kursk. Hitler was determined to destroy it. The stage was set for one of the most savage battles of World War II and the greatest clash of armour in history. Into this maelstrom were thrown the crack divisions of the Waffen-SS.

Hitler's motivation in deciding to extinguish the Kursk salient, bulging into the German lines, was threefold. Politically, it would give the Germans the initiative once again in the East, boost morale among his east European allies and, Hitler hoped, encourage Turkey to enter the war on Germany's side. Militarily it would dramatically shorten the length of front the German armies were forced to defend, the bulge being just 160km (100 miles) across its base. A successful offensive would eliminate up to 15 Soviet armies and net hundreds of thousands of enemy prisoners, who could be used as forced labour for the benefit of the German war effort. German troops would then be released from the Eastern Front to face the anticipated Allied invasion of southern Europe.

Hitler's enthusiasm for the offensive was not matched by corresponding approval from all of his generals. Two of Germany's finest soldiers, Field Marshal Erich von Manstein and General Heinz Guderian, argued against the plan, suggesting that it would be better for Germany to allow the Soviets to go on the offensive, withdraw gradually to allow them to over-extend themselves, and then hit back with full fury. This would repeat the success that had occurred at Kharkov (see previous chapter). Hitler would hear none of it, though, and insisted that planning for the offensive, to be codenamed Operation 'Citadel' ('Zitadelle' in German), be carried forward with all haste.

Facing the German forces were the Soviet armies of the Central Front, under General Rokossovsky, and the Voronezh Front, commanded by General Vatutin. Airborne support came from the 2nd and 16th Air Armies under Air Marshals Rudenko and Krasovski respectively.

Quite apart from the massive strength in the salient itself – 11 entire armies – the Soviets had a massive third force, the Steppe Front, commanded by Colonel-General Konev, held in reserve. Reserve air support was provided by 5th Air Army under Colonel General Goryunov. All in all, the Soviets could field over 1,300,000 troops, with 3300 tanks, 20,000 pieces of artillery and 2000 aircraft.

GERMAN STRENGTH AT KURSK

Facing this awesome might were Army Group South, under the command of Field Marshal von Manstein, and Army Group Centre, under the command of Field Marshal von Kluge. Army Group South comprised Panzer Group *Kempf*, commanded by General Kempf, and the Fourth Panzer Army under Colonel General Hoth. Panzer Group *Kempf* fielded XI Corps under General Raus, comprising the 106th and 320th Infantry Divisions; XLII Corps under General Mattenklott, with the 39th, 161st and 282nd Infantry Divisions; and III Panzer Corps under General Breith, comprising the 6th, 7th and 19th Panzer Divisions and 168th Infantry Division. Hoth's Fourth Panzer Army comprised II SS Panzer Corps under SS-Obergruppenführer Paul Hausser, made up of the 1st SS Panzer Division *Leibstandarte*, 2nd SS Panzer Division *Das Reich* and 3rd SS Panzer Division *Totenkopf*; XLVIII Panzer Corps under General von Knobelsdorff, with the 3rd and 11th Panzer Divisions, 167th Infantry Division and Panzergrenadier Division *Grossdeutschland*; and LII Corps under General Ott, the with 57th, 255th and 332nd Infantry Divisions. Air support was provided by General Dessloch's Air Fleet IV.

To the north, Field Marshal von Kluge's forces consisted of Colonel-General Model's Ninth Army, XLI Panzer Corps under General Harpe, XLVI Panzer Corps under General Zorn, XXIII Corps under General Freissner, and XLVII Panzer Corps under General Lemelsen. Air support was provided by Colonel-General von Greim's Air Fleet VI.

The total German force was some 900,000 soldiers, with around 2700 tanks and 10,000 guns. Around 2000 Luftwaffe aircraft would supply air cover. Hausser's Waffen-SS represented less than 10 per cent of the German total, but

> **The total German force was some 900,000 soldiers, with around 2700 tanks and 10,000 guns**

would play a disproportionately large part in the fighting. In view of the fact that at Kharkov the Germans had taken on and defeated a Soviet force eight times its own size, the forces opposing each other at Kursk might have seemed reasonably well matched.

Most of the German tanks used at Kharkov were of the old Mk IV type, or even updated versions of the even older Mk III. This would still be the case at Kursk four months later. A number of the more powerful Mk VI Tiger types had been used at Kharkov and more of these were now available, but the Germans put their greatest hopes on the newest of their tanks, the Mk V Panther medium tank, which would be making its operational debut at Kursk. Also to be employed were some examples of the Ferdinand assault gun, which was based on a version of the Tiger chassis.

Above: One of Germany's finest armoured strategists, General Heinz Guderian (second from right), inspects a Tiger heavy tank of the *Leibstandarte* Division in the days prior to the Kursk offensive.

Unfortunately for the Germans, so extensive were the movements required to assemble their armies in preparation for this great offensive, that the Soviets could hardly fail to detect the enemy build-up. As well as the physical movement of troops and equipment, radio traffic increased dramatically. Intelligence sources provided further information, some of it passed on to the Soviets by the British, from the results of their code-breaking operations.

Stalin had been keen for the Red Army to take the offensive, which would have suited the plan of action envisaged by von Manstein and Guderian. His high command and his generals in the field, however, persuaded him that the better course of action would be to prepare first-class defensive systems, draw the German armies into the salient, allow them to bleed themselves white attempting to smash through the extensive Soviet defence works, then counterattack.

The Red Army drafted in around 300,000 local civilians, who were put to work on producing the most extensive defensive systems ever created for a single battle. Eight lines of anti-tank ditches running for a total of 5600km (3500 miles) were constructed. Over half a million mines were laid, skilfully arranged to channel any attacking vehicles into carefully prepared killing grounds covered by thick belts of anti-tank weapons.

The Red Army drafted in around 300,000 local civilians to work on the defences

THE OPENING MOVES

The Soviets assumed that the Germans would concentrate their attack on the northern part of the salient. Therefore, three Soviet armies were crammed into a defence front just 80km (50 miles) wide. Almost 4000 anti-tank and 4400 anti-personnel mines were laid along each kilometre of the front, the defensive belt stretching back for several kilometres. The Soviet assumptions were wrong, however. The German offensive would in fact be more powerful on the southern side of the salient, and in the spearhead, as ever, would be the armoured formations of the Waffen-SS: the *Leibstandarte*, *Das Reich* and the *Totenkopf*.

In the northern sector the offensive began at 0430 on 5 July 1943, when Army Group Centre launched a massed artillery barrage intended to soften up the enemy positions. When the barrage ended and the German troops began their assault, they found the Soviet defences far from being smashed, and the Red Army units very much alive and kicking. German troops immediately came under heavy mortar and gun fire. When they tried to take cover in the tall grass prevalent in this area they found that the terrain was saturated with anti-personnel mines. German losses were heavy. By the end of the first day German troops on the western flank had advanced only a few kilometres and their push was already beginning to bog down. A little to the east German armoured units had effected a slightly more successful penetration of the Soviet defences, with the 20th Panzer division and 6th Infantry Division pushing into the salient to a depth of around eight kilometres (five miles). Despite having local air superiority, the Germans were also suffering badly from enemy air attacks. Although the heavy Tiger tanks and Ferdinand tank destroyers were able to wreak havoc upon the lighter Soviet T-34s, an alarming attrition rate was suffered by German armour, due mainly to Soviet minefields.

The strength and tenacity of the Soviet defenders had come as a nasty shock to the Germans. The Soviet assumption that the main German push would come from the north, and the subsequent concentration of their defences there, led to Army Group Centre meeting far greater resistance than had been anticipated. Progress was very slow and very costly. The furthest penetration achieved on the northern sector during the entire offensive was only 16km (10 miles). The distance from the frontline to Kursk, the objective, was around 80km (50 miles).

In the south, the Soviets had learned from the interrogation of POWs that the German attack was imminent and launched their own pre-emptive artillery barrage, from over 600 guns. The German artillery then responded with a barrage of incredible intensity along the entire front. The weight of shells fired during this barrage actually exceeded the entire weight fired by the German artillery during the whole of the Polish and French campaigns! Luftwaffe air support was also far more effective in the south. This was caused in part by a Soviet attempting to launch a pre-emptive strike on German air bases. The approaching Soviet aircraft were detected by German radar and intercepted.

Hoth's Fourth Panzer Army had as its initial objective the town of Oboyan. The left flank of the attack was covered by XLVIII Panzer Corps, and the

Above: Horse-drawn German supplies are moved up to the front on the eve of 'Citadel'. The offensive was originally scheduled to take place in mid-May, but Hitler insisted that it be postponed in order to equip his armoured units with new Panther and Tiger tanks. However, this also aided the enemy, as Manstein stated: 'the longer one waited, the more armour the Russians would have.'

Right: A German soldier takes the opportunity to write letters to loved ones far away before the fighting begins. Unknown to him, he is about to attack the strongest and deepest defence lines in the world.

Hoth decided that the Soviet reserves would have to be dealt with to avoid putting the German flank at risk

German units made good initial progress, with the 3rd and 11th Panzer Divisions and Panzergrenadier Division *Grossdeutschland* swiftly overcoming the first lines of the Soviet defences around Cherkasskoye by the end of the first day. This success was not without its costs, however. For example, 10 Panzer Brigade, equipped with the new Panthers, ran into extensive Soviet minefields and lost 36 of its tanks.

Hoth decided that the Soviet reserves would have to be dealt with sooner rather than later to avoid putting the right flank of the German advance at risk.

After breaking through the Soviet defence lines, therefore, he ordered that an attack towards the northeast be launched, to eliminate the enemy reserves. The task of smashing the enemy reserves fell to Hausser's II SS Panzer Corps, with its massive armoured spearhead consisting of nearly 350 tanks and 200 self-propelled guns. Each of the SS divisions had its own integral Tiger unit, making the SS Panzer Corps one of the most powerful weapons in the German arsenal.

Hausser's troops set off at 0400 on 5 July, passing easily through the first sets of minefields, which had been efficiently swept by the SS engineers. The point of the German advance was taken by the massive Tiger tanks, flanked by the only slightly lighter Panthers. The Panthers were in turn flanked by the standard Mk IV and Mk III types, as well as the Sturmgeschützen (assault guns). This armoured wedge, or Panzerkeil, swiftly smashed its way through the enemy defences, and by the end of the first day Hausser's men had penetrated up to 19km (12 miles) into the salient.

THE *TOTENKOPF* ADVANCES

The *Totenkopf* Division, on the right flank of II SS Panzer Corps, slammed into the Soviet 52nd Guards Division which was overwhelmed after bitter fighting and, by the end of the first day, had captured the village of Yakovlevo, taking the command post of the Soviet 69th Army with numerous high-ranking staff officers. The division continued its rapid advance on the second day, penetrating almost 32km (20 miles) into the salient and crossing the main Belgorod-Oboyan road. Soviet resistance stiffened, however, and progress began to slow.

The *Totenkopf* continued its slow but steady progress on the next day. By then the division had increased its penetration of the salient up to 48km (30 miles) or so, cutting several vital road and rail links. The *Totenkopf* received important assistance from ground-attack aircraft, including the tank-busting Stukas of Ground-Attack Wing 2 Immelmann (the Stukas having had 37mm anti-tank cannon slung under each wing, thus turning obsolete aircraft into potent tank killers). By this stage in the battle the Soviet 6th Guards Army had been split in two. For the drive to continue, however, the *Totenkopf* had to be released from its task of covering the corps' flank. It was therefore replaced in this role by the 167th Infantry Division from the Army. The *Totenkopf* troops spent most of 8 July awaiting the arrival of their replacements.

At this point General Vatutin ordered II Guards Tank Corps to launch a counterattack on the Germans from a point to the northeast of Belgorod. The line of attack would have carried this powerful enemy force straight into the flanks of the *Totenkopf* Division and II SS Panzer Corps. However, the Soviet move was detected and a massed attack by Luftwaffe bomber and fighter-bomber aircraft decimated the Soviet force before it could reach the *Totenkopf*'s positions.

On 9 July the *Totenkopf* began to smash its way through yet more Soviet defence lines, which began crumbling within hours of the German onslaught. On 10 July the division reached the River Psel. The Soviets were now becoming greatly alarmed by the extent of the German advance, and so the decision was made to bring the 5th Guards Tank Army and two tank brigades from their

On 9 July the *Totenkopf* began to smash its way through yet more Soviet defence lines

reserve locations to the northeast of Prokhorovka to smash the German arm—oured spearhead once and for all. To the south of the *Totenkopf*, the *Leibstandarte* Division had set off on 5 July making fast initial progress, but once it had smash—ed through the first line of Soviet defences, resistance began to stiffen and the advance slowed. The troops of Hitler's bodyguard division, however, consid—ering themselves the élite of the élite, would allow no obstacle to stand in their way, and redoubled their efforts.

On 5 July SS–Obersturmführer Georg Karck, in command of 9 Company, SS Panzergrenadier Regiment 2, at the head of his men stormed two strongly

The *Leibstandarte* had set off on 5 July, making fast initial progress

Right: 5 July 1943 – the assault begins. A member of the *Leib-standarte* wrote on this first day: 'I saw our leading Tiger sections roar away and vanish almost completely in the peculiar silver-grey tall grass which is a feature of the area.'

defended Soviet positions on high ground overlooking the surrounding terrain. During the battle which ensued, Karck personally neutralised five Soviet bunkers using only his machine pistol and hand grenades. Once taken, the positions were successfully defended against Soviet attempts to retake them. Although himself wounded in the head, Karck once again led his men in driving the enemy back. For his distinguished leadership and personal gallantry, Karck was decorated with the Knights Cross of the Iron Cross on 3 August.

Karck was typical of the type of officer to be found in the *Leibstandarte* at that time. Although he was a distinguished member of the premier Waffen-SS unit, he nevertheless hated politics, and particularly despised the so called 'Golden Pheasants' of the Nazi Party. (Party functionaries, so called because of their pre-dilection for gaudy uniforms bedecked with gilt braided insignia.) When he received home leave after the Kursk offensive ended, Karck knew that the local Party officials would have laid on a civic welcome for him, in which he knew he would have to endure the long and pompous speeches they loved to deliver. He thus got off his train at an earlier stop and made his way home across country, leaving the assembled dignitaries to meet an empty carriage. This brave and popular leader was killed in a motoring accident on the Normandy front when his vehicle collided one night with a truck carrying a full load of munitions.

Above: A *Leibstandarte* Panzer IV at Kursk. The division made good progress on the first day of the offensive, overrunning the first Russian defensive belt with ease. But then massed enemy artillery fire and minefields halted progress. On the second day the Waffen-SS met determined resistance, including Red Army battalions made up of civilians without weapons, who nevertheless mounted human-wave attacks.

Above: Armoured personnel carriers and soft-skinned vehicles of the *Leibstandarte* Division photographed during the Kursk battles. The first day of the offensive cost the division over 600 killed and wounded, the next day another 450 more. Worse, Russian resistance was intensifying.

The battles around Kursk also saw the rise to fame of a young officer who was destined to become the most successful tank commander in history, SS-Untersturmführer Michael Wittmann. Wittmann's Tiger unit was in fact initially deployed in support of the panzergrenadier regiment which contained Karck's company. Wittmann and his crew knocked out eight enemy tanks on the first day of the offensive. When they were finally able to snatch some rest at the end of the day, Wittmann found that one of his crew members, who was supposed to be on watch, had fallen asleep, utterly exhausted. Instead of reprimanding him, Wittmann simply sent him off to rest and took over guard duty himself. By the time the offensive was over, Wittmann had destroyed 30 enemy tanks and 26 anti-tank guns.

On 5 July SS-Unterscharführer Kurt Sametreiter, serving as a platoon leader in the heavy company of the *Leibstandarte*'s tank-destroyer battalion, located a

large Soviet armoured force lying in a depression near the village of Stalinsk. Knowing that sooner or later this powerful force would set off to attack, Sametreiter skilfully positioned his four heavy anti-tank guns to cover the exit from the village and waited. At dawn the sound of the Soviet tanks drew nearer. Approaching Sametreiter's tiny force of four guns, with their crews and a handful of infantrymen, were 40 heavy tanks.

Sametreiter's guns opened fire from the flanks of the enemy force. Working as fast as humanly possible to reload, aim and fire before the Soviets spotted their positions, the Waffen-SS gunners knocked out 24 tanks before the remainder fled. This was not the end of the matter, however, as an infantry force about two battalions strong next advanced on Sametreiter's positions. Undeterred, the daredevil NCO gathered his gun crews and his small infantry support unit and, with machine pistols and hand grenades, launched an immediate attack on the approaching enemy troops, throwing them back. Sametreiter was decorated with the Knights Cross of the Iron Cross on 31 July 1943 for this considerable achievement. He survived the war and is still alive today.

WAFFEN-SS LOSSES

Many such acts of distinguished leadership and courage were carried out by soldiers of the *Leibstandarte*, and indeed the other Waffen-SS divisions during the opening days of Kursk, but such successes were offset by considerable losses. On the first day of the offensive, for example, the *Leibstandarte* lost 97 men killed in action and 522 wounded. By the second day of the offensive, the *Leibstandarte*'s total losses had risen to 181 killed and 906 wounded. Some 10 per cent of the division's personnel had become casualties in just two days of fighting. This was, of course, nothing to the casualty rates being suffered by the Soviet units, some of which had been effectively wiped out. The Soviets, however, seemed to have limitless amounts of manpower from which to make up losses, a luxury not available to the Germans.

Despite their losses, the Waffen-SS divisions continued to advance even as the Army units to the flanks on Hausser's II SS Panzer Corps became bogged down. Tank losses were also very serious for, by the end of the third day, the corps had only 40 Panthers left from a starting total of 200.

The Tiger tank was proving to be a formidable weapon, with its ability to destroy Soviet tanks well before they could close in to a range at which their own weapons would be effective against the Tiger's massive armour. Its newer companion, the Panther, although displaying tremendous future potential, was

Despite their losses, the Waffen-SS divisions continued to advance, but the Army got bogged down

still being dogged by mechanical teething troubles. Even worse than the Panther's problems were those of the Ferdinand, a massive tank destroyer, bigger even than the Tiger, and with awesome destructive capabilities. Lack of foresight had led to its designers failing to arm the Ferdinand with a machine gun for close defence work. Some 90 of these monsters served with Army Group Centre in the northern wing of the offensive. Their crews soon found that, once these behemoths had overrun the Soviet positions, they were easy meat for enemy 'tank-hunting' teams, who picked them off with satchel charges, or Molotov cocktails. It is said that desperate Ferdinand crews were reduced to trying to shoot individual Soviet infantrymen with their main 8.8cm guns.

On 7 July, the *Leibstandarte* pushed forward once again with Teterevino and Oboyan as its main objectives. Here Wittmann added seven more enemy tanks and 19 anti-tank guns of the Soviet 29th Anti-Tank Brigade to his growing tally. However, as the Waffen-SS Panzers pushed on towards Psyolknee the enemy launched a powerful armoured counterattack.

THE ADVANCE TO PROKHOROVKA

During this action, SS-Oberscharführer Franz Staudegger, a 20-year-old Tiger tank commander in 13 Company of SS Panzer Regiment 1, found himself facing 50-60 T-34s which were attempting to manoeuvre into the rear of the regiment. Without a second's hesitation, Staudegger gave battle to this huge force. Working at a furious pace to reload and fire the deadly 8.8cm cannon of their Tiger, Staudegger and his crew blasted huge gaps in the enemy ranks. When the Tiger's ammunition racks finally lay empty, 22 T-34s lay blazing on the battlefield. The remaining T-34s, which were also now being attacked by German troops armed with Teller mines, beat a hasty retreat. Staudegger was immediately recommended for the Knights Cross, which was granted on 10 July 1943.

The 2nd Battalion of Panzer Regiment 1, under the command of SS-Sturmbannführer Martin Gross, had, meanwhile, destroyed around 90 T-34s in three hours of battle. In addition, 30 more enemy tanks had been taken out by SS Panzergrenadier tank-hunting groups. The area around Teterevino had become a veritable graveyard of T-34s.

On the *Leibstandarte*'s right flank, *Das Reich* was facing determined resistance. Although the division's assault troops had infiltrated enemy lines prior to the launch of the offensive, and were thus quickly able to neutralise the first lines of the enemy defences, the Soviet barrage which followed the initial German advance caught many of the division's second wave, causing many casualties. One problem was that the panzergrenadiers had to toil forward through terrain turned into a boggy morass by heavy rains. The soft ground also delayed their heavy support vehicles, leaving them without any tank support.

Das Reich's principal target on the first day of the offensive was to attack and capture the village of Beresov. Supported by Stuka dive-bombers, the division's troops stormed past the village, then swung round and attacked the enemy positions from the rear. The advance then swept onwards to seize the ridge of high ground beyond the village. The division successfully secured its objectives,

Das Reich grenadiers had to toil forward through terrain turned into a boggy morass by heavy rains

Left: A Waffen-SS grenadier talks to displaced Russian civilians in the ruins of Belgorod. The town had been subjected to a sustained artillery and aerial bombardment on the first day of the offensive, and had suffered accordingly. The Red Army also took a pounding during the subsequent days. For example, the War Diary of II SS Panzer Corps recorded that on 8 July alone 290 Russian tanks were destroyed. And yet the Russians carried on fighting.

but the decision was taken to press on and exploit the success. The assault finally began to run out of steam when it ran into the extensive belt of minefields beyond Beresov. On the following day, the Waffen-SS grenadiers struggled on through the mud, breaking through the Soviet lines and opening the main road to Lutschki. The division's armour them poured through the breech.

The SS panzer corps continued its push northwards, led by the *Totenkopf*, smashing aside the Soviet forces to the west of Prokhorovka. Just to the east of the town the main Soviet reserve, the 5th Guards Tank Army, was preparing its

Above: A 150mm gun of the *Totenkopf* Division pounds Russian positions around Prokhorovka. The fearful encounter at that place left the division battered and bleeding. By 15 July, for example, it was estimated that it had lost half its tanks and vehicles to enemy action.

own offensive, aimed at halting the rampaging SS corps, when Hausser's Waffen-SS divisions arrived and disrupted the Soviet preparations. Hausser's divisions wheeled eastwards, the *Totenkopf* on the left flank, the *Leibstandarte* in the centre, and *Das Reich* to the right. Desperate Soviet counterattacks just managed to hold the Germans to the west of the town, as the Luftwaffe pummelled the defenders with incessant air attacks.

This German advance set the Soviets a problem. If they delayed their counterattack until all of their units were fully deployed, this would also give the Germans time to bring up their own reinforcements. The Soviets were well aware that III Panzer Corps, with its 300 or so additional tanks, was pressing northwards along the right flank of Hausser's men. When this force arrived in the area around Prokhorovka, the balance of armoured strength would swing in the German's favour. The Soviets therefore decided that their best chance lay in an immediate attack on Hausser's corps, while a blocking force of two mechanised brigades, a mechanised Guards corps, an armoured brigade and a Guards rifle division were sent to halt, or at least slow, the progress of III Panzer Corps. The the rest of 5th Guards Tank Army would then meet II SS Panzer Corps head on.

On 12 July the German attack was renewed with a massive bombing raid by the Luftwaffe on all identifiable Soviet positions. The Waffen-SS divisions once again formed their highly effective Panzerkeil, with the formidable Tigers to the front, flanked by lighter Panthers, Mk IVs and Mk IIIs. The Luftwaffe's aerial bombardment was complemented by a massed artillery barrage intended to complete the softening up of the enemy positions.

The Soviets were well aware of the awesome destructive capabilities of the heavy tanks which spearheaded the German armoured formations. The T-34s, which formed just over 50 per cent of the Soviet armoured strength, were fast, manoeuvrable and dependable, but their 76mm gun was no match for the Tiger unless it could approach to within dangerously close range and hit the Tiger in its thinner flank or rear armour. The Tiger, on the other hand, could kill a T-34 at ranges of 2000 metres or more. It should be remembered, however, that only one company, the heavy company, of each SS panzer regiment at Kursk was equipped with the Tiger. This represented a total of less than 50 serviceable Tigers available for battle at Prokhorovka. The greatest percentage of German tanks were either Mk IVs or the even older, obsolescent Mk IIIs armed with 50mm guns.

As the German artillery barrage ended, the Soviet tanks broke cover and drove towards the astonished Germans at full speed, with the sun behind them, blinding their opponents. Many Soviet tanks fell victim to the experienced German gunners, but others did succeed in reaching the lines of German tanks. Battles were soon being fought at virtual point-blank range, where the effect of a hit from even a smaller calibre weapon could be devastating. Tanks receiving direct hits, and there were many of them on both sides, literally blew apart, with turrets weighing many tonnes being thrown in the air as if they were made of paper.

THE GERMAN TIDE IS STEMMED

The death rate among German tanks crews in World War II was over 80 per cent, second only to losses in the U-Boats. Death was never a pleasant proposition for any soldier, but for tank crews the end could come in so many slow and agonising ways that those who were killed instantly when their tank was hit were often the lucky ones. Many photographs of the Kursk battlefield show the blackened and charred bodies of tank crews in or around their burned-out vehicles. Many Soviet tank crews fought with almost superhuman and often suicidal bravery, deliberately ramming the enemy once their ammunition had run out. The effect of a 30-ton T-34 hitting an enemy tank at top speed was devastating.

On the left flank of II SS Panzer Corps, the *Totenkopf* Division was hit by two Soviet corps, XXXI Guards Corps and XXIII Guards Rifle Corps. By noon the division's advance had been checked and the *Totenkopf* was forced on to the defensive. *Das Reich* likewise was facing tough opposition against the weight of II Guards Tank Corps.

By afternoon the battle was reaching its crescendo but the outcome was still very much in the balance. Unfortunately for Hausser and the Waffen-SS, however, III Panzer Corps had been halted by the blocking force and was now

As the German artillery barrage ended, the Soviet tanks broke cover and drove towards the Germans

struggling to make headway. Although it would eventually batter its way through, it would not arrive in time to influence the outcome of the battle at Prokhorovka. Meanwhile, the *Leibstandarte* and *Das Reich* Divisions had regrouped for a final all-out attempt to swing the result in their favour. The Soviets anticipated this and committed the very last of their own reserves to the battle. Fighting raged on for the rest of the day, finally petering out as darkness began to fall, both sides badly battered and utterly exhausted.

The day had seen over 300 German tanks lost. The Soviets, too, had suffered drastic losses, but had remained in command of the battlefield. Their tanks could thus be recovered and repaired wherever possible. To the Germans, however, a damaged tank was as good as destroyed. Throughout 13-15 July, fighting continued, though the Germans now realised that they had no chance of success.

'CITADEL' IS ABANDONED

Hitler, meanwhile, was becoming increasingly worried over developments in the Mediterranean theatre, and the Allied landings in Sicily (which began on 10 July 1943) finally persuaded him that it was here that the greatest danger to Germany lay. In his opinion, only the fighting qualities of his élite Waffen-SS divisions could be depended upon to strengthen the Italian Front sufficiently. On 13 July, therefore, Hitler decided to suspend 'Citadel', finally ending any possibility of achieving even a limited success. By withdrawing the Waffen-SS divisions, he seriously weakened the German forces in the Kursk area to the extent that they would be unlikely to withstand a Soviet counterattack. All the territory gained during the offensive would simply have to be given up once again and, in the event, it was all retaken by the Soviets by 23 July.

Field Marshal von Manstein argued that by scaling down the objectives and continuing pressure on the Soviets, the offensive could be relaunched with at least some chance of limited success. Hitler was adamant and the order for the withdrawal of the *Leibstandarte*, *Das Reich* and the *Totenkopf* from the Eastern Front sounded the final death knell for 'Citadel'. German losses during the offensive were estimated at around 100,000 men. Soviet losses were kept secret for decades and only after the collapse of the Soviet system in Russia did the true figures come to light – over 250,000 killed and 600,000 wounded. The Soviets also lost around 50 per cent of their entire tank strength. The German losses, in both men and in tanks, were catastrophic for their forces and were a disaster from which the Wehrmacht would never recover. More importantly, the initiative on the Eastern Front had been lost and would never be regained.

Although the ultimate effects of German losses at Kursk were enormous, in Hitler's eyes the Waffen-SS divisions had once again proved themselves outstanding. Waffen-SS units at Kursk were still advancing even at the last moment before the offensive was called off and as Army units on their flanks were being held or beaten back.

The Waffen-SS divisions were initially moved to an area near Kharkov for a brief rest period before their intended transfer to the West. In the event, General Malinovsky launched a counterattack against the German forces in the Donetz

> **The Waffen-SS divisions were intially to move to Kharkov for a brief rest period**

basin on 25 July, smashing into Field Marshal von Manstein's forces along the Mius river and overrunning the German positions. The *Totenkopf* and *Das Reich*, together with the Army's 16th and 23rd Panzer Divisions, were rushed south to Stalino and thrown into the fray on 30 July. After three days of vicious fighting, the Soviet advance was halted and the front stabilised. The situation in Russia, however, was still too serious to allow the Waffen-SS divisions to be withdrawn to Italy as three whole Soviet fronts next smashed into the Germans in two attacks, around Belgorod and towards Orel, ripping huge gaps in the German lines. The *Totenkopf* and *Das Reich* Divisions were rushed northwards once again to cover the left flank of von Manstein's forces. Only the *Leibstandarte* could be spared and was duly transported from the Eastern Front to Italy.

From here on until the end of the war, the German armies in the East would be fighting a predominantly defensive war, being driven slowly but inexorably out of the Soviet Union, through Eastern Europe and to the gates of Berlin itself. The divisions of the Waffen-SS would be used time and time again to plug a gap or retrieve a desperate situation, and for a while the front would be stabilised. However, not even Himmler's supermen could alter the final outcome of the war. The only questions were how long the conflict would it last, and what would be the price in terms of blood?

Above: A knocked-out T-34 at Prokhorovka. Though the Red Army suffered tank losses of 50 per cent at Kursk, by blunting the German offensive the Russians had gained the initiative on the Eastern Front. Waffen-SS losses were high. On 16 July, for example, Hausser's command was down to 30 Tigers, 69 Mk IVs, 80 Mk IIIs and four Mk IIs. In addition, the SS soldiers were exhausted.

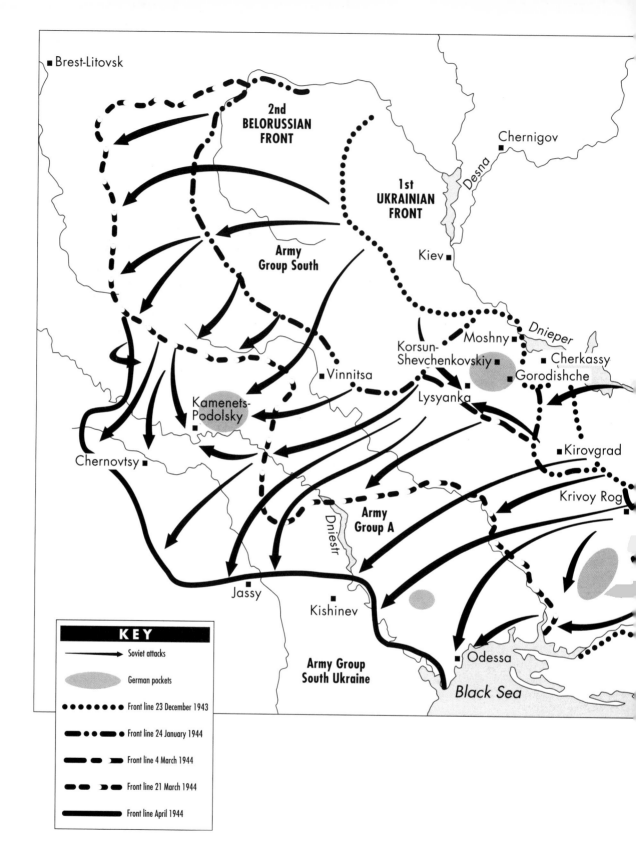

Brest-Litovsk

2nd BELORUSSIAN FRONT

Chernigov

Desna

1st UKRAINIAN FRONT

Army Group South

Kiev

Korsun-Shevchenkovskiy

Moshny

Dnieper

Cherkassy

Gorodishche

Vinnitsa

Lysyanka

Kamenets-Podolsky

Chernovtsy

Kirovgrad

Krivoy Rog

Army Group A

Dniestr

Jassy

Kishinev

Army Group South Ukraine

Odessa

Black Sea

KEY

→ Soviet attacks

German pockets

•••••••• Front line 23 December 1943

•–•–•– Front line 24 January 1944

– – –▶ Front line 4 March 1944

▬ ▬ ▬▶ Front line 21 March 1944

▬▬▬ Front line April 1944

2nd UKRAINIAN FRONT

Dnepropetrovsk

3rd UKRAINIAN FRONT

4th UKRAINIAN FRONT

Sea of Azov

The Cherkassy Pocket

In the second half of 1943, the Soviets went on the offensive along the whole of the Eastern Front. In the south, for example, they hurled 2,000,000 men, 51,000 artillery pieces, 2400 tanks and assault guns and 2850 combat aircraft against the weakened Germans. As 1943 came to a close, the Red Army had liberated thousands of square kilometres of previously occupied territory. In addition, it had trapped 75,000 German troops, including Waffen-SS, in the Cherkassy Pocket. It was determined to destroy them, but the Waffen-SS troops in the pocket had other ideas...

Towards the end of December 1943, the Red Army forces in the southern sector of the Eastern Front renewed their push westwards from Kiev. The Soviet offensive had been halted only a few weeks earlier by the combined efforts of German Army and Waffen-SS troops under the command of LVII Corps. Now the Soviet advance quickly regained its momentum. Zhitomir was rapidly overrun and German forces found themselves being swept westwards by the rampaging Soviets. Some German units were pushed back by as much as 160km (100 miles) before Field Marshal von Manstein's battered and greatly outnumbered divisions began to re-assert themselves by sheer determination.

Kirovgrad was assaulted by the combined forces of First and Second Ukraine Fronts under the command of Vatutin and Konev respectively. German resistance had stiffened and the city fell to the Soviets only after bitter fighting, a

Right: A *Wiking* Division Panzer IV in the Cherkassy Pocket. The division's tanks would sacrifice themselves to enable the trapped German soldiers to escape from the Red Army.

The enemy was making all possible efforts to encircle the Germans around Cherkassy and Korsun

determined defence having been put up by 12 divisions from the First Panzer Army and Eighth Army. These forces included the *Wiking* Division and the Walloon volunteer unit, Sturmbrigade *Wallonie*.

Although pushed out of Kirovgrad, these units still posed a considerable threat to First Ukraine Front's southern flank and the northern flank of Second Ukraine Front. As Soviet units to the north and south continued to press forward with their offensive, a German-held salient was formed, centred around the town of Korsun.

Reconnaissance patrols from the *Wiking* Division soon established that enemy armour had begun to penetrate areas behind the German lines both at Kanew to the northeast of the salient, and at Smela to the south. To the west, at the northern edge of the neck of the salient, Soviet armoured units had overrun the town of Boguslaw. On 28 January 1944, reports were received that divisional elements near Olschana in the southwest of the salient were also coming under heavy attack. Clearly the enemy was making all possible efforts to encircle the German forces around Cherkassy and Korsun.

As the ring around the German forces began to close, it fell to a *Wiking* Division battle group under the command of SS-Hauptsturmführer Eberhard Heder to hold open the ever-constricting neck of the salient in the area near the town of Olschana. To accomplish this task Heder had only the divisional supply troops, normally non-combatants, although trained to fulfil a combat role whenever necessary. Heder's battle group, reinforced by Estonian SS volunteers from the *Narwa* Battalion and one company of the division's engineer battalion, held off vastly superior enemy forces around Olschana until 5 February, when they were ordered to withdraw. Then Soviet forces then broke through near Olschana, capturing the towns of Schanderowka and Kwitki on 5 February and pressing on eastwards into the pocket.

With the encirclement of the German divisions around Korsun and Cherkassy complete the Red Army had succeeded in trapping nearly 75,000 enemy troops. At first the Luftwaffe was able to keep the trapped units supplied by air, but an unexpected thaw once again turned the frozen landscape into a boggy morass. The ground on which the only airfield in the pocket was located became so soft that all flying operations had to be cancelled. At this stage 35 Soviet divisions were pitted against the Germans, and constant pressure by this vastly superior force saw the pocket being gradually whittled down in size until, by 9 February, it measured only 100 square kilometres (40 square miles).

THE BREAK-OUT BEGINS

Hitler saw the situation as mirroring that which had occurred at Demyansk, and once again he refused all requests for permission to be given to the trapped formations to break out westwards, ordering their commander, General Stemmermann, to hold on until Field Marshal von Manstein could assemble a large enough relief force and fight his way through. Stemmermann knew that this was an impossible task and seemed ready, with the agreement of some of his divisional commanders, to accept the inevitability of surrender negotiations. SS-Gruppenführer Gille, commander of the *Wiking* Division, however, had other ideas, and was adamant that he would not countenance any notion of surrender.

It soon became clear that the main German forces in the sector were in no fit condition to launch offensive operations and, somewhat surprisingly, Hitler was finally persuaded to give his permission for a break-out attempt to be made. On 7 February, Eighth Army signalled General Stemmermann that he should shorten his front lines and begin concentrating his forces in the west of the pocket, ready to begin a break-out when the order was given. As the German units began redeploying, their movements were detected by the Soviets. The Soviets read these as an indicator that the German defences were crumbling and soon began to announce the imminent destruction of the Cherkassy Pocket. They were particularly gleeful in their claims that the *Wiking* Division was about to be annihilated.

Meanwhile, the Germans had set about destroying all non-essential equipment and supplies. Only food and ammunition were kept. When the break-out was made, the German troops would take only the clothes they stood up in and such equipment as they could carry in light fighting order. Speed would be essential and the

Below: A letter from home brings a smile to the face of a member of the *Germania* Regiment encircled in the Cherkassy Pocket. *Germania* was instrumental in retaking several villages in the west of the pocket, the German possession of which was essential if the break-out was to be successful.

Germans could not afford to be burdened by superfluous equipment. Every man, fit or otherwise, would be needed. In *Wiking*'s Panzer Regiment, for example, all non-tank crew members (including mechanics and other personnel) were grouped together to form an infantry company, armed only with small arms and hand grenades. During the break-out, this improvised company would suffer 25 per cent casualties.

Once again, it would fall to the Waffen-SS to take the lead role in the operation. As the only armoured unit available, the *Wiking* Division would lead the break-out. The Soviets would make an all-out attempt to crush the Germans as soon as they became aware that a break-out was being attempted, so the task of acting as rearguard and covering the retreat of the bulk of the German forces was also one which could only be undertaken by troops of the utmost reliability, as this could end up being little more than a suicide mission. Needless to say, that task fell to the Waffen-SS, specifically the Belgian Sturmbrigade *Wallonie*.

Meanwhile, the villages on the western edge of the pocket, only lost to the enemy a few days earlier, would have to be retaken. The *Germania* Regiment from the *Wiking* Division succeeded in recapturing Schanderowka and Komarowka, while the Army's 72nd Infantry Division retook Novaya-Buda and Chishinzy. Once Novaya-Buda had been retaken, the Army troops were relieved by the Sturmbrigade *Wallonie*, which held the village against ferocious Soviet counterattacks. During these defensive battles, the brigade commander, Lucien Lippert, was killed and the Belgian fascist Rexist leader, SS-Hauptsturmführer Léon Degrelle, took command.

SS-Untersturmführer Kurt Schumacher

During fighting to the southeast of Novaya-Buda, one of the *Wiking* Division's daredevil tank commanders, SS-Untersturmführer Kurt Schumacher, commander of 3 Company of the Panzer Regiment, was to win the Knights Cross of the Iron Cross for outstanding gallantry. During this action, two Soviet battalions broke through the German positions. With only two tanks, Schumacher advanced and drove the enemy out of the village. Undaunted, the Soviets counterattacked, this time with support from a force of around 15 T-34s. Schumacher returned to the fray once again, destroying eight T-34s which had penetrated the village. Then, emerging from the outskirts, he knocked out two more. The Soviets were determined to drive the Germans back, however, and re-launched their attack on the following day, this time supported by 11 tanks. One of Schumacher's tanks had been damaged, leaving his own vehicle as the only opposition to the Soviet armour, yet, without hesitation, he launched a flank attack on the advancing Soviets, destroying seven of them. With no armour-piercing ammunition left, Schumacher continued his attack with high-explosive shells. Ineffective against the armour of the T-34s, they nevertheless caused great consternation to the Soviet tank crews, who assumed they had been hit by armour-piercing rounds and baled out. The arrival of another German tank gave Schumacher cover to finish the destruction of the abandoned T-34s by setting them on fire. His tally for the day was not yet complete, however, as

> **With only two tanks, Schumacher attacked and drove the Soviets out of the village**

a final T–34 was spotted, attempting to work its way around his flank and attack from the rear. This T–34 went the same way as its companions, though, bringing Schumacher's score over the two days to an amazing 21 Russian T–34s destroyed. Although Schumacher received the Knights Cross for this action, like most tank commanders he looked upon the decoration as being an award not just to himself, but to the whole crew he commanded, for only by all crew members pulling together and working to peak efficiency could success be achieved in such actions.

Meanwhile, thousands of German vehicles crammed the roads leading westwards. The soft, boggy terrain made cross-country travel impossible and the congested roads made superb targets for Soviet ground-attack aircraft. German losses were horrendous. Left with no alternative, the remaining vehicles were torched to prevent their capture by the enemy, and the weary Germans continued their trek to the western edge of the pocket by foot. On 10 February 1944, the town of Korsun was evacuated. As the town held the only airfield available to the Germans there could be no further aerial supply of food or ammunition to the men on the ground (appalling conditions on the ground had in fact already greatly curtailed the Luftwaffe's supply operations).

Above: *Wiking* **Division grenadiers and tanks near Korsun, early February 1944. During the Cherkassy battles the Soviets tried to induce the Waffen-SS soldiers to surrender with leaflets and loud-speakers at the front. It was an appeal that fell on deaf ears.**

Above: 'Without food or drink we had survived since morning on a few handfuls of snow. But the snow has made us more thirsty. We huddled together as close as possible for warmth.' (Léon Degrelle at Cherkassy)

As the German concentration in the west of the pocket continued, Field Marshal von Manstein was faced with the daunting task of mounting a relief operation to smash through to the trapped forces. The Soviets had concentrated two entire Guards tank armies in the area between the pocket and the German forces to the west. Eight panzer divisions were rapidly assembled to face them. There was little doubt that, on paper at least, the German relief force was well capable of smashing through the Soviets, but von Manstein was to be frustrated by interference from the Army High Command, which insisted in switching around some of the units involved. Ultimately, von Manstein took matters into his own hands and gave General Stemmermann the order to break out.

Even as the operation was set to begin, there was a brief panic when Soviet armoured units burst through the German rearguard positions between the 57th and 88th Infantry Divisions. Within just one hour, Schanderowka had again been overrun. A handful of the few remaining panzers of the *Wiking* Division turned back and hurled themselves at the enemy in a desperate attempt to stem the Russians. In his memoirs Léon Degrelle recalled seeing the proud young tank commanders, in their black panzer uniforms, standing in the cupolas of their tanks as they rolled calmly towards the enemy and certain death. The battle which ensued gained time for the evacuation westwards of thousands of German infantrymen who would otherwise certainly have been captured or killed. However, not one single *Wiking* panzer survived.

DEATH IN THE SNOW

The final break-out began on 16 February. On the northern flank was the 112th Infantry Division, in the centre the 72nd Infantry Division and, in the south, the *Wiking* Division. The assembly area was around the village of Chilki. The Soviets were at first taken by surprise and the lead elements of the German force made good initial progress. As they approached the higher ground to the west, however, the Russian units in that part of the ring were waiting for them.

In order to maintain the element of surprise, it had been impossible for the Germans to attempt any form of softening-up barrage by their artillery on the enemy positions. In any case, all artillery and anti-tank guns had been spiked and abandoned prior to the break-out commencing. Thus the Germans were faced by full-strength Soviet units determined to halt their escape, and without anti-tank guns with which to counter the Soviet tanks being thrown against them. The progress westwards was halted. As the main body began to catch up with the spearhead elements they came under attack from Soviet armour, mostly T-34s but including a number of the newer JS-II Stalin tanks, which were a match for any German tank, including the Tiger. Without heavy anti-tank weapons, the German infantrymen were forced to attack the Soviet armour using only hand-held weapons, and German losses were enormous. One battle group from the *Germania* Regiment destroyed 24 T-34s in close-quarter battle using only satchel charges and Teller mines.

Fortunately for the Germans, at around midday on 16 February heavy snow began to fall, whipped up by strong winds into almost blizzard conditions.

> **One battle group from the *Germania* Regiment destroyed 24 T-34s in close-quarter combat**

Above: Awaiting the next Soviet attack. The abandonment of the tanks and vehicles meant the Germans were terribly exposed during their break-out attempts. One who survived wrote: 'Four T-34s drove to within a few hundred metres of the tightly packed mass of men and fired with HE [high explosive]. Horrible.'

Burdened by thousands of wounded and large numbers of female signals auxiliaries, the Germans slowly made their way westwards under the cover of the snowstorms. The break-out was continued mostly on foot, the bulk of the German vehicles by now having been abandoned and destroyed. Meanwhile, the pocket was being crushed ever further, and within a few days over 54,000 German troops were contained within an area measuring only some 100 square kilometres (40 square miles).

One particular episode which occurred during the break-out illustrates particularly well the incredible determination shown by the Waffen-SS grenadiers in the course of these difficult actions. During the fighting around Novaya Buda, one of the tanks under SS-Untersturmführer Schumacher's command was hit in the engine compartment and burst into flames. As the crew abandoned their stricken vehicle they were all wounded to some degree or other, mostly by small-arms fire. The tank commander was SS-Oberscharführer Fiebelkorn. He, too, was injured, breaking an ankle when he jumped from his burning tank. The entire crew managed to make their way safely back to their own lines and were ordered to report to the battalion medical officer. The first aid posts were already

Left: A signaller of
Sturmbrigade *Wallonie*
tunes his radio.
Degrelle's men managed
to escape from the
pocket, but the price
was heavy in terms of
casualties: 1400 killed
or wounded.

The Germans slowly made their way westwards under cover of the snowstorms

full to overflowing with wounded and dying men, and Fiebelkorn and his crew were sent back to their unit after having their wounds dressed.

It had been decided that each unit would be responsible for evacuating its own wounded during the break-out. For Fiebelkorn and his crew this meant that they and the other injured soldiers would be evacuated using the battalion's 18-ton half-tracked tank recovery vehicles. One such half-track was equipped with machine guns to give cover, while the remaining three were to carry the wounded. Not long after they set off, the half-track in which Fiebelkorn was travelling was hit by anti-tank fire, killing the commander and wounding many of the passengers yet again. The wounded were removed from the damaged vehicle and loaded onto horse-drawn carts. Next, while passing through wooded terrain near Dshurshenzy, the column came under attack once again and the wounded were forced to take cover among the trees, while the panzers at the head of the column gave battle to the enemy tanks.

Once the enemy had been beaten off, one of Fiebelkorn's comrades arranged a horse-drawn wagon and driver to take him on. Fiebelkorn had hardly gone another kilometre when his driver abandoned him to his fate and made off, attempting to save his own skin. The wounded NCO crawled into cover, to lie there, exhausted, for many hours. Eventually he summoned up the energy to continue and crawled onwards, meeting two other wounded soldiers, who joined him. Next morning, Fiebelkorn realised that they were lost and in the midst of enemy positions. The heavy snow which was falling hid them as they dug themselves into a snow-hole to await the cover of darkness. Shortly after setting off once again, both of Fiebelkorn's comrades died. The determined NCO did not give up, though, and crawled on alone across the snow-covered battlefield, finally reaching the safety of a German outpost, suffering from severe

Below: A German machine-gun team opens up against Red Army targets during the retreat to the west side of the pocket. Though 34,000 Germans and their allies eventually escaped, 20,000 were killed or captured.

frostbite in both of his hands, his knees and his feet. He collapsed into uncon-
sciousness just after reaching safety.

Eventually the main German retreat reached the stream at Gniloi-Tilkitsch.
Only two metres (6 feet) deep, the stream would not normally have presented
much of an obstacle, but heavy rain and now snow had turned it into a raging
torrent. There was no bridge in the area, so an 18-ton half-track was driven into
the stream to make a crude ford. So great was the force of water, however, that
even this was swept away.

Meanwhile, Soviet units, supported by tanks, were rapidly closing on both
flanks of the German columns. The Germans had no option but to try to swim
across the freezing waters. An attempt was made by SS-Gruppenführer Gille to
form a human chain, with swimmers helping their non-swimming comrades.
Gille took his place in the chain along with his men, but even some of the

**Above: A *Wiking*
messenger and senior
officer in the snow near
the crossing at Gniloi-
Tilkitsch. Though
normally only a stream,
the heavy snows and
rains had turned the
last obstacle before
freedom into a raging
torrent. Many drowned
attempting to cross it.**

strongest swimmers found themselves swept away to their deaths. Thousands of German soldiers were drowned attempting to cross, though many did succeed, principally by using branches hewn from nearby trees as floats. Even on reaching the opposite bank, however, their ordeal was far from over. In soaking wet clothes and in temperatures of minus 10 degrees, their sodden uniforms soon froze solid on their bodies.

The Soviets were now well aware that a major break-out was under way, and launched a murderous barrage of artillery and rocket fire on the helpless escaping German soldiers.

The Sturmbrigade *Wallonie*, meantime, was suffering appalling casualties as it battled to hold the pursuing Soviets at bay. At Novaya-Buda, for example, the Belgian volunteers had to fight their way through Soviet cavalry units before reaching Gniloi-Tilkitsch, where around 3000 survivors hid in the nearby woods to await the cover of darkness before attempting to cross. The entire area was by then crawling with Soviet cavalry, infantry and armour. With considerable good luck, Degrelle's surviving grenadiers were able to cross without further losses. With them they brought the body of their fallen commander, Lucien Lippert, determined that his remains would not fall into Soviet hands. General Stemmermann, commander of the encircled pocket, was also killed in action at this time, near the village of Potschapinzy.

THE SURVIVORS OF CHERKASSY REGROUP

Despite the ferocity of the fighting, and the atrocious conditions, fully 70 per cent of the troops encircled within the Cherkassy Pocket were saved, more than 34,000 German troops reaching the safety of German-held territory. Despite this achievement, it is still a sobering thought to consider that well over 20,000 troops had been killed or captured in just one day of fighting. Very few of those who went into Soviet captivity ever returned.

The survivors of the once mighty *Wiking* Division regrouped near Risino. The weary grenadiers possessed only what clothes they stood up in, plus their weapons and a few rounds of ammunition. All vehicles and equipment had been left behind. The very least that the battered survivors hoped for was a spell of home leave in order to regain their strength, but even that was to be denied to all except the seriously wounded. The deteriorating situation for the Germans all along the Eastern Front meant that, even in its battered state, the *Wiking* Division was sorely needed.

As a reward for the accomplishments of his division, SS-Gruppenführer Gille was awarded the Swords, Oak Leaves and Diamonds to his Knights Cross of the Iron Cross, while Léon Degrelle, somewhat of a favourite of Hitler's, received the Knights Cross. Degrelle was also able to gain Hitler's approval for a brief spell of home leave for the remnants of his Sturmbrigade *Wallonie*.

For Gille and his division further problems loomed. It had been decided that reforming and rearming would be carried out at Kowel. This city, located within the Pripet Marsh region, was defended only by an under-strength garrison and looked likely to be the object of an enemy attack in the near future. By station-

The weary grenadiers possessed only the clothes they stood up in, plus their weapons

Right: A weary Norwegian NCO of the *Wiking* Division stares at the camera. Men such as him had spent over two and a half years at the front fighting the Russians. Even after their escape from Cherkassy there would be no respite, for Kowel had to be saved.

ing the *Wiking* Division there while it reformed, so the theory went, the city would be given some degree of protection when the attack came.

On 16 March, the *Germania* and *Westland* Regiments began their movement to Kowel, while Gille and his staff travelled to the city by air. The garrison troops were delighted at being reinforced by a Waffen-SS panzer division, not realising that, even if it reached the town unmolested, the *Wiking* was now a division in

Above: Some of Degrelle's men photographed after the battles in the Cherkassy Pocket. Sturmbrigade *Wallonie* continued to fight well in the East, and it was upgraded to a division in the autumn of 1944.

name only. None of its heavy weapons had been replaced nor had its manpower losses been made up. Gille was also soon worried by the non-arrival of his two regiments. Eventually, a message came in, to the effect that the trains transporting them to the city had run into Soviet units. It appeared that at least four Soviet divisions had now surrounded Kowel and the two regiments found it impossible to fight their way through, weakened as they were after their escape from Cherkassy, and without heavy equipment or armour.

Gille and his staff were trapped in the city, which Hitler quickly declared a 'Fortress' and insisted must be defended at all costs. Kowel was in fact an important road and rail junction, the loss of which would be seriously damaging for the Germans. It once again fell to the Luftwaffe to supply the encircled troops

by air. Unfortunately the city had no airfield so supplies had to be dropped by parachute. Over 250 supply missions were flown by the Luftwaffe in support of Kowel's beleaguered garrison. Gille was declared Fortress Commandant and immediately set about training the Army troops under his command in the art of close-quarter battle against enemy tanks. Fortifications around the city were strengthened, as were all minefields.

A relief force was quickly assembled, including the *Germania* and *Westland* Regiments, now finally with their heavy weapons and armoured personnel carriers, and the Army's 131st Infantry Division and Assault Gun Brigade 190. Time was rapidly running out for Kowel's defenders, however. Over 2000 troops had already been wounded holding off the Soviet attackers. It was clear the city could not hold out for too much longer.

THE RELIEF OF KOWEL

It was therefore decided to launch an immediate direct attack through the Red Army's front along the main Cholm–Kowel railway line. The attack was to be led by 8 Company of SS Panzer Regiment 5, newly equipped with 16 of the latest model of the excellent Panther medium tank. This armoured force, under the command of SS-Obersturmführer Karl Nicolussi-Leck, would be supported by a battle group from the *Germania* Regiment with 10 assault guns, under SS-Sturmbannführer Franz Hack. In addition, the 1st Battalion, Grenadier Regiment 434 from the Army, under Hauptmann Bolm, with seven self-propelled guns, would also lend a hand.

The attack made good progress and the town of Czerkasy was swiftly overrun, with over 300 Soviet prisoners being taken. Colonel Naber, commander of Grenadier Regiment 434 and nominally in command of the whole attack force, refused to agree to the retreating Soviets being pursued and ordered the assault force to remain in Czerkasy as darkness approached. Nicolussi-Leck, however, did not wish to lose the initiative and, with Bolm's agreement, decided that the attack should be carried forward at first light.

Nicolussi-Leck's Panthers met little serious resistance, but two tanks were lost to Soviet mines and some delay was experienced while engineers cleared the minefield. Bolm had now received direct orders to proceed no further, but Nicolussi-Leck had no intention of halting and pressed on with his advance. The going was extremely difficult, with Nicolussi-Leck's tanks struggling over boggy ground. Resistance began to stiffen and losses began to reach serious proportions. When only two kilometres (1.25 miles) from Kowel, and with only around half

> **Over 250 supply missions were flown by the Luftwaffe in support of Kowel's garrison**

of his force remaining intact, Nicolussi-Leck received orders to halt. However, as his tanks were already in action against Soviet units barring the entrance to the west of the city, he once again disobeyed and continued his attack, punching his way through the Soviet units and destroying a number of tanks and anti-tank guns in the process. Pushing on into the city itself, he eventually reported to Gille's headquarters.

Although he had broken into the city, and his Panthers would be a welcome addition to Kowel's defences, as soon as he had entered the ring around the city closed once again, with Nicolussi-Leck having done little more than join the trapped garrison.

The remainder of the relief force, meanwhile, had run into serious opposition from Soviet units ranged around the west of Kowel. The small town of Czerkasy, so recently taken, came under heavy pressure, and in fact changed hands several times until the arrival of another company from SS Panzer Regiment 5 finally swung the balance in the Germans' favour.

It was rapidly becoming clear that the forces available were not strong enough to fight their way through to Kowel, and accordingly Army Group Centre took a hand in matters. Conscious of the importance of the city, it detached LVI Panzer Corps, with its two constituent armoured units, the 4th and 5th Panzer Divisions, with orders to relieve the city with all speed. Just after midnight on 4 April 1944, a preparatory artillery barrage smashed into the Soviet units west of Kowel. The subsequent assault was spearheaded by the 4th Panzer Division, which included a battle group from SS Panzer Regiment 5. Contact was made with some of Kowel's defenders on the following day and German tanks penetrated into the city from the north, bursting through the Soviet anti-tank positions between Moszezona and Dobowaja on the afternoon of the same day.

AWARDS FOR THE SURVIVORS

On 6 April the evacuation of German wounded from Kowel began while, at the same time, a battle group from the *Germania* Regiment, supported by 7 Company of SS Panzer Regiment 5, thrust its way out of the western districts of Kowel to link up with the 131st Infantry Division outside the city. By 10 April Soviet units on the eastern side of the city had also been cleared, their attempts to counterattack held off by the tanks of the 4th Panzer Division and SS Panzer Regiment 5. With the relief of Kowel achieved, the weary soldiers of the *Wiking* Division would now be given some respite, albeit brief, to complete the process of refitting and reforming.

The *Wiking* Division had already earned itself a considerable reputation for combat élan, even winning the grudging respect of the Soviets. The break-out from the Cherkassy Pocket and the subsequent battle at Kowel only served to enhance this reputation further. Twelve of the division's soldiers were decorated with the Knights Cross of the Iron Cross for actions in these two battles.

For his invaluable contribution to the defence of Kowel, SS-Hauptsturm-führer Nicolussi-Leck was decorated with the Knights Cross on 9 April 1944. Nicolussi-Leck's comrades from the Panzer Regiment, SS-Hauptsturmführer

The remainder of the relief force, meanwhile, had run into stiff opposition

Willi Hein, SS-Obersturmführer Kurt Schumacher and SS-Obersturmführer Otto Schneider, also received the Knights Cross for actions at Cherkassy and Kowel. From the *Germania* Regiment, SS-Obersturmbannführer Ehrath, SS-Hauptsturmführer Werner Meyer, SS-Obersturmbannführer Franz Hack and SS-Standartenoberjunker Biegi were similarly honoured. Also rewarded with this high decoration were SS-Standartenführer Richter from the Armoured Artillery Regiment, SS-Unterscharführer Fischer from the Tank-Destroyer Battalion, SS-Hauptsturmführer Debus from the Armoured Reconnaissance Battalion, and SS-Obersturmbannführer Schonfelder from the divisional staff.

SS-Hauptsturmführer Léon Degrelle, who had taken over command of Sturmbrigade *Wallonie* after the death of Lucien Lippert, was decorated with the Knights Cross on 20 February 1944. Six months later he added the Oak Leaves to his decoration, ultimately reaching the rank of SS-Standartenführer and commander of the 28th SS-Freiwilligen Panzergrenadier Division *Wallonien*. After a number of further adventures, Degrelle survived the war and died in Spain in 1994 following a long illness, still popular with Walloon veterans of the Waffen-SS, many of whom kept in regular contact with him and regularly visited their old commander.

Above: Survivors from Cherkassy make their way west. In terms of manpower the operation had been a success. However, the two German corps that had been trapped in the pocket had ceased to exist as fighting formations. All that remained were exhausted men without tanks and heavy equipment. The Waffen-SS soldiers were shadows of their former selves.

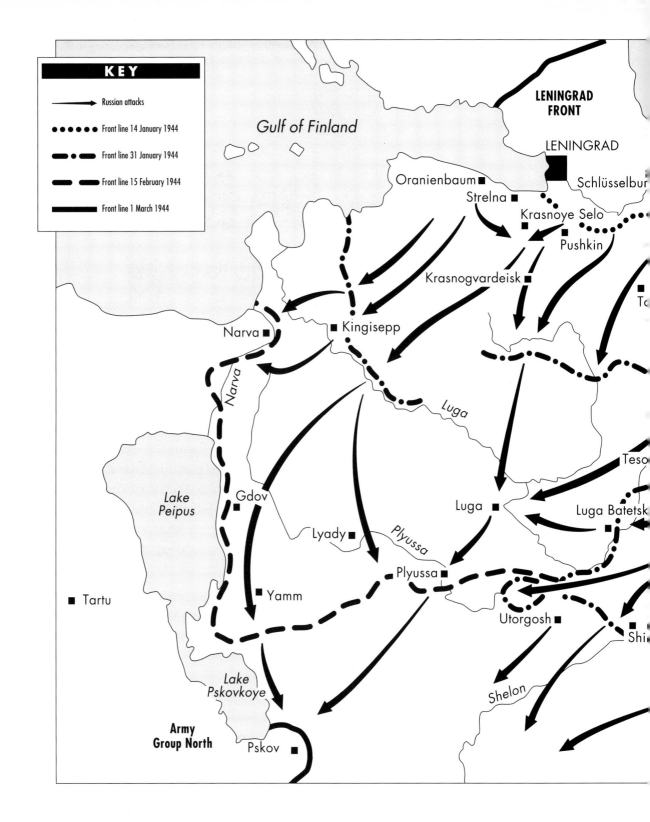

KEY

Russian attacks

•••••• Front line 14 January 1944

—·—·— Front line 31 January 1944

— — — Front line 15 February 1944

—— Front line 1 March 1944

Gulf of Finland

LENINGRAD FRONT

LENINGRAD

Schlüsselbur

Oranienbaum ■

Strelna ■

Krasnoye Selo

Pushkin

Krasnogvardeisk ■

To

Narva ■

Kingisepp ■

Narva

Luga

Lake Peipus

Gdov ■

Teso

Luga ■

Luga Batetsk

Lyady ■

Plyussa

Tartu ■

Yamm ■

Plyussa ■

Utorgosh ■

Shi

Lake Pskovkoye

Shelon

Army Group North

Pskov ■

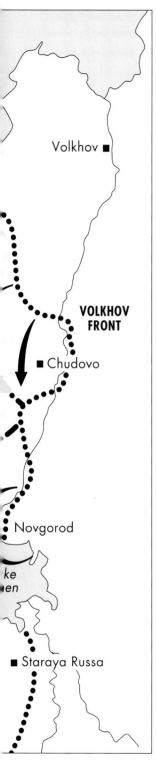

Volkhov ■

VOLKHOV FRONT

■ Chudovo

Novgorod

ke
en

■ Staraya Russa

The Defence of Narva

By early 1944 the Germans were suffering serious reverses on the Eastern Front. The Soviets had finally raised the siege of Leningrad and had driven the German armies westwards into Latvia and Estonia. In this particular sector of the front were to be found the bulk of the non-German volunteer divisions of the Waffen-SS. These foreign volunteers made a stand at Narva, and in an epic defence held up the Red Army for six months.

The principal volunteer formation was SS-Gruppenführer Felix Steiner's III (germanisches) SS Panzer Corps, comprising the 11th SS-Freiwilligen Panzergrenadier Division *Nordland* and the SS-Freiwilligen Panzergrenadier Brigade *Nederland*. As the name implies the latter was composed principally of Dutch volunteers. The former, however, was a truly international unit. Its principal combat formations were SS Panzergrenadier Regiment 23 *Norge*, SS Panzergrenadier Regiment 24 *Danmark* and SS Panzer Battalion 11 *Hermann von Salza*. Principally made up of Scandinavians, a number of Dutch, French, Estonian, Swiss and even a few British volunteers (from the minuscule 'Britische Freikorps') also served within its ranks.

Operating in the same sector were the 15th Waffen-Grenadier Division der SS (lettische Nr 1) and 19th Waffen-Grenadier Division der SS (lettische Nr 2), both Latvian volunteer Divisions; the 20th Waffen-Grenadier Division der SS (estnische Nr 1), an Estonian unit; the Flemish volunteers of SS-Freiwilligen Sturmbrigade *Langemarck* and Léon Degrelle's Sturmbrigade *Wallonien*.

Above: The old Germanic fort at Narva. This photograph was taken before the Russian assault, which reduced the town and the castle to rubble. Note the destroyed bridge.

Throughout January the Germans were driven remorselessly westwards and, by the end of the month, the Red Army was approaching the German defensive positions at the ancient city of Narva. Narva had a great significance for the Nazi mythologists, for it was here that the Teutonic Knights had fought against the Eastern tribes. It was here, too, that the Bolsheviks had been repulsed on numerous occasions during the Estonian War of Independence in 1919-20. Significantly, the panzer battalion of the *Nordland* Division was named after the Grand Master of the Teutonic Knights who had defended Narva centuries before.

III SS Panzer Corps had been transferred to the Leningrad Front in December 1943, to bolster the defences in an area only weakly held by inexperienced troops of the Luftwaffe's 9th and 10th Divisions. It was put into the line along the western edge of the Oranienbaum Pocket, held by the Soviets to the west of Leningrad on the Baltic coast. Initially only the *Nordland* Division was available for action, the *Nederland* Division still being en route from its previous location in Croatia. The *Nordland* Division consisted of only 11,500 troops, yet it was obliged to hold a front line extending for some 29km (18 miles). The *Nederland* finally arrived towards the end of December and was quickly fed into the front line to the north of the *Nordland*.

The Red Army's formation's within the Oranienbaum Pocket had been receiving considerable reinforcements for some time and, on 14 January 1944, the Soviet 2nd Shock Army burst out of the pocket and smashed into the 9th Luftwaffe Division. The Luftwaffe troops were cut to pieces, the few survivors fleeing in disarray. Only the engineer battalion from the *Nordland* Division, which had been inserted into this most forward part of the front, near Ropscha, to bolster the weaker Luftwaffe units, offered any form of resistance. To be fair to the Luftwaffe troops, many were former aircrew rendered redundant by the lack of aircraft and fuel, who had been shoved into hastily formed and inadequately trained ground combat units. Despite the best efforts of the SS engineers, however, the task facing them was all but impossible and, although they drove the attacking Soviets off in panic by their ferocious defence on more than one occasion, such localised successes could only delay the inevitable and they were gradually pushed back.

Within one week of the start of the Soviet offensive, III SS Panzer Corps had committed its last reserves and was desperately trying to hold defensive positions along the line from Vitino to Klopizy as German Army units, decimated in the savage fighting around Leningrad, fled west. Although combined Army and Waffen-SS efforts in the south of the sector succeeded in rebuffing enemy attacks and the Waffen-SS units in Vitino itself were successful in holding off the enemy, the Soviets made gains to the north and south of the town and the SS troops evacuated to avoid encirclement.

The front was becoming increasingly fragmented, and many units found themselves having to break out of enemy encirclements but, although Steiner's panzer corps was being gradually forced westwards, it was by no means a rout.

> **III SS Panzer Corps had committed its reserves and was trying to hold defensive positions**

On numerous occasions over-confident Red Army units, assuming the Germans were in full retreat, found themselves confronted by SS armour, which attacked vastly superior enemy forces without hesitation. At Gubizany, for example, a force of over 60 Soviet tanks entered the town to find themselves facing a small detachment from Armoured Reconnaissance Battalion 11 from the *Nordland* Division. The Germans attacked immediately, and destroyed nearly 50 enemy tanks without loss. The remaining Soviet tanks pulled back.

However, localised successes could not alter the strategic situation, and by 26 January a full scale withdrawal was underway, which saw the Germans mount a fighting retreat all the way back to the line of the Luga river, up to 100km (60 miles) from their start points.

Steiner's III SS Panzer Corps was tasked by Field Marshal Model, commander of Army Group North, with defending the northern sector of the Luga River defence line. Steiner was unhappy about his orders, arguing that Soviet penetrations of the defence line further to the south had already rendered pointless any commitment of major forces to holding this line. Steiner argued that it would be far wiser to withdraw further west and defend the much shorter line running from Narva to the northern edge of Lake Peipus, and from the southern edge of this vast lake, which provided the Germans with an excellent natural

Below: Reichsführer-SS Heinrich Himmler watches Latvian SS units undertake an anti-tank exercise near Narva, early 1944. The Latvian SS volunteer units performed consistently well in the East, and they came forward in sufficient numbers to form two SS divisions.

barrier, to Nevel in the south. This would allow greater concentrations of German troops to be spread over a much shorter line. Hitler would not agree, and so Steiner was overruled.

Steiner was soon to be proved correct when Red Army units smashed their way through the German lines near Hungerburg on the Gulf of Finland, attacking through terrain the Germans had assumed to be all but impenetrable, and had thus only defended with weak forces. Despite determined efforts by the *Norge* and *Danmark* Regiments to keep the Soviets at bay, their pressure began to tell.

Near the town of Padoga, a local counterattack was launched by 5 Company, SS Panzergrenadier Regiment 24 *Danmark*, commanded by SS-Obersturmführer Walter Seebach, which succeeded in driving back the Soviet attackers, albeit temporarily. When his exhausted troops returned to their own lines, Seebach was informed that seven of his men, all of whom had been wounded, were missing. Seebach knew what their fate would be if they were found by the Soviets, and immediately led his men out once again and succeeded in recovering all of his wounded comrades. Seebach was awarded the Knights Cross of the Iron Cross on 12 March 1944 for his courageous actions.

THE DEFENCES AT NARVA

The Soviets soon renewed their offensive, and one by one the defensive strongpoints held by the Waffen-SS were overrun. By 1 February all of the bridges over the Luga had been blown to delay the Soviet advance, and the Germans began retreating towards the Narva river defence lines as Steiner had proposed.

At the city of Narva itself stood two ancient fortresses. On the west bank lay the old Germanic Hermannsburg Castle, and on the east bank the old Russian fortress of Ivangorod. The river running between them was spanned at that point by the main bridge carrying road traffic into the city. The railway bridge lay some way farther to the south. On the eastern banks of the Narva river, the northern outskirts of the city were defended by the engineer battalion of the *Nederland* Division. Between the river and the village of Lilienbach, SS Panzergrenadier Regiment *De Ruiter* was positioned, with its sister regiment from the *Nederland* Division, SS Panzergrenadier Regiment 48 *General Seyffardt*, defending the eastern approaches to the central part on the city. The southeastern approaches were defended by SS Panzergrenadier Regiment 24 *Danmark* from the *Nordland* Division. On the western banks of the river, Narva's northern edge was defended by SS Artillery Battalion 54 from SS-Freiwilligen Brigade *Nederland*. The main central part of the city was held by the engineer battalion of the *Nordland* Division, while the division's artillery regiment was positioned on the southern edge of the city. The southwestern approaches to the city were protected by SS Panzergrenadier Regiment 23 *Norge*. As well as these Waffen-SS units, there were also a number of small battle groups formed from the fragmented remnants of a number of Army infantry divisions, as well as some polizei units.

The German defenders came under Soviet artillery bombardment almost as soon as they had reached their positions. The ancient city of Narva was soon reduced to a sea of rubble. So great was the destruction that the commander of

Red Army units smashed their way through the German lines near Hungerburg

the *Nordland* Division, SS-Brigadeführer Fritz von Scholz, is said to have set up his command post in a battered civilian bus, thus giving him the opportunity to move whenever circumstances dictated.

Two Soviet attempts to cross the Narva river in early February were quickly repulsed by Waffen-SS troops, including the reconnaissance platoon from the *Nordland*'s armoured battalion, the *Hermann von Salza*. On 12 February, however, the Soviets did succeed in pushing a sizeable force across the river near Ssivertsi on the northwestern outskirts of the city. The situation quickly became critical and all available troops were soon being rushed to this area.

ERADICATING THE BRIDGEHEAD AT MEREKULA

As the Germans battled to throw back the Soviet attackers at Ssivertsi, more Red Army troops came pouring across the frozen waters of the Narva river just to the south. The combat engineers of SS Engineer Battalion 54 succeeded in driving back this second attack. The SS artillery then began to shell the frozen waters of the Narva river, breaking up the ice to prevent any further attempts by the Soviets to cross. The arrival of reinforcements diverted from the defence of the city itself finally allowed the Germans to encircle the Soviets at Ssivertsi. The Soviet bridgehead on the west bank of the Narva was finally eliminated by a determined attack by the newly arrived Estonians from the 20th Waffen-Grenadier Division, the decisive assault on the Soviet positions being led by Waffen-Unterscharführer Harald Nugiseks, who became the first Estonian to be decorated with the Knights Cross of the Iron Cross for gallantry displayed during this action. Nugiseks had received multiple wounds during the battle but continued to lead his men in close-quarter fighting with the Soviet defenders. He was captured by the Soviets just a few days later. He survived several years in a Siberian labour camp and still lives in his native Estonia.

A further attack by the Soviets was made on the night of 12/13 February, when a small fleet of ships landed assault troops at Merekula on the Gulf of Finland in an attempt to outflank the defenders of Narva. The Soviets had reasoned that this move deep into the German rear would force the withdrawal of some of Narva's defenders and, with the city's defences thus weakened, would allow the Red Army to storm over the river and seize Narva.

Although the town of Merekula itself was soon occupied by the Soviets, the defenders were quick to react and soon had the area sealed off. The Soviets were then hit by Luftwaffe Stuka dive-bombers, but not before the aircraft had mistakenly bombed a small area of the town still held by German troops. The arrival of an armoured force from the reconnaissance battalion of the *Nordland* Division allowed the Germans to mount a two-pronged pincer offensive on Merekula, which finally crushed the Soviet enclave. Almost 400 Soviet prisoners were taken, and around 250 killed in the fighting.

Some distance to the south of Narva, at Krivasso, the Soviet 8th Army had established a strong bridgehead from which to launch an attack northwards toward Narva. The area around the bridgehead was held by élite troops from the Army's *Feldherrnhalle* Division, along with the 61st, 170th and 227th Infantry

---

The Soviet bridgehead on the west bank of the Narva was finally eliminated

Left: Waffen-SS soldiers at Narva await the next Soviet armoured attack. Note the Panzerfaust anti-tank weapon in the foreground, which fired a 3kg (6.6lb) hollow-charge projectile and could knock out any enemy tank then in service, though it only had a range of around 50m (164ft).

Divisions. On 24 February, a Soviet attack was launched which pushed aside weak Army resistance and looked set to sweep up into the rear of III SS Panzer Corps. A German blocking force was hastily formed from elements of both the *Norge* Regiment and the *Hermann von Salza* Panzer Battalion from the *Nordland* Division, supported by Tiger tanks from Panzer Battalion 502. Soviet forces established two bridgeheads, around Vaivara and at Lipsusig. A counterattack was

Above: The commander of the *Nordland* Division, SS-Brigadeführer Fritz von Scholz, on a tour of his division's defences at Narva. Scholz's command post was located in a civilian bus, which allowed him to move it at will. It also meant it could be moved away from those areas receiving treatment from the Red Army's artillery.

launched against them but, although it made good early progress, it soon bogged down after its commander was seriously wounded. A second force which sought to exploit this initial success also ran into trouble when its commander was killed in action. The Soviets then struck back, and fighting soon degenerated into vicious hand-to-hand combat. Only the arrival of some Tiger tanks allowed the Germans to disengage and withdraw safely. The tenacious defence subsequently put up by this blocking force, and by the *Feldherrnhalle* Division held the Soviets at bay for several weeks to come.

In late March grenadiers from the *Norge* Regiment were able to stabilise the sector of the front around Vaivara and recapture large tracts of territory from the Soviets. Back at the city of Narva itself, the beginning of March had seen a considerable increase in the intensity of Soviet bombardments. On 7 March the city had suffered a particularly savage aerial bombardment lasting for 12 hours, followed by an equally ferocious artillery barrage. Fortunately the civilian inhabitants had already been evacuated and the defenders were firmly established in well prepared bunkers. Although casualties were, in comparison to the severity of the bombardment, relatively light, a considerable amount of damage was done to the defenders' vehicles, guns and equipment.

The bombardment was followed up by a concentrated Soviet attack on the bridgehead on the east bank of the Narva river, held by the *General Seyffardt* Regiment. The tenacious Dutch volunteers held off each and every Soviet attack and were even able to launch their own counterattack, driving the Soviets back in panic. The regimental commander, SS-Obersturmbannführer Wolfgang Joerchel, was decorated with the Knights Cross in recognition of these achievements.

The next Soviet thrust was directed against the *De Ruiter* Regiment around the village of Lilienbach. Here the Soviets succeeded in breaking into the German lines with armoured support. A rapidly assembled counterattack force, composed of elements of the *Norge* and *Danmark* Regiments of the *Nordland* Division, hurled itself at the Soviets and drove them back, retaking German defensive positions that the Soviets had earlier overrun.

Despite these impressive defensive successes, it was becoming clear that Soviet pressure on the Lilienbach sector was increasing and that eventually the Germans would be swamped. This indeed almost occurred when Soviet tanks smashed through the German lines and began driving rapidly towards Ivangorod and the main bridge over the Narva. Only the arrival of 1 Company of the *Hermann von Salza* Panzer Battalion, equipped with Panther medium tanks, saw the Soviets halted. One Waffen-SS tank commander, SS-Oberscharführer Philipp, Wild received the Knights Cross of the Iron Cross for his fearless attacks on superior numbers of Soviet tanks during this action.

THE LULL BEFORE THE STORM

On the night of 13/14 March, the *De Ruiter* Regiment began to evacuate its positions at Lilienbach. The Soviets detected the enemy's movements and attacked in strength while the Germans were withdrawing. The regiment suffered serious losses, with some companies being forced to counterattack to cover the withdrawal of their comrades. Eventually the regimental front was stabilised again just to the southwest of Lilienbach. Shortly afterwards, this new line came under heavy enemy attacks, which penetrated the German lines. Once again the situation was resolved only by a rapidly assembled blocking force being thrown in against the enemy. After vicious close-quarter fighting, the Soviets were repulsed and the German line once again restored.

During the coming weeks, the Waffen-SS units on the Narva front concentrated on consolidating their defensive positions as much as possible. The actions being fought were of a minor nature, intended to keep the Germans under pressure and deny them the chance to rest, rather than being serious attempts to oust them from their positions. Artillery bombardments of the German lines continued unabated, causing a gradual increase in German casualties.

On 7 June, the Soviets began a concerted effort to eliminate the defensive positions on the southeastern approach to the city, held by the *Danmark* Regiment. Attacks and artillery bombardments grew in intensity until around noon on 12 June, when the Soviets made their attempt to storm the German positions

On 7 June the Soviets began a concentrated effort to eliminate the defensive positions

Right: A Waffen-SS 80mm sGrW 34 mortar in action at Narva. German mortar crews were especially adept at getting their weapons in and out of action quickly, a flexibility that gave them the edge in battle.

after a massive artillery barrage, which concluded with salvoes of smoke shells to cover the advance of the Russian troops.

Despite the determined efforts of the Danish volunteers, Soviet units penetrated the German defences, although losing many men to SS artillery fire. One particular strongpoint, codenamed 'Sunshine', a key part of the defences in the southeast, was overrun and occupied. A Danish NCO, SS-Unterscharführer

Egon Christofferson, serving as a squad leader with 7 Company of the *Danmark* Regiment, was alert to the crisis which was developing and quickly assembled an assault group from the scattered survivors of his company. Without hesitation Christofferson and his men charged into the enemy, and in fierce hand-to-hand fighting succeeded in ousting the Soviets from the German strongpoint. Christofferson was decorated on the spot with the Iron Cross First Class by his battalion commander for his quick thinking and initiative. This award was followed shortly thereafter by the Knights Cross of the Iron Cross.

Despite such localised successes, it was clear that the German defences on the Narva front were becoming increasingly weakened and vulnerable to Soviet attacks. The Germans had realised that the time would come when the situation at Narva would become untenable, and had thus begun construction of another defensive line some 24km (15 miles) farther west. Built on high ground, giving the defenders a good field of fire, the positions were known as the Tannenberg Line. By mid-June, German intelligence had detected Soviet preparations for a massive new offensive against the city of Narva. It was felt unlikely that the defensive positions in front of the city itself would be able to withstand such an assault, and so it was decided that III SS Panzer Corps would have a far better chance of holding the offensive at the Tannenberg positions.

On 24 July the Soviet Third Baltic Front, comprising some 20 Red Army divisions, was launched against the Narva defences. Although some German units had begun to withdraw towards the Tannenberg Line, a rapidly executed Soviet pincer movement saw the bulk of III SS Panzer Corps threatened with encirclement. Although the Army's 11th Infantry Division had held fast in the south, to the north the 20th SS Division was pushed back, allowing the Soviets to swing round behind the city.

THE WITHDRAWAL FROM THE EAST BANK

Waffen-SS units began withdrawing from the east bank of the Narva as the race to complete the withdrawal before Narva was completely encircled began. In the early hours of 26 July, SS engineers blew the main bridge between Hermannsburg and Ivangorod. As the smoke and dust cleared, the German infantry nearby were horrified to see that the bridge still stood. The engineers had already returned to their accommodation to begin their evacuation and were unaware of the disaster which was about to unfold. Their commander, SS-Sturmbannführer Gunther Wänhofer, had, however, stayed behind to observe the bridge's destruction. Now he could only watch in horror as Soviet troops charged onto the intact bridge. Wänhofer sped off to gather his men and bring them back, but his vehicle broke down and he was forced to make his way on foot. However, other German troops withdrawing through the area had seen what had happened at the bridge and called down mortar fire on the Soviet advance. The accuracy of the German fire succeeded in driving the Soviets off the bridge and back onto the eastern bank of the river.

When Wänhofer and his engineers returned to attach additional charges to the bridge they were met by a furious hail of fire from the Soviet troops on the

As the smoke and dust cleared, the German infantry were horrified to see that the bridge still stood

eastern bank, determined to prevent the destruction of this vital river crossing. Despite the intensity of the Soviet fire, Wänhofer's men succeeded in their task. This time the bridge collapsed into the Narva river.

Meanwhile, the bulk of III SS Panzer Corps was withdrawing in stages towards the Tannenberg defences. While most of the units succeeded in reaching their assigned positions in the defensive network, the *General Seyffardt* Regiment was overtaken by the rapidity of the Soviet advance and found itself cut off behind enemy lines. Attempts by a relief force to reach the beleaguered Dutch troops failed. The remnants of *General Seyffardt* then split up into small groups to try to make their way back to the German lines independently. Only around 20 per cent returned, the remainder being killed or captured by the Soviets.

No sooner had the Germans reached the Tannenberg Line positions than the Soviet attack hit them with full fury. The southeastern part of the Tannenberg defences was held by the *Danmark* Regiment, and the Danish volunteers came in for terrible punishment, with the Soviets penetrating their lines at several locations. The Soviets were eventually pushed back and the German lines stabilised, but only after the intervention of the *Norge* Regiment.

HOLDING THE LINE

Fortunately for the Germans, the line had been well chosen and the terrain in the area favoured their defence. German positions were concentrated in front of a ridge of high ground running from the coast and known as the Swedish Wall, and around three strategically vital hills: Hill 69.9, Grenadier Hill and Orphanage Hill, which ran in a virtually straight line from west to east. In position in front of the Swedish Wall were the engineer battalion and the *De Ruiter* Regiment from the *Nederland* Division, which covered the area south as far as the main highway to the Estonian capital, Tallinn. Running roughly parallel to this road, but farther south still, was the main railway line. The ground between the two was held by the *Danmark* Regiment. The defence lines then ran along the south side of the rail line and were manned by elements of the *Danmark* and *Norge* Regiments, and the artillery regiment of the *Nordland* Division. The area around Orphanage Hill was held by the Flemish volunteers of Sturmbrigade *Langemarck*. In addition, a number of Army units and even naval infantry were to take part in the defence of the Tannenberg Line. These last, lacking in combat experience, were to suffer heavy casualties in the days to come.

It was against the zone held by the naval infantrymen that the first Soviet attacks were launched. With tank support, the Soviets swiftly overran the German positions and seized the eastern slopes of Orphanage Hill. An immediate counterattack was launched by the *Danmark* Regiment, sending in troops mounted on motorcycles and armed with Panzerfaust anti-tank weapons. In a brief but vicious battle the Soviet tanks were destroyed and the front restored.

The next day saw the launch of a massed Red Army attack along the whole Tannenberg front. A force of some 30 Soviet tanks attacked the sector held by 10 and 11 Company of the *Danmark* Regiment. The Danish SS men calmly waited until the Soviets had come within extremely close range before they opened

> **The Soviets swiftly overran the German positions and seized the slopes of Orphanage Hill**

fire with their Panzerfausts. Within minutes almost half the tank force lay in flames and the remainder fled. The success was short lived, though, for under cover of darkness Soviet troops infiltrated the German lines and the two Danish companies were cut off and annihilated.

The whole front was now ablaze. At Orphanage Hill, SS-Sturmmann Remi Schrijnen, a young Flemish volunteer serving with the anti-tank detachment of the *Langemarck* Brigade, watched with horror as he saw a large Soviet armoured force sweep by to the north in an attempt to outflank his unit. Despite being wounded, he managed to manoeuvre his 7.5cm anti-tank gun into a position from which he could bring it to bear on the enemy tanks on his flank. Several fell victim to his excellent marksmanship before the Soviets withdrew.

Schrijnen would later receive the Knights Cross and promotion to SS-Unterscharführer, not for this feat but for an amazing action just three days later. When all the other guns in his troop had been knocked out, and the other crew members of his own gun had been killed, Schrijnen single-handedly continued to battle against a force of up to 30 Soviet tanks, many of them the latest Josef Stalin II type. Schrijnen knocked out at least 11 tanks before his own position received a direct hit and he was seriously wounded.

By 27 July the situation was looking very bleak for III SS Panzer Corps. Casualties had been severe, most units having lost anything up to half their strength

Above: A German MG34 machine-gun team scan the horizon for signs of the next Soviet attack. In the distance can be seen a number of knocked-out T-34 tanks, testimony to the ferocity of the fighting. Both sides fought with much gallantry at Narva.

Right: Waffen-Unterscharführer Harald Nugiseks, who became the first Estonian to be decorated with the Knights Cross for his part in eliminating the Soviet bridgehead at Ssivertsi, to the north-west of Narva.

On 16 September 1944, the front around the Tannenberg Line once more erupted into violence

and some having been completely wiped out, including tanks. Obergruppen-führer Steiner made up for his shortage of tanks in part by concentrating all his available artillery at critical points. The battered German units were now faced by at least 17 Red Army divisions, of which six were armoured. The Soviets had also repaired the bridges over the Narva, which meant that their strength was increasing by the hour.

On 28 July the relentless Soviet pressure finally forced the Germans from Orphanage Hill, the survivors barely reaching safety at the next strongpoint, Grenadier Hill to the west. The victorious Soviets then turned south and smashed into the positions held by the *Danmark* Regiment. Only the intervention of the massed German artillery units finally halted the Soviet drive. A subsequent attempt by SS troops to regain Orphanage Hill failed, however, and on 29 July the Soviet attack continued with massed artillery and aerial bombardments.

A last-ditch counterattack was launched by SS Panzer Battalion 11 *Hermann von Salza* with its few remaining battle-worthy tanks. Led by SS-Obersturmbannführer Paul Albert Kausch, the panzers hurled themselves at the Soviets and, despite being greatly outnumbered, the sheer ferocity of their attack, combined with the marksmanship of the SS tank gunners, saw the Germans prevail and their enemy retreat. The remaining days in July were filled with Soviet attacks and successful German counterattacks. Despite their overwhelming numerical superiority, the Red Army troops were unable to dislodge the SS troops from their defensive strongpoints.

On 3 August, a determined Soviet attack succeeded in penetrating the German positions on Grenadier Hill and was only thrown back after the timely intervention of a combat group formed from men from the corps' penal company. These disgraced Waffen-SS soldiers succeeded in throwing the Soviets off the hill in vicious hand-to-hand fighting.

Above: SS-Obersturmführer Helmut Scholz, commander of 7 Company, SS-Freiwilligen Panzergrenadier Regiment 49 *De Ruiter*, who was awarded the Knights Cross for his actions at Narva.

Following the failure of this latest Soviet attack, a brief spell of calm followed as both sides gathered their strength to continue the battle. For a week or so only small-scale raiding parties, some with tank support, proved themselves a nuisance to the Germans. On 12 August, however, larger attacks were made on the German lines but, having had time to rebuild their defences during the preceding lull, the Waffen-SS troops were successful in fending these off. These were to be the last attacks on the Tannenberg Line for some time as both sides contented themselves with sporadic artillery barrages of each other's positions.

On 16 September 1944, the front around the Tannenberg Line once more erupted into violence when the Soviet Third Baltic Front began a new drive. Unfortunately for Steiner and his men, Hitler had come to the decision that the corps was expendable and was prepared to sacrifice it in an attempt to deny Estonia to the Soviets. Despite Hitler's wishes, however, Colonel-General Ferdinand Schörner, the commander of Army Group North, was prepared to ignore his orders and permit the evacuation of Army Group Narva. By the late evening of 18 September, all Waffen-SS units had been pulled out of the front line and withdrawn towards western Estonia. The exceptional performance of the volunteer divisions on the Narva front resulted in 29 Knights Crosses being awarded to Waffen-SS personnel for actions during these battles. But no amount of medals could hide the fact that time was running out for the Germans in the East.

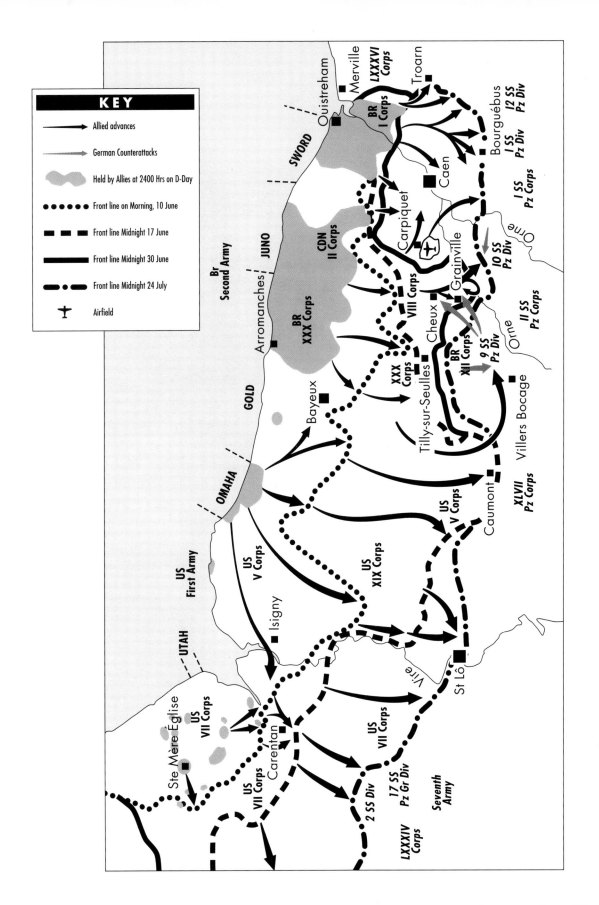

KEY

→ Allied advances

→ German Counterattacks

Held by Allies at 2400 Hrs on D-Day

•••••• Front line on Morning, 10 June

▄▄▄ Front line Midnight 17 June

▬▬▬ Front line Midnight 30 June

▄▬▄▬ Front line Midnight 24 July

✈ Airfield

Merville

Ouistreham

SWORD

BR I Corps

LXXXVI Corps

Troarn

Bourguébus

I SS Pz Div

12 SS Pz Div

Caen

I SS Pz Corps

Carpiquet

Grainville

10 SS Pz Div

II SS Pz Corps

JUNO

Br Second Army

Arromanches

CDN II Corps

VIII Corps

Cheux

BR XII Corps

9 SS Pz Div

Orne

BR XXX Corps

GOLD

XXX Corps

Tilly-sur-Seulles

Villers Bocage

OMAHA

Bayeux

US V Corps

Caumont

XLVII Pz Corps

US First Army

US V Corps

US XIX Corps

St Lô

Vire

Isigny

UTAH

Ste Mère Église

US VII Corps

US VII Corps

Carentan

US VII Corps

2 SS Div

17 SS Pz Gr Div

Seventh Army

LXXXIV Corps

Normandy and Arnhem

When the Allied invasion of France took place on 6 June 1944, some of the finest Waffen-SS divisions were committed to the battle. However, though both the Wehrmacht and SS fought well, the Normandy fighting bled them white, and they were forced out of northern France and pushed back towards the German frontier.

Occupied western Europe was divided between two German army groups: Army Group B, commanded by Field Marshal Rommel in the north, and Army Group G, commanded by Colonel-General Blaskowitz, in the south. Each comprised two armies, Army Group B having the Seventh Army under Colonel-General Dollmann and the Fifteenth Army under General Salmuth, while Army Group G had the First Army under General Chevallerie and the Nineteenth Army under General Sodenstern.

Only a limited number of armoured units were available to counter the Allied invasion and, as Hitler was uncertain as to where it would take place, they were held inland ready to be dispatched to whichever area most required them. Army Group B was given 2nd, 21st and 116th Panzer Divisions, while the 1st SS Panzer Division *Leibstandarte*, 12th SS Panzer Division *Hitlerjugend* (*Hitler Youth*), 17th SS Panzergrenadier Division *Götz von Berlichingen* and the excellent *Panzer Lehr* Division from the Army were held in reserve, only to be committed to action with Hitler's personal approval.

The *Leibstandarte* was located in the area around Bruges in Belgium, enjoying a period of rest and refit. The *Götz von Berlichingen* was stationed to the

Right: Reichsführer-SS Heinrich Himmler inspects soldiers of the *Hitlerjugend* Division just days before the D-Day invasion.

News of the landings soon reached the headquarters of the *Hitlerjugend* Division

southwest, in Tours, in the area of responsibility of Army Group G. This newly formed division was still something of an unknown quantity, being untested in battle. Although it included a panzer battalion in its order of battle, the division did not in fact possess any tanks, their place being taken by assault guns. With the powerful 2nd SS Panzer Division *Das Reich* located near Toulon to guard against any invasion on France's southern coast, this left only the untried *Hitlerjugend* Division in a position where it could rapidly be moved against any Allied landings. It was located near Dreux in the area between Paris and Caen.

INITIAL GERMAN MOVES

In the early hours of 6 June 1944, Allied airborne troops landed on the European mainland. News of the landings soon reached the headquarters of the *Hitlerjugend* Division. As no sign had yet been seen of any Allied invasion fleet off the French coast, it was assumed these airborne drops were simple probing attacks intended to establish the state of the German defences, or were feints, designed to draw German attention away from a real attempt to be made somewhere else. By 0130, however, news of seaborne landings was beginning to arrive and the division was quickly put on the alert.

At just after 0400, the *Hitlerjugend*, *Götz von Berlichingen* and *Panzer Lehr* Divisions were ordered to a state of immediate readiness. The armoured reconnaissance battalion of the *Hitlerjugend* Division had in fact already been sent towards the coast to ascertain the true state of affairs. It reported back that the Allied

invasion was indeed taking place, and so at 0700 the 12th SS Panzer Division finally received its marching orders, and set off for Lisieux around 1000 under the
fortuitous cover of low cloud and rain.

At first the High Command refused to sanction its committal to battle, but as
it had already begun to move it was allowed to continue to Lisieux, but *Panzer
Lehr* and *Götz von Berlichingen* were ordered to hold their positions. None of the
three divisions was permitted to go into action. Not until 1430 were both the
Hitlerjugend and *Panzer Lehr* finally released. By this time, the German forces
along the coast were in dire straits.

On arriving at the front, the *Hitlerjugend* and *Panzer Lehr* Divisions were to
join forces with the 716th Infantry Division and 21st Panzer Division, under the
banner of I SS Panzer Corps, to form a strike force intended to launch an immediate counterattack and throw the invaders back into the sea. As far as the *Hitlerjugend* was concerned, the considerable time and effort put into planning and
preparation for commitment to battle had been well spent. The division had been
expertly broken down into sub-unit battle groups, each fully capable of acting
independently, and with its own allocated artillery and tank support.

Under constant attack by Allied fighter-bombers, the division had arrived in
the area around Caen by the evening of 6 June. Its losses to Allied air attack had
not in fact been too severe, but the delays caused by these attacks had been
considerable. The first major combat unit to arrive at the front was SS Panzergrenadier Regiment 25, which reached the outskirts of Caen, already ravaged by
Allied bombing raids, at around 2200. The regimental commander, SS-Oberführer Kurt Meyer, immediately sent out patrols and discovered that the outskirts
of the city, including the vital Carpiquet airfield, were virtually undefended.
Shortly afterwards Meyer received orders from SS-Brigadeführer Fritz Witt, the
divisional commander, explaining that the he must hold Caen and the airport.

ATTEMPTS TO HOLD CAEN

Meyer's panzergrenadier battalions would be supported by artillery from the 3rd
Battalion, SS Artillery Regiment 12, and by Panzer IV tanks from the 2nd Battalion, SS Panzer Regiment 12. In addition, each of his battalions was accompanied
by its own artillery detachment and a section of half-track-mounted quadruple
20mm Flak guns. These were intended for anti-aircraft defence but were also
highly effective in the ground role.

The sister regiment to Meyer's 25th, SS Panzergrenadier Regiment 26, commanded by SS-Obersturmbannführer Wilhelm Mohnke, had not yet caught up
with the remainder of the division and was still somewhere to the east of the
Orne river. The other battalion of SS-Obersturmbannführer Max Wünsche's
Panzer Regiment 12, equipped with the more powerful Mk V Panther, was also
east of the Orne, stranded temporarily for want of fuel. It had been intended that
Mohnke's Regiment would attack on the left flank of Meyer's group.

During the morning of 7 June, the British and Canadian units approaching
Caen made good progress, advancing inland through les Buissons and Buron and
reaching the village of Authie about noon. An attempt by Canadian infantry to

**The first major
unit to arrive
at the front
was SS
Panzer-
grenadier
Regiment 25**

progress further, through the village of Franqueville, began to run into fiercer opposition. The Canadians therefore decided to withdraw into Authie and dig in. Before they could do so, however, they were hit by the *Hitlerjugend* Division.

Both the German Mk IVs and the Canadian M4 Shermans were armed with 75mm cannons and were thus reasonably evenly matched for firepower. The Sherman, however, had an alarming habit of bursting into flames when hit, due largely to its use of high octane petrol as fuel. Despite these faults, the Sherman was reasonably fast and manoeuvrable, and in this case put up a good show against the Mk IVs of the *Hitlerjugend*, several of which were knocked out. Nevertheless the ferocity of the German attack soon saw the Canadians retreat from Authie. The SS battle group then pushed on towards Buron. German casualties were remarkably light in the initial stages of the attack. When they reached Buron, however, they came within range of Canadian artillery, which began a fierce bombardment, supported by gunfire from Allied tanks and self-propelled artillery. Casualties on both sides began to escalate rapidly, but the Germans slowly but surely pushed the Canadians out of Buron. In desperation, the Canadians launched an immediate counterattack supported by their few remaining tanks and succeeded in driving the *Hitlerjugend* grenadiers back.

HOLDING THE LINE

The Canadians had suffered considerable casualties and, although they had retaken Buron, they had insufficient strength to consolidate and defend their positions. As the light began to fade during the evening of 7 June, therefore, they withdrew to les Buissons, around 1500m (just under one mile) to the north.

Meanwhile, Meyer had committed the 1st and 2nd Battalions of his regiment to the attack, on the 3rd Battalion's right flank. On the extreme right flank, the 1st Battalion pushed northwards for around 6km (3.75 miles), reaching the small village of Cambes. When it exited to the north of the village, it ran smack into the British 3rd Infantry Division. The Germans had only five Mk IVs from 8 Company of SS Panzer Regiment 12. Despite being outnumbered, the tanks went into action as soon as SS-Obersturmführer Hans Siegel in command realised that the attack by the *Hitlerjugend* troops was beginning to bog down. One tank suffered a mechanical breakdown almost immediately. Siegel's own tank was hit by a falling tree and its turret was jammed. Two others received hits and were disabled and the last was put out of action when it slid into a shell crater.

The Waffen-SS tank men were somewhat disconcerted to see tanks from 21st Panzer Division sitting watching the events unfold, and made no effort to help them. In addition to losing their tanks, the SS men suffered the loss of their artillery liaison observer and thus their artillery support also. In view of the circumstances, the battalion commander, SS-Sturmbannführer Waldmuller, pulled his men back through Cambes to the south of the village, where they dug in.

From his command post and vantage point in the Abbey Ardenne on the outskirts of Caen, Meyer could see that powerful Allied forces were moving into the area. Realising that he could not realistically hope to continue his advance, he ordered his units to dig in where they stood and prepare to defend their gains.

German casualties were remarkably light in the initial stages of the attack

Left: Grenadiers of the *Leibstandarte* Division take shelter during an Allied barrage near Caen. The intensity of enemy air and artillery strikes came as a great shock to Hitler's bodyguard in Normandy. As an Army officer who fought alongside the *Leibstandarte* at Caen wrote: 'it had no experience of fighter-bomber attacks on this scale.'

The young grenadiers of the *Hitlerjugend* Division had come through their first serious combat action. Losses had been considerable, though, with Meyer's regiment suffering some 300 casualties in just a few hours of combat. A dozen Mk IVs had also been destroyed and 43 tank crewmen killed or wounded.

During the early hours of 8 June, Mohnke's SS Panzergrenadier Regiment 26 finally reached its positions to the west of Meyer's battle group, thus closing a dangerous gap some 10km (six miles) wide in the line. Mohnke's orders were to launch an immediate attack towards the villages of Norrey-en-Bessin, Bretteville-l'Orgueilleuse, Brouay and Putot-en-Bessin, all of which lay around the im-

Above: Waffen-SS troops in action against British forces during Operation 'Goodwood', July 1944. German resistance accounted for 200 British tanks, and resulted in the operation being abandoned.

portant Bayeux–Caen road, which I SS Panzer Corps would need to use in its intended strike towards the coast. At around 0300, Mohnke's 1st Battalion began its advance. Under the command of SS-Sturmbannführer Krause, the SS men initially made good progress, but soon ran into murderous artillery fire, forcing them to halt and dig in. The 2nd Battalion, under SS-Sturmbannführer Siebken, fared somewhat better at first and, despite taking heavy Allied fire, pressed home its attack and succeeded in driving the Canadian troops of the Royal Winnipeg Rifles out of Putot-en-Bessin. A Canadian counterattack, with armoured support, was launched almost immediately. Battered by an artillery barrage and lacking in anti-tank weapons, Siebken's troops were gradually forced to retreat. The

Regiment's 3rd Battalion, under SS-Sturmbannführer Olboeter, launched its attack on the left flank of the 2nd Battalion, the objective the village of Brouay.

SS Panzergrenadier Regiment 25 was, meanwhile, enjoying a short respite from enemy action. From his vantage point in the old tower of the Ardenne Abbey, Meyer could see that there was no immediate likelihood of an Allied advance and thus decided to attack himself, in the direction of Bayeux, taking some of the pressure off Mohnke's regiment.

At around 2200 on 8 June, Meyer moved off with a battle group from his own regiment supported by Panther tanks from 1 and 4 Company of SS Panzer Regiment 12. The German force made rapid progress until it reached the village of Bretteville-l'Orgueill-euse, where the German tanks came under heavy fire. A furious battle then ensued, in darkness, in which the SS grenadiers succeeded in forcing their way into the villages. One Panther reached the building in which the Canadian battalion headquarters was located before being put out of action. Losses on both sides were heavy. Meyer himself was almost killed when the fuel tank of his motorcycle combination was hit and he was enveloped in flames. Luckily some of his men spotted him and helped douse the flames, Meyer escaping with only light burns. Frustrated at being unable to oust the Canadians, SS-Sturmbannführer Max Wünsche, the commander of SS Panzer Regiment 12, ordered his 1 Company to skirt around the village and try to outflank its defenders. This ended in disaster, though, as several Panthers were knocked out.

By 10 June 1944, any thoughts of the *Hitlerjugend* Division leading a counterattack to drive the Allied invaders back into the sea had been forgotten, as Allied men and materiel poured ashore. The division and its companion units in 1 SS Panzer Corps, the 21st Panzer and *Panzer Lehr* Divisions, were now very much on the defensive. The *Hitlerjugend* Division now covered a 16km (10-mile) stretch of front to the west of Caen, with *Panzer Lehr* on its left flank and 21st Panzer to the right. The *Hitlerjugend* Division was supported by corps elements and had been joined by its own Nebelwerfer battalion, equipped with the deadly multi-barrel rocket launchers, some of which were mounted on half-tracked armoured trucks.

On the morning of 11 June, elements of the 6th Canadian Armoured Regiment advanced towards the *Hitlerjugend*'s positions from Norrey-en-Bessin. Directly opposing them were the combat engineers of SS Engineer Battalion 12,

> **On the morning of 11 June, elements of the 6th Canadian Armoured Regiment advanced**

Above: A heavily camouflaged German StuG III self-propelled gun awaits its prey in the bocage. Such camouflage was necessary in Normandy, as the total Allied air superiority made daylight movement hazardous. For example, the *Leibstandarte*, while moving in daylight in early August, suffered a 35 per cent daily wastage rate due to air attacks.

who had only been driven back from Norrey with heavy losses on the previous day. This time the SS men would have their revenge. Well deployed in cunningly concealed defences, the combat engineers waited until the Canadian tanks, with infantry riding on their decks, were almost among their positions before opening up with concentrated machine-gun fire. The Germans then attacked the tanks with grenades and magnetic charges at close-quarters. Tanks from SS Panzer Regiment 12 joined in the fray and one Canadian tank after another suffered fatal hits. Almost 40 Canadian tanks were destroyed, for the loss of just four German panzers

Also on 11 June, an attack was made on the *Hitlerjugend* by Royal Marines from 46 Commando, supported by M4 Sherman tanks from the 10th Canadian Armoured Regiment. The attack made swift initial progress through the villages of Cairon, Lasson and Rosel to the west of Caen, before running into Waffen-SS troops in the village of Rots. Furious close-quarter battle ensued in which the Marines succeeded in ousting the SS troops from the village, but took heavy casualties in doing so. An immediate counterattack was launched, supported by Panthers from SS Panzer Regiment 12, which swiftly drove the Marines out of the village and destroyed several Shermans. However, the Marines attacked again with fresh armoured support. Fighting raged on into the night and through the morning of 12 June before the SS were finally forced out of the village. Losses were heavy on both sides.

For the next two weeks the main thrust of the Allied attack was diverted to other parts of the front, and the position around Caen quietened down. One particularly spectacular engagement did occur, however, which involved I SS Panzer Corps' heavy tank battalion, SS Panzer Battalion 101. Serving in this unit, equipped with the formidable Mk VI Tiger, was SS tank ace SS-Obersturmführer Michael Wittmann. The battalion arrived at the front on 12 June, and on the following day Wittmann took a small force, numbering four Tigers and one Mk IV, on a reconnaissance towards the village of Villers Bocage, where he quickly spotted an advancing group of Allied armoured vehicles. In the subsequent encounter he knocked out 27 Allied tanks and over 20 half-tracks and other vehicles, and escaping unscathed when his panzers were later ambushed.

THE LOSS OF CAEN

On hearing of Wittmann's exploits, SS-Obergruppenführer 'Sepp' Dietrich recommended the award of the Swords to his Knights Cross with Oak Leaves, an award which was swiftly authorised, together with promotion to SS-Hauptsturmführer. It was a fitting reward, for Wittmann's solo effort had all but eliminated the British 22nd Armoured Brigade.

This notable success for I SS Panzer Corps was tempered on the very next day when the commander of the *Hitlerjugend* Division, SS-Brigadeführer Fritz Witt, was killed when a British warship lying off shore successfully bombarded the division's headquarters position. Command of the division then passed to Meyer. 'Panzermeyer' became the youngest divisional commander in the German armed forces, at just 33 years of age.

On 26 June, the Allies launched a major offensive towards the west of Caen, codenamed 'Epsom'. The attack, by the British XXX and VIII Corps, was intended to cut off Caen's defenders and signal an Allied break-out from Normandy. VIII Corps, made up of the 43rd (Wessex) Division, 11th Armoured Division, 15th (Scottish) Division and two brigades of tanks, was to strike into the German line between Caen and Tilly, cross the Odon and Orne rivers and capture the ground between Bretteville and Bourguebus. Some 60,000 troops were available to VIII Corps, as well as over 600 tanks and around 700 pieces of artillery.

The attack commenced at 0730 with a massive artillery barrage and considerable air support. The attack was led by the 15th (Scottish) Division, with tank support, and their path was barred initially by two battalions from the *Hitlerjugend* Division. Although the Germans suffered heavy casualties from the Allied bombardment, sufficient numbers survived to inflict considerable losses on the attackers. Despite bad weather preventing effective air support, the sheer numerical superiority of the attacking troops saw the Waffen-SS positions being overrun.

As pressure on the *Hitlerjugend* Division continued to mount, every available soldier was thrown into the line in a desperate effort to hold back the Allied

> **The attack commenced at 0730 with a massive artillery barrage and considerable air support**

attack. The Panzer Regiment's 2nd Battalion successfully halted the advance of the 11th Armoured Division at Gavrus on the Odon river. The 11th Armoured Division made much better progress near Mouen, and was on the point of over-running elements of SS Panzergrenadier Regiment 25 when the arrival of a single Tiger tank turned the tables against the British Shermans.

By the end of that day, the *Hitlerjugend* Division had succeeded in holding the British offensive, albeit with horrendous losses in both men and in tanks. Over 700 men had been killed and SS Panzer Regiment 12, once boasting around 150 tanks, now had only 47 remaining. When night fell, both sides took advantage of a lull in fighting, the British to consolidate and prepare to continue the next day, and the *Hitlerjugend* to strengthen and reorganise its defences.

The *Leibstandarte* Division had by now arrived at the front from its former base in Belgium, and the decision had also been made to transfer the formidable new II SS Panzer Corps from Poland to Normandy. This formation comprised the the 9th SS Panzer Division *Hohenstaufen* and 10th SS Panzer Division *Frundsberg*. Although the *Hitlerjugend* Division was badly battered and seriously weakened by its dreadful losses, it had no option but to hold the line in an attempt to gain time until the arrival of these fresh forces.

The remnants of SS Panzer Regiment 12 were tasked with defending Hill 112

II SS PANZER CORPS

In addition to II SS Panzer Corps, elements of the 2nd SS Panzer Division *Das Reich* had begun to reach the invasion front, having travelled from the Toulouse area in the south of France. Along the way it had butchered the population of the village of Oradour-sur-Glane, allegedly in reprisal for partisan attacks. The first elements to arrive in the Normandy area were formed into a battle group and placed under the command *Hohenstaufen* in II SS Panzer Corps.

On 27 June the British offensive continued, with the 15th (Scottish) Division leading the way, supported by tanks from the 11th Armoured Division. The British soon pushed the weak SS forces back and advanced towards the lower slopes of Hill 112, which dominated the area. The remnants of SS Panzer Regiment 12 were tasked with defending Hill 112 and the nearby town of Fontaine. Despite being greatly outnumbered, the *Hitlerjugend*'s remaining panzers held the British attackers. On the following day the fighting continued. Despite their superiority in numbers, the Allied tanks were unable to gain a firm hold of this strategic spot and the British had to satisfy themselves with consolidating their bridgeheads over the Odon.

Although the British had penetrated German-held territory by up to 8km (five miles), the corridor they had created was seldom more than 3.2km (two miles) wide. On 28 June General Dollmann, commander of the Seventh Army, decided to launch II SS Panzer Corps against this corridor. On the following day, however, the weather began to clear and Allied fighter-bombers appeared in considerable numbers and, together with British artillery fire, wreaked havoc among the SS panzer units.

When the German attack finally began II SS Panzer Corps made good progress, slicing into the British corridor. Once more the sheer mass of Allied troops facing the Waffen-SS units, acconpanied by their almost unlimited artillery and air support, forced the German advance to slow and eventually halt. On the following day the Germans resumed their advance and made initial progress. By the afternoon, however, the attack began to run out of steam.

The situation had become so perilous that von Rundstedt requested permission to pull back from positions around Caen. Hitler refused absolutely and von Rundstedt's reward was to be relieved of his command, along with his subordinate, General Geyr von Schweppenburg, commander of Panzer Group West.

Operation 'Goodwood'

On 7 July, in preparation for a new ground offensive, the RAF carried out a concentrated bombing raid on Caen with a force of almost 500 bombers. On the following morning I British Corps began an all-out frontal advance on Caen, supported by a concentrated artillery barrage. By evening the Allies had crushed all resistance. A desperate counterattack by a few Panthers from SS Panzer Regiment 12, with infantry in support, only halted the

Above: The Waffen-SS's greatest tank ace: SS-Hauptsturmführer Michael Wittmann, who detroyed a total of 138 enemy tanks and 132 anti-tank guns during a two-year career. Killed in action south of Caen on 8 August 1944, 'Sepp' Dietrich said of him: 'He was a fighter in every way, he lived and breathed action.'

Allied push at the very walls of the Abbey Ardenne. Despite Hitler's orders, the situation had become so critical that Meyer decided that his only chance lay in abandoning that part of the city to the north and west of the River Orne. His fresh-faced youths who had marched confidently into action just a few weeks previously were now exhausted and filthy, with emaciated faces and sunken eyes. In Meyer's own words, his men 'presented a picture of deep human misery'.

During the hours of darkness the *Hitlerjugend* began to pull back over the Orne. Caen had at last fallen. As the division was completing its withdrawal from Caen, the remaining units of the *Leibstandarte* arrived in the area and, on 11 July, relieved the exhausted *Hitlerjugend* survivors.

Within just a few days of taking over from the *Hitlerjugend*, the *Leibstandarte* took the full brunt of the new British offensive, codenamed 'Goodwood'. After the usual ferocious aerial and artillery bombardments, the British attack began on the morning of 18 July. The *Leibstandarte* reacted immediately, launching a desperate counterattack with the 21st Panzer Division. Although overwhelming British pressure gradually forced the Germans back, waiting for the attackers was a line of 8.8cm guns from III Flak Corps. Tank after tank fell victim to the deadly 88s. A new counterattack, which threw back the British with loss. It is estimated that the British lost around 200 tanks. On the following day the British had their revenge, and completely wiped out one of the *Leibstandarte*'s panzergrenadier battalions in vicious close-quarter fighting around the town of Bras.

On 20 July, the Canadians managed to punch their way through the 272nd Infantry Division on the Vassières ridge before being stopped by a battle group from the *Leibstandarte* and the 2nd Panzer Division. 'Goodwood' was called off. By the second half of July 1944, *Das Reich* and the other divisions in LXXXIV Corps were beginning to lose ground. Constant combat attrition on the German side, coupled with the growing strength of the units within the Allied bridgehead as reinforcements continued to pour ashore, ensured that the Germans were gradually pushed back.

On 25 July, the Americans launched Operation 'Cobra', a major offensive led by VII Corps under General Collins which was intended to lead to an American break-out from the Cherbourg peninsula. Confusion reigned at LXXXIV Corps headquarters and a stream of conflicting instructions was issued. These resulted in Waffen-SS troops making long difficult marches under cover of darkness only to receive fresh orders to move again once they had reached their initial objectives. These subsequent movements often had to be made in daylight, attracting the unwelcome attention of Allied fighter-bombers and causing serious losses. By the time they reached their final destinations, the Germans often found them to be already occupied by the Americans and were forced to mount furious attacks before they themselves could dig in.

The attack had been launched during a spell of thick fog which prevented Allied air operations

THE FALAISE POCKET

In early August the Germans struck back, launching a thrust codenamed Operation 'Luttich' towards Avranches. The first wave was to include part of the *Leibstandarte*, together with *Das Reich*, the 116th Panzer Division and parts of *Götz von Berlichingen*. The second assault wave would comprise the remaining elements of the *Leibstandarte*, plus the *Hohenstaufen* and *Frundsberg* Divisions.

The attack began on 7 August and ran into trouble almost straight away. For example, the attack had been launched during a spell of thick fog which prevented Allied air operations but, as the sky cleared, the air filled with fighter-bombers, which proceeded to wreak havoc among the German armour. The offensive fell apart, and by 9 August the Germans had lost the initiative. The Americans immediately renewed their advance. The Waffen-SS troops could not hold the Americans back, and so they carried out a fighting withdrawal over the following week, moving gradually towards the area around Falaise.

Meanwhile, as the British and Canadian forces continued to bear down from the north, and the Americans drove eastwards from Mortain and Vire and north from Alençon towards Argentan, the bulk of the German forces in Normandy were rapidly being constricted in a salient, the neck of which was a narrow gap between Falaise and Argentan. This gap, some 32km (20 miles) wide, was the sole avenue of escape for up to 24 German divisions located nearby, trapped in what was already being referred to as the Falaise Pocket. The *Hitlerjugend* held open the northern edge of the gap, to the south of Falaise, while *Das Reich* was located at the southern edge, to the east of Argentan. The *Hohenstaufen* Division faced units of the British Second Army in the northwest corner of the pocket, while *Frundsberg* faced elements of the US First Army in the southwest corner.

Though over 20,000 trapped German soldiers were able to escape, some 50,000 German troops went into captivity in the Falaise Pocket, and over 5000

German armoured vehicles were destroyed. Fortunately for the Waffen-SS, the *Hohenstaufen*, *Leibstandarte*, *Götz von Berlichingen* and *Das Reich* Divisions had all been pulled out of the pocket before the neck was finally sealed. The *Hitlerjugend* and *Frundsberg* Divisions, however, suffered considerable losses. The former had lost over 9,000 men during the whole of the fighting in Normandy, well over 40 per cent of its strength.

All of the Waffen-SS divisions which had taken part in the Normandy battles had performed exceptionally well, but none more so than youths of the *Hitlerjugend* Division. From here on, however, the Germans would be on the defensive on all fronts, and with Allied superiority growing by the day, none of the senior Waffen-SS commanders had any doubts about the final outcome. For at least two of the Waffen-SS panzer divisions, however, there was still considerable action to come. After the battering it had taken in Normandy, II SS Panzer Corps, comprising the *Hohenstaufen* and *Frundsberg* Divisions, was moved to Holland for a spell of rest and reorganisation. Unknown to the Germans, the area around Arnhem, where the two Waffen-SS formations were resting, was the

Above: Knocked-out British Sherman tanks in Normandy. Allied tanks were markedly inferior to the German Panther and Tiger models. In the hands of crews that had learnt their trade on the Eastern Front, German armoured formations wreaked havoc in Normandy.

Above: Waffen-SS soldiers taken prisoner during the initial Allied airborne assault at Arnhem. The photograph clearly illustrates the youth of some of those serving in the armed SS at this time.

chosen site for the airborne part of a major new Anglo-American offensive, codenamed Operation 'Market-Garden', designed to punch into Germany itself. The British Second Army and part of the US First Army provided the ground assault forces, while First Allied Airborne Army provided the airborne element. Specifically, the US 101st Airborne Division was tasked with the capture of the bridge at Eindhoven, the US 82nd Airborne Division with the capture of the bridge at Nijmegen, and the British I Airborne Corps, comprising the 1st Airborne Division, 1st Polish Independent Parachute Brigade and 52nd (Lowland) Division, with the capture of the bridge at Arnhem.

When the airborne assault began on 17 September the Germans were taken completely by surprise. The commander of Army Group B, Field Marshal Walter Model, immediately placed his forces on the alert. The *Hohenstaufen* was despatched to halt the British airborne troops who had landed just outside the city, while the *Frundsberg* was sent to Nijmegen to halt the progress of Allied ground units, including the British XXX Corps under Lieutenant-General Brian Horrocks. As well as the remnants of the two SS panzer divisions, other minor SS units and a battalion of Dutch SS police were committed to the fray.

By the end of the first day British airborne troops under Lieutenant-Colonel John Frost had reached the bridge and secured its northern end. Overnight, some elements of the 1st Parachute Brigade arrived, bringing Frost's forces up to a strength of around 600 men. While strong enough to hold the northern edge of the bridge, Frost had insufficient strength to capture the entire bridge, the southern end of which was firmly held by Waffen-SS troops. And the latter had heavy weapons and armoured vehicles, neither of which Frost had.

The other British units found themselves in trouble almost immediately. Elements of SS Battle Group *Hohenstaufen* began their advance from the north of the city, while SS Battle Group *Spindler* moved into the Oosterbeek area to the west. Troops from 16th SS Stammbataillon, under SS-Hauptsturmführer Krafft, were positioned between the main landing area and the city itself.

The Germans quickly realised that dislodging Frost's troops from the northern end of the bridge would be no easy task. A direct assault over the bridge from its southern end by a force from SS Armoured Reconnaissance Battalion 9, under SS-Hauptsturmführer Grabner, was a disaster, with Grabner himself being killed and over 20 of the unit's armoured personnel carriers and armoured cars being left shattered and blazing on the bridge. The Germans withdrew to lick their wounds while armour and artillery reinforcements were brought in.

Frost was, by now, beginning to run low on ammunition and food supplies and the 1st Parachute Brigade, on its way to relieve his beleaguered troops, was being held by the Germans some way to the west of the bridge. The arrival of a second wave of British airborne troops brought little relief while, to the south, XXX Corps was still bogged down a good distance from Arnhem with little chance of bringing imminent relief to the airborne strike force.

THE END AT ARNHEM

On 19 September, elements of both the 1st and 4th Parachute Brigades tried to push forwards to the bridge under the cover of a heavy fog. The fog lifted before they could reach their objective, however, exposing the British to the full fury of the German guns, and the attack was routed. To the west of the city, elements of Major-General Stanislaw Sosabowski's Polish Parachute Brigade landed in the area between that held by the two British parachute brigades and that held by Krafft's 16th SS Stammbataillon and were virtually cut to pieces. The ill-fated arrival of the Poles was followed by one of a number of disastrous supply operations, with only about 30 tons, of 400 tons dropped, reaching the British troops.

By now Frost's troops on the northern end of the bridge were coming under attack from SS Battle Group *Knaust* (although a titular SS formation, this unit was in fact commanded by a highly experienced Army officer, Colonel Hans-Peter Knaust). By this time Frost had only around 250 unwounded men at his disposal. The western edge of his shrinking perimeter was also being hit by SS Battle Group *Brinkmann*. Despite his precarious situation, a German call for Frost to surrender was swiftly rejected.

By 20 September the situation had reached a virtual stalemate. British forces were fragmented and disorganised but the Germans themselves were weakened after their recent combat in Normandy, and did not yet have sufficient reinforcements to allow them to overrun their enemy. British-held perimeters had been squeezed considerably, however, and their first aid stations could not be sited out of the line of German fire. A local agreement was reached with the Waffen-SS troops, in which the British withdrew slightly, allowing the Germans to take the buildings in which the wounded were housed, and thereafter the British were treated alongside the German wounded.

> **To the south, XXX Corps was still bogged down a good distance from Arnhem**

Frost's ammunition and rations, especially water, were now critically low. Frost himself had been badly wounded and at around 1800 on the 20th four Tiger tanks attached to SS Battle Group *Knaust* forced their way over the bridge from the north, joining the *Frundsberg* troops on the south bank. Although the Tigers were able to cross the bridge, the tenacity of the British defenders prevented any of Knaust's other armour from following. As the evening wore on, a temporary truce was arranged which allowed the Germans to evacuate over 200 British wounded, including Frost himself.

At around 0900 on the following morning, the remnants of Frost's now greatly depleted force, under the command of Major Gough, attempted to break out towards the north, through the area held by Battle Group *Knaust*. The British force was fragmented into a great many small groups, many of whom were captured but several remained 'at large' for at least two more days, continuing to fight the Germans.

Further west, the shrinking British enclave at Oosterbeek was surrounded by two German forces, SS Battle Group *Hohenstaufen* and Battle Group *Tettau* (under the command of Lieutenant General Hans von Tettau). Although the Germans were able to contain the British, they still had insufficient strength to eliminate the Oosterbeek pocket.

Battle Group *Knaust* had meanwhile reached Elst, to the southwest of Arnhem, where it formed a blocking force to hold off the approaching British XXX Corps, which had crossed the Waal at Nijmegen. From there Arnhem was within artillery range, and XXX Corps was now able to give much-needed fire support to the airborne troops around Oosterbeek.

On 24 September II SS Panzer Corps agreed to a truce with the British in the pocket to allow over 700 wounded airborne troops to be evacuated by the Germans, with a further 500 being evacuated in the same manner on the next day. The lives of many airborne soldiers were saved thanks to the efforts of one of the medical officers of the *Hohenstaufen* Division, SS-Sturmbannführer Dr Egon Skalka and a British medical officer, Dr Warrack.

The stalemate was finally broken by the arrival of the King Tigers of Heavy Panzer Battalion 506. Two companies, each of 15 tanks, were sent to aid the blocking of the advancing XXX Corps at Elst, while the remainder went into action against the eastern flank of the Oosterbeek pocket. At this point the order for the evacuation of the remaining troops from the pocket was issued by the British Second Army. At 2100 on 25 September, a massed artillery barrage by

On 24 September II SS Panzer Corps agreed a truce with the British

XXX Corps began, giving cover while some 37 assault boats from both British and Canadian engineer units crossed the River Rhine to evacuate the men of the 1st British Airborne. The Germans made no real effort to strike at their withdrawing enemy, who blew up their ammunition stocks and spiked their remaining guns before they left their positions. The evacuation had ended by first light on 26 September. Operation 'Market-Garden was over'.

The Allies sustained 17,000 casualties at Arnhem. German losses were put at around 3300, though it is probably higher. Nevertheless, after the losses suffered in Normandy, the result at Arnhem was a much-needed propaganda coup, and showed once again that even in a weakened and battered state, the Waffen-SS was capable of achieving successes.

Above: A German StuG III at Arnhem. The defeat of 'Market-Garden' meant there would be no quick end to the war in the West. But for the Wehrmacht and the Waffen-SS, the future held only the prospect of defeat and annihilation.

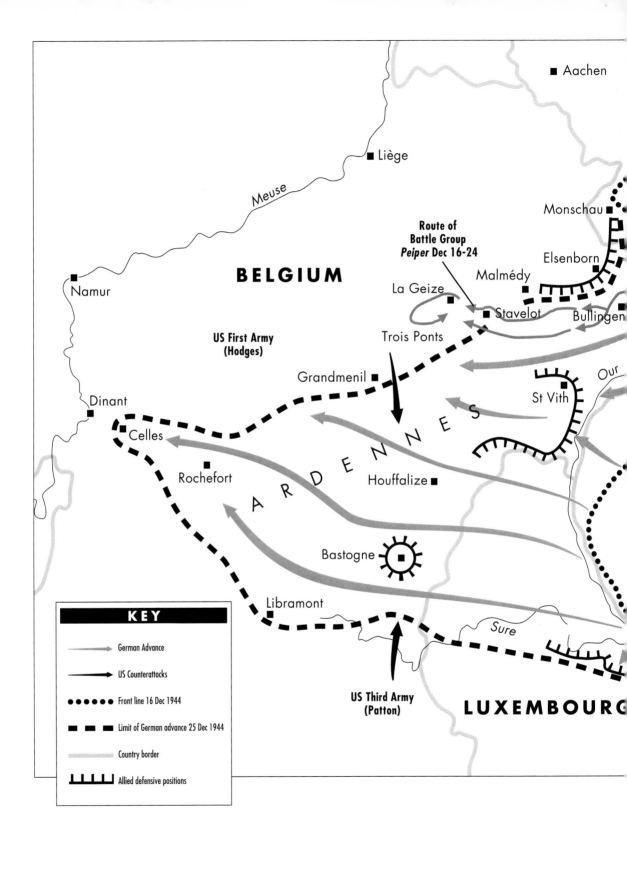

■ Aachen

■ Liège

Meuse

BELGIUM

Monschau ■

Elsenborn

Malmédy

**Route of
Battle Group
Peiper Dec 16-24**

■ Namur

La Geize ■

Stavelot

Bullingen

**US First Army
(Hodges)**

Trois Ponts

Grandmenil ■

Our

Dinant

St Vith

A R D E N N E S

Celles

Houffalize ■

■ Rochefort

Bastogne

Libramont

Sure

**US Third Army
(Patton)**

LUXEMBOURG

Sixth SS
Panzer Army
(Dietrich)

osheim

SCHNEE
EIFEL

Panzer Army
(Manteuffel)

GERMANY

eventh Army
(andenberger)

Echternach

The SS Ardennes Offensive

Operation 'Wacht am Rhein' was designed to regain the initiative in the West by cutting through the Allied armies and taking the strategically important port of Antwerp. The grandly titled 6th SS Panzer Army was the main component of the German force, but when the offensive was launched even the vaunted Waffen-SS could not give Hitler the victory he so badly wanted. The end result was a costly battle of attrition the Germans could ill afford.

Even as the German armies were on the retreat after the mauling they had received in Normandy, Hitler was planning a last, all-out attack in the West, under the codename 'Wacht am Rhein', which was aimed at splitting the British and American forces by driving four entire German armies westwards through the Ardennes from the German border to the coast at Antwerp. Hitler counted on the panic and confusion this would cause between the Western Allies, allowing him to transfer a sizeable portion of his reserves to the Eastern Front to deliver a similar devastating blow against the Soviets.

Most of Hitler's senior commanders, including Field Marshal Gerd von Rundstedt and Field Marshal Walther Model, Commander-in-Chief West and commander of Army Group B respectively, were horrified at Hitler's ridiculously optimistic and grandiose plans, arguing to no avail for more modest objectives. An entire new army, the 6th SS Panzer Army, was formed specifically for the Ardennes Offensive and placed under the command of one of Hitler's favourite generals, SS-Oberstgruppenführer Josef 'Sepp' Dietrich. Dietrich's army would

Right: SS panzer-grenadiers hitch a ride on a StuG III self-propelled gun during the build-up for the Ardennes Offensive. Hitler believed that his attack would overwhelm and separate the Allied armies, allowing him to destroy them piece-meal. In 1940, an offensive from the Ardennes had resulted in the British evacuation at Dunkirk and the eventual fall of France. But at the end of 1944 the Wehrmacht was inferior to the Allies in terms of men and materiel, and the enemy controlled the skies. The omens for success were not good.

The main effort on the northern flank would come from the 6th SS Panzer Army

include I SS Panzer Corps, commanded by SS-Gruppenführer Hermann Priess and comprising the *Leibstandarte* and the *Hitlerjugend* Divisions, as well as the Army's 12th and 277th Volksgrenadier Divisions and the Luftwaffe's 3rd Para-troop Division; II SS Panzer Corps, commanded by SS-Obergruppenführer Willi Bittrich, comprising the *Das Reich* and the *Hohenstaufen* Divisions; and LX-VII Corps, commanded by Lieutenant-General Otto Hitzfeld, comprising the 272nd and 326th Volksgrenadier Divisions. In addition, a number of independent battalions of assault guns, Tiger tanks, Jadgpanthers, combat engineers, artillery and other troops were allocated to the 6th SS Panzer Army.

As well as Dietrich's powerful force, one of Germany's top panzer generals, Hasso von Manteuffel, had command of the Fifth Panzer Army for the offensive. Manteuffel's army comprised LXVI Corps, under General Walter Lucht, with the 18th and 62nd Volksgrenadier Divisions; LVIII Panzer Corps, under General Walther Kruger, with the 116th Panzer Division and 560th Volks-grenadier Division; and XXXXVII Panzer Corps, under General Heinrich von Luttwitz, with the 2nd Panzer Division, *Panzer Lehr* Division and 26th Volks-grenadier Division. As well as the two panzer armies, other formations available for the offensive included the Seventh Army under General der Panzertruppe Brandenberger, and the Fifteenth Army. In addition, the High Command also retained control of additional reserve forces, such as the 9th and 167th Volks-grenadier Divisions and 3rd Panzergrenadier Division, some of which would eventually join the attack.

The front along which the advance would be made stretched for some 135km (85 miles), and was held by just four American divisions. The main effort on the northern flank of the offensive would come from the 6th SS Panzer Army, which would attack along a relatively narrow front between Monschau and Losheim and race for the Meuse river on the stretch between Liège and Huy. Four days had been allocated to reach these objectives. Spearheading 6th SS Panzer Army's move would be I SS Panzer Corps. The *Hitlerjugend* Division would attack from start points at Hollerath, Udenbreth and Losheim, heading for the northern half of the area between Liège and Huy, while the *Leibstandarte* struck from Losheim and Manderfeld, aiming for the southern half of the target area. In the event, things would begin to go wrong for the Germans within just a few hours of the offensive being opened.

At first light on 16 December 1944, a massed barrage of artillery shells and rocket projectiles hit the American positions all along the front. Opposite I SS Panzer Corps were just a handful of relatively inexperienced US infantry battalions. However, the Americans put up a determined defence and, in an offensive where time was of the essence, managed to cause a significant delay to the attackers. By the end of the first day, the German forces had signally failed to achieve a decisive breakthrough, and even American units with little combat experience had held their positions.

BATTLE GROUP *PEIPER*

One of the main spearhead units of the German forces during the Ardennes offensive was Battle Group *Peiper*, commanded by SS-Obersturmbannführer Joachim Peiper. Often described as the personification of the ideal Waffen-SS soldier, Peiper was tall, blond, handsome, young and fanatically loyal. He had already displayed great gallantry on a number of occasions and had been highly decorated. Peiper's battle group comprised some 5000 élite troops composed of 1 Battalion, SS Panzer Regiment 1; heavy SS Panzer Battalion 501, equipped with the formidable King Tiger; 3 Battalion, SS Panzergrenadier Regiment 2; 2 Battalion, SS Armoured Artillery Regiment 1; a company of armoured engineers; and Luftwaffe support in the form of anti-aircraft troops. Because of the difficulties expected in breaking through the American lines, a spearhead unit of paratroops had been dropped ahead of Peiper's battle group to clear the roads.

Peiper was well aware of the problems facing him. His route lay along narrow winding roads, with many steep hills and deep gullies, through wooded terrain ideal for defensive ambushes. Even small numbers of determined defenders could cause havoc with the German timetable in such ground. As Peiper advanced, he was infuriated to find that roads which should have been cleared of mines had not been touched and was forced to clear them himself. Two half-tracks were destroyed in the process, but the road was opened and Peiper pressed onwards. On reaching the village of Lanzerath, Peiper found the 'spearhead' paratroopers resting, awaiting the coming of full daylight before advancing. No sentries had been posted and the village seemed deserted. Peiper stormed into the paratrooper's command post and berated the colonel in command, demanding that he release one of his battalions to Peiper to press on with the advance.

In the early hours of 17 September, Peiper reached the village of Buchholz, which turned out to have been abandoned by the Americans. Pressing on, the

> **One of the main spearhead units of the German forces during the offensive was Battle Group *Peiper***

battle group reached Honsfeld just before dawn broke and ran into its first opposition. A fierce battle ensued, and almost immediately the Germans came under attack from Allied fighter-bombers. Though the Luftwaffe's flak gunners drove off the enemy planes, Peiper could not afford the time to eliminate the American defenders, and so left a handful of tanks behind to support the para-troops while they seized Honsfeld. Peiper pressed on, his objective an American fuel dump at Buellingen (the numerous delays and congested roads had meant that his tanks were already beginning to run low on fuel). Fortunately for Peiper, Buellingen was captured intact, before the Americans could fire the fuel dump, and the battle group was able to fill its fuel tanks before continuing. Schoppen, Ondenval and Thirimont were captured by midday on 17 December.

THE MALMÉDY MASSACRE

Some way ahead of the main body of the battle group, the spearhead element, a pair of Mk V Panther tanks, had surprised an American convoy at Baugnez and immediately opened fire. The Americans were quickly overwhelmed and a number of prisoners, from the 285th Field Observation Battery, were taken. The prisoners were grouped in a field at the main crossroads in Baugnez and subsequently shot. The Malmédy Massacre resulted in 40 disarmed and surrendered American soldiers dying in a hail of fire. The incident resulted in yet another stain on the already blackened reputation of the Waffen-SS.

While the Malmédy incident was in progress, Peiper himself had left the scene, racing on to Ligneuville. A captured American officer had revealed that a US divisional staff, complete with commanding general, was located in the village and Peiper was intent on capturing them. He arrived, in fact, just a few minutes after the Americans had departed in a great rush, abandoning the meals they were about to enjoy. So narrow was their escape that their food was still hot when the Germans captured the hotel in which they had been billeted.

Peiper remained in the town for a short period to confer with the *Leibstandarte*'s commander, SS-Oberführer Wilhelm Mohnke, while the battle group continued on. Without its charismatic commander, however, Battle Group *Peiper* was less aggressive. On the road leading into Stavelot, for example, a small force of American troops had established a roadblock. In the fading daylight, the lead tanks of the battle group reached the roadblock, only to come under fire from an American bazooka. Unaware that their opponents were so small in number, the Germans retreated out of range and halted for the night.

By the next morning Peiper had returned, and after a barrage from the battle group's artillery, he led his men into the attack, swiftly smashing through the weak US forces in the town. Once again, however, pressure of time precluded a full-scale hunt through Stavelot to eject all of its American occupiers, and Peiper had to satisfy himself with driving on and leaving a small contingent to secure the route through the town. His next objective was the small town of Trois Ponts, so named because of the three bridges crossing the rivers Salm and Amblève at this location. A planned attack on these vital river crossings came to naught when the Americans blew the bridges over both rivers.

Left: A Panther tank moves forward during the opening phase of the offensive. The Germans amassed 1200 tanks and assault guns for the attack in the Ardennes. However, this figure is less impressive when it is remembered that the Germans only had a quarter of the fuel they regarded as the absolute minimum. As a result, many tanks simply ground to a halt.

The German column came under attack from American fighter-bombers

Peiper was forced to turn towards La Gleize, which was reached without incident. Pressing onwards, the battle group discovered an intact bridge over the Amblève near Cheneux. Shortly after crossing, however, the German column came under attack from American fighter-bombers and was forced to take cover in the nearby woods for several hours until weather conditions worsened and halted Allied air operations. Although the damage sustained in this attack was

Right: Joachim Peiper, photographed earlier in the war. Often described as the epitomy of the Waffen-SS officer, he and his men performed well in the Ardennes. They also displayed other attributes of the SS: a disregard for life and the shooting of prisoners out of hand.

As it drew near to the river crossings at Neuf Moulin, the bridge was blown up before it could be secured

minimal, precious, irredeemable hours had been lost, and Battle Group *Peiper* was falling ever further behind schedule.

The battle group ploughed on, reaching the River Lienne. As it drew near to the river crossing at Neuf Moulin, though, the bridge was blown up before it could be secured. Smaller bridges were captured to both the north and south of the main bridge, but these were incapable of taking Peiper's heavier armour. A small force of armoured infantry in half-tracks did cross and investigated the area on the opposite bank, only to come under fire from American tank destroyers and be forced to retreat. With no heavy bridging equipment available to him, Peiper was forced to withdraw into the woods near Stoumont for the night, leaving a detachment to guard the bridges.

At Stavelot, meanwhile, armoured reinforcements had reached those American troops still occupying parts of the town, and the troops Peiper had left behind to hold the route open were now in grave danger of being cut off. Despite support arriving from the *Leibstandarte*, the Germans were unable to clear the Americans from Stavelot and, by the end of 18 December, the town was all but back in American hands. A small supply column had, however, managed to reach the main body of Battle Group *Peiper* at La Gleize, boosting the morale of the Waffen-SS troops.

Peiper's force had made by far the most substantial gains of any of the Waffen-SS units and so the corps commander, SS-Gruppenführer Hermann Priess, now ordered the *Leibstandarte* to concentrate on assisting Peiper. Despite the best efforts of the *Leibstandarte* elements struggling to oust the Americans from Stavelot and clear the route towards Peiper's troops at La Gleize, the Americans held on tenaciously to the town. Elements of 2 Battalion of the *Leibstandarte*, under SS-Sturmbannführer Schnelle, did, however, make their way through to La Gleize on the morning of 20 December. At dawn on that same day, Peiper had launched his attack on Stoumont and succeeded in sweeping the American defenders out of the village. The Americans suffered around 250 casualties in the fight, and had some 100 or so of their soldiers taken prisoner.

PEIPER ABANDONS THE ADVANCE

Peiper immediately sent a pursuit group after the retreating Americans, only to have it run into an American tank and infantry force, which was itself preparing to counterattack his battle group. Three Panther tanks were destroyed at close range, and the Germans withdrew rather than risk further losses as concentrated American artillery fire also began to fall. Peiper, once again running low on fuel and supplies, was forced to give up thoughts of advancing any further, and concentrate instead on securing the areas he already held. Unfortunately for the Germans, Battle Group *Peiper* had been halted just a few kilometres away from a US Army fuel dump containing around two million gallons of fuel!

Elements of Battle Group *Peiper* were now stretched out over a considerable distance, and the point units with Peiper himself were not only running short of supplies but also facing US formations which were slowly but gradually increasing in strength. A number of small supply columns which attempted to reach Peiper were intercepted and destroyed. Continuing attempts by German troops to oust the Americans from Stavelot and re-open the supply lines to Peiper were also foiled. It was becoming apparent to I SS Panzer Corps that a situation might well arise in which Battle Group *Peiper* would have to fight its way back out of an American encirclement. However, 6th SS Panzer Army refused to countenance a retreat, and insisted on the *Leibstandarte* continuing its attempts to reinforce Peiper's group. This was easier said than done.

Three Panther tanks were destroyed, and the Germans withdrew rather than risk further losses

Peiper was soon being compelled to shorten his perimeter in the face of the growing strength of American attacks, and concentrate all his forces around La Gleize and the river crossing near Cheneux. American attacks increased in intensity, losses were mounting and ammunition was running perilously low. The Luftwaffe attempted a supply drop on 22 December, but around 90 per cent of the vital material landed in American-held territory.

La Gleize itself had by now been turned into a sea of rubble by constant American shelling. It was clear that Peiper's positions in the town had become totally untenable by this stage, and so I SS Panzer Corps finally gave permission for a break-out to be attempted. The lack of fuel precluded any attempt at a fighting break-out, so the remaining panzers were destroyed and Battle Group *Peiper* withdrew stealthily, under the cover of darkness, leaving all their heavy equipment and wounded behind.

A small rearguard was left behind to destroy the last vehicles, and the medical officer attached to the battle group, SS-Obersturmführer Dittman, volunteered to remain behind with the wounded. Although they became involved in several skirmishes with American units, the bulk of the battle group reached the safety of the German lines in the early hours of 25 December. Despite the ultimate failure of his mission, Peiper and his battle group had made the greatest penetration of enemy territory and had come closest of all the German units to achieving its objectives. Peiper was duly rewarded with the Swords and Oak Leaves clasp to his Knights Cross of the Iron Cross.

By 20 December, Field Marshal Model had decided to shift the responsibility for the main thrust of the German attack from the 6th SS Panzer Army to the Fifth Panzer Army, in part because of the difficulties encountered by Peiper at the head of the advance. II SS Panzer Corps was therefore deployed to support 6th SS Panzer Army's new role, that of providing cover to the northern flank of von Manteuffel's Fifth Panzer Army.

The American defenders of the crossroads were finally driven out by the Waffen-SS grenadiers

THE OFFENSIVE BEGINS TO FALTER

Some indication of the chaotic nature of the conditions prevailing can be judged from the fact that, although the *Hohenstaufen* Division was formally committed to battle on 18 December, it took four days struggling through congested roads to reach the front. Attacking northwest from Houffalize towards Manhay, the route taken by the Waffen-SS troops had been detected by the Americans and a blocking force intercepted them at a crossroads by Baraque de Fraiture. Extreme fuel shortages, coupled with a brief improvement in weather conditions which allowed US fighter-bombers to take to the air, forced the Germans into a whole day of almost total inactivity, and allowed the Americans precious time to bring up reinforcements. Fuel supplies finally arrived on 22 December and, by the early morning of the next day, the *Hohenstaufen* Division was ready to roll. The American defenders of the crossroads were finally driven out by the Waffen-SS grenadiers after several hours of bitter fighting.

From Manhay, meanwhile, the *Das Reich* Division wheeled left, heading towards Grandmenil and sweeping aside an American blocking force with ease.

Grandmenil fell soon afterwards. Attempts to move farther westwards, however, were halted by a fresh US infantry regiment. With the lead German armour having outrun its infantry support, caution prevailed and the panzers withdrew. The Americans were now bringing up their 3rd Armored Division, whose troops suffered the indignity of being mistaken for Germans and were therefore bombed and strafed by their own fighter-bombers. On their arrival some elements did manage to penetrate into Grandmenil itself, but were immediately ejected by the determined Waffen-SS grenadiers. Subsequent attempts to oust the Germans as dark fell were also rebuffed.

On 26 December 1944, by pure coincidence, a fresh German attempt to advance from Grandmenil was launched just as the Americans made yet another assault on the town. One arm of the two-pronged German attack met the Americans head-on on the Grandmenil-Erezee road. In the furious battle which developed, the German were halted, but only at terrible cost to the Americans, who were left with only two battle-worthy Sherman tanks after the fighting had ceased. The other German armoured column advanced along narrow roads through heavily wooded terrain. It made good progress until it and found its route blocked by felled trees. It then came under well-aimed American artillery fire, which forced it to withdraw.

Above: Allied tanks in the Ardennes. As this picture shows, the snow and ice on the ground made road movement slow and hazardous for both sides. However, the Germans also had to contend with Allied air superiority, which meant they often had to move their vehicles at night to avoid being strafed by enemy aircraft.

Later that same day the Americans renewed their efforts to capture both Man-hay and Grandmenil, and launched heavy aerial and artillery bombardments against both towns. Overwhelmed by the sheer weight of US firepower, the Waffen-SS troops were forced to retreat and, by 27 December, both towns were in American hands again. The Germans were then gradually pushed back towards the crossroads at Fraiture.

The *Das Reich's* companion in II SS Panzer Corps, the *Hohenstaufen* Division, had gone into action to the north of *Das Reich*, advancing via St Vith towards Poteau and Halleux and reaching as far as Villettes and Bra, where it was finally held by the US 82nd Airborne Division. Halted here, it turned south in the opening days of the new year to take part in the effort to eliminate the American pocket holding out at Bastogne, where it joined the *Hitlerjugend* and the *Leibstandarte*. Bastogne was held by elements of the US 101st Airborne Division. The German attempts to take Bastogne were to prove fruitless and instead an American counteroffensive to relieve the town rapidly grew in strength.

FAILURE AT BASTOGNE

By this stage the *Hohenstaufen* Division had only 30 tanks remaining, and some of its battalions numbered only 150 or so men, little more than company strength. Many sub-units of the Waffen-SS divisions, such as the *Hitlerjugend's* artillery regiment, had been left stranded along the route of the offensive for lack of fuel. Although the Waffen-SS troops still retained a surprisingly high level of morale, in their weakened state they were unable to overcome the stout defence put up by the Americans, who included élite units such as the 101st Airborne Division. Several penetrations into the American perimeters were made, mostly by the Waffen-SS divisions, but the Germans were just too weak to carry their attacks through. General George Patton himself said of the Waffen-SS troops at this stage of the battle: 'They are colder, weaker and hungrier than we are, but they are still doing a great piece of fighting.'

On 1 January 1945, the battered remnants of the *Leibstandarte* were withdrawn from the front and ordered into reserve, to be followed on 6 January by the *Hitlerjugend*. It was obvious that the offensive was all but over and, with a major Soviet advance brewing in the East, Hitler ordered the withdrawal of the Waffen-SS panzer divisions for transfer to the crumbling Eastern Front. The *Hohenstaufen*, the last to depart, completed its withdrawal on 24 January.

Before closing, mention should be made of one further infamous unit which participated in the offensive. Its successes in purely physical, military terms, were modest, but in terms of the effect it had on Allied morale, it can be said to be one of the most successful of all participating units: Panzerbrigade 150. This unit, commanded by SS-Obersturmbannführer Otto Skorzeny, was to be equipped with captured American vehicles and manned, wherever possible, by English-speaking Germans. In the event, insufficient captured vehicles were available and the Germans had to make do with disguising their own vehicles with additional plating to alter their distinctive outlines, painting them in US Army olive green, and adding large white star Allied markings. In addition, squads of German commandos, dressed in American uniforms and posing as US military police, carried out reconnaissance missions behind the enemy lines and caused considerable disruption by mis-directing American convoys and so on.

Although the armoured elements of Panzerbrigade 150 achieved only limited success, their disguised vehicles rarely fooling the enemy, Skorzeny's commandos did sow widespread panic behind the enemy lines. Once it became known that Germans dressed in American uniform were operating behind the American lines, an air of paranoia rapidly emerged, almost every US soldier worrying whether the next 'American' he met might be an impostor. Several unfortunate US soldiers were shot by their own side in cases of mistaken identity. All sorts of rumours began to spread like wildfire, including one which had the German commandos on a mission to strike deep behind Allied lines and mount an assassination attempt on General Eisenhower. These rumours were given credence by Eisenhower's staff, who increased security precautions to such an extent that the general himself complained at the restrictions on his freedom of

Above: One German who got something from the Ardennes Offensive: SS-Obersturmführer Georg Preuss. He was awarded the Knights Cross for his leadership of 10 Company, SS-Panzergrenadier Regiment 2, *Leibstandarte* Division.

movement. Successful as these operations had been, they could amount to little more than nuisance value in overall terms. Needless to say, Skorzeny's men were breaching the rules of war, and any who were captured were executed as spies.

By 10 February 1945, all of the German units were back on the east bank of the Rhine. The offensive had been a total and absolute failure and had achieved only the squandering of the Wehrmacht's carefully husbanded and irreplaceable reserves. The battle had been costly for both sides. The Allies had lost approximately 75,000 men dead, captured or wounded, the Germans only slight less than this. The German had lost some 600 or so tanks in the action, though a large number of those had actually been destroyed by their own crews to prevent them falling into Allied hands after they had run out of fuel. The Allies are estimated to have lost between 700 and 800. For the Allies, however, replacement of these material losses was simple. For the Germans, the loss of so much armour at this stage in the war was catastrophic.

On the German side, some 66 soldiers were decorated with the Knights Cross of the Iron Cross for gallantry or distinguished leadership, of which 11 were from the Waffen-SS: seven from *Das Reich*, three from the *Leibstandarte*, and one from the *Hitlerjugend*. More significant was the fact that at this stage of the war not even the Waffen-SS could halt the military reverses the Third Reich was suffering in ever-greater numbers. Indeed, during the Ardennes Offensive it had been Army units that had made the greatest advances. The supermen were failing.

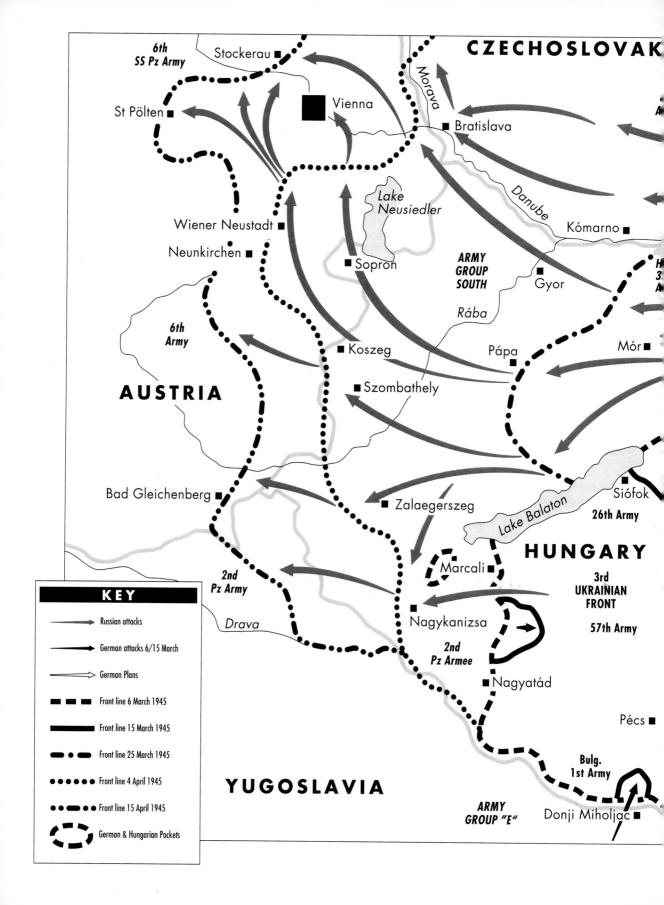

CZECHOSLOVAK

6th
SS Pz Army

Stockerau

Morava

St Pölten

Vienna

Bratislava

Danube

Lake
Neusiedler

Kómarno

Wiener Neustadt

ARMY
GROUP
SOUTH

Gyor

Neunkirchen

Sopron

Rába

6th
Army

Koszeg

Pápa

Mór

AUSTRIA

Szombathely

Bad Gleichenberg

Zalaegerszeg

Siófok

Lake Balaton

26th Army

HUNGARY

2nd
Pz Army

Marcali

3rd
UKRAINIAN
FRONT

Drava

Nagykanizsa

57th Army

2nd
Pz Armee

Nagyatád

Pécs

Bulg.
1st Army

YUGOSLAVIA

ARMY
GROUP "E"

Donji Miholjac

KEY

→	Russian attacks
→	German attacks 6/15 March
⇾	German Plans
▬ ▬ ▬	Front line 6 March 1945
▬▬▬	Front line 15 March 1945
▬ ·▬· ▬	Front line 25 March 1945
• • • • •	Front line 4 April 1945
▬• ▬• ▬•	Front line 15 April 1945
⬭	German & Hungarian Pockets

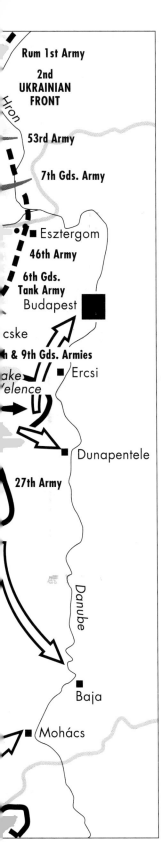

Rum 1st Army

2nd
UKRAINIAN
FRONT

Hron

53rd Army

7th Gds. Army

Esztergom

46th Army

6th Gds.
Tank Army

Budapest

cske

h & 9th Gds. Armies

ake
elence

Ercsi

Dunapentele

27th Army

Danube

Baja

Mohács

Operation 'Spring Awakening'

The second half of 1944 had seen disaster after disaster for Hitler on the Eastern Front. Most of his east European allies had either been overrun by the Soviets or had changed sides and were now fighting against him. Hitler was determined to reverse the dire situation in the East, and chose his Waffen-SS divisions to be the spearhead of what was to be the last German offensive of World War II. However, the weather and Hitler's ludicrously inflated expectations combined to turn the attack into a rout.

The Hungarian capital, Budapest, was defended by units from General Otto Wöhler's Army Group South, including the 8th and 22nd SS Cavalry Divisions *Florian Geyer* and *Maria Theresa*, as well as the 18th SS-Freiwilligen Panzergrenadier Division *Horst Wessel*. Although Budapest was strongly defended, and the Red Army was all but exhausted after its pell-mell advance through eastern Europe, it would clearly be only a matter of time before the combined strength of two complete Red Army Fronts, Second and Third Ukrainian, was gathered to smash into the German defenders.

Initially unable to break through the strong German defences to the south of the Hungarian capital, between Budapest and Lake Balaton, Marshal Tolbukhin swung his armies north, by-passing the eastern edges of Budapest, and renewed his attack from the northeast. The German defences here were swiftly overrun and the main roads between Budapest and Vienna were cut. The Soviets then turned south along the west bank of the Danube, isolating Budapest.

Right: The newly appointed pro-German Hungarian defence minister, Marshal Beregfy, inspects defensive positions of the *Florian Geyer* Division on the outskirts of Budapest, late 1944. The division was destroyed during the attempted break-out from the city.

The German garrison in the capital held back all Soviet attempts to drive them out of the city

On 26 December IV SS Panzer Corps, comprising at this time the élite 3rd SS Panzer Division *Totenkopf* and 5th SS Panzer Division *Wiking*, was diverted from its positions around Warsaw in an attempt to burst through the Soviet positions around the north of Budapest and relive the beleaguered city. The attack was a total failure, with the Red Army's own counterattack forcing the Germans onto the defensive.

The German garrison in the capital held back all Soviet attempts to drive them out of the city, but the end was inevitable. SS-Obergruppenführer Pfeffer-Wildenbruch, commander of the defence forces, authorised a break-out from the Hungarian capital on 11 February 1945. The city garrison, some 70,000 men strong, was split into three assault groups in an attempt to drive through to the west. The Soviets anticipated the move and opened up with all their artillery and rocket launchers on the forces attempting to escape.

The badly shaken German and Hungarian units were then mopped-up by the Red Army. Of the 70,000 men who attempted to escape the city, only 790 reached German lines. Nine entire German divisions had ceased to exist.

Once Budapest had been taken, a considerable number of Soviet divisions were then released to take part in a new offensive aimed at capturing the German held oil-fields at Nagykanizsa. This was now one of the very few sources of fuel left to Hitler's rapidly contracting Third Reich, and their loss would be catastrophic. Only 80km (50 miles) separated the Soviets from the vital oil-fields, and Hitler decided that only a powerful new offensive could be counted upon to throw the Soviets back over the River Danube, stabilise the situation in Hungary, and defend the approaches to Vienna.

PLANS FOR 'SPRING AWAKENING'

Hitler decided to entrust this new operation, codenamed 'Spring Awakening', to his finest remaining divisions, and thus ordered the removal of the 6th SS Panzer Army from the Ardennes front for immediate transfer to the East. Orders were issued for I SS Panzer Corps, comprising the *Leibstandarte* and *Hitlerjugend* Divisions, and II SS Panzer Corps, with the *Das Reich* and *Hohenstaufen* Divisions, to move to the so-called 'Margarethe' positions located in Hungary.

The move, at Hitler's insistence, was to take place in absolute secrecy. All identifying insignia were to be removed from uniforms and vehicles, all units were given cover-names, and corps headquarters were not permitted to become operational until their constituent divisions were in place. The measures became ludicrous. For example, the commander of the 6th SS Panzer Army, SS-Oberstgruppenführer 'Sepp' Dietrich, was not permitted to enter the operational area until just before the offensive was launched for fear his presence might be detected by Soviet spies.

Hitler's plan involved a combined attack by Army Group South and Army Group Southeast. General Wöhler's Army Group South, comprising the 6th SS Panzer Army, Sixth Army, Eighth Army and the Hungarian Third Army, would strike south between Lake Balaton and Lake Velence, while Army Group Southeast, with the Second Panzer Army, would attack from west of the Soviet lines. It was hoped that Marshal Tolbukhin's Third Ukrainian Front, which comprised the 4th Guards Army, 26th and 57th Armies, as well as the 1st Bulgarian Army, would thus be crushed.

The Germans had good reason to expect the ground in this region to be frozen solid in early March. However, the spring thaws had come much earlier than normal and the usual iron-hard ground was instead a soft boggy morass. Into this sea of glutinous mud, Dietrich's heavy panzers would sink all the way up to their axles and even, in a few extreme cases, all the way up to their turrets.

> Hitler decided that only a powerful new offensive could be counted upon to throw the Soviets back

Right: Waffen-SS troops fighting in Budapest, December 1944. Note the soldier on the left is armed with an MP43 assault rifle, which first saw service at Kursk in July 1943.

By the time the SS troopers reached their launch points, they were already soaking wet

Prior to the opening of the offensive proper, I SS Panzer Corps had launched an attack aimed at smashing a Soviet bridgehead at Gran, northwest of Budapest, in a lightning assault. The attack was a complete success, but had the effect of forewarning the Soviets that powerful Waffen-SS units had arrived in the area. The Soviet High Command correctly predicted that this meant that a major offensive was imminent, and also correctly predicted the target area would be the land bridge between the two great lakes. The Soviets therefore began strengthening their defences in this area. Massive new minefields were rapidly laid and a myriad of tank traps hastily constructed. The Germans were totally unaware of these developments, because Hitler's insistence on secrecy had even prevented individual units from sending out reconnaissance patrols lest they be intercepted and the parent formations identified. In effect, the attackers were going in blind, and would suffer accordingly.

On the opening day of the offensive, 6 March, snow began to fall, further compounding the already atrocious ground conditions. To preserve the element of surprise, and not knowing that the Soviets were well aware of the coming attack, some Waffen-SS grenadiers had been dropped off as much as 18km (11 miles) from their start points lest the sound of their trucks alert the enemy to their presence. By the time the SS troopers reached the launch point for their attack, they were already soaking wet, freezing and exhausted. Many did not reach the start line in time. This was disastrous, for with no powerful and immediate infantry attack to follow the barrage from the German artillery, the Soviets had ample time to recover. In several cases the armoured support for the Waffen-SS troops had become so hopelessly bogged down in the German rear that the infantry were forced to launch their attacks without it, and suffered horrendous casualties as a result.

Despite their problems, the Waffen-SS troops threw themselves into battle with their customary élan. These Waffen-SS divisions were no longer the mighty formations of two years before. Combat attrition had cost them many of their best troops, and the quality of the replacements they received could not hope to match that of those they had lost. Nevertheless, even the greenest of the inadequately trained replacements were aware of the combat reputations of the divisions in which they now served, and gave their utmost in the uneven battle which developed. Unfortunately, such enthusiasm counted for little against the well-equipped and highly professional Red Army units.

THE OFFENSIVE MAKES LITTLE HEADWAY

The *Hitlerjugend* ran into trouble almost immediately. On the right flank of the *Leibstandarte*, its main objective was the seizure of the Sio Canal. The advance hit heavily defended Soviet positions at Odon-Puzsta, and these were only the first line of the Red Army defences. Only after a full day of bitter fighting and with the assistance of an attack by Luftwaffe fighters did the division break through the Soviet lines. The *Das Reich* Division arrived several hours late at its start point, thus losing the advantage of the preparatory artillery barrage, and was further disadvantaged by having to attack without armoured support. Despite this, the SS grenadiers characteristically stormed into the first line of defences and captured several important objectives.

Below: Red Army troops fight their way into Budapest, January 1945. The attempt by the *Wiking* and *Totenkopf* Divisions to relieve the city was a failure. The Hungarian capital fell on 13 February 1945.

Soviet counterattacks were launched almost immediately. German losses suffered in successfully beating these off left them too weak to press forward again as planned. However, by 11 March the town of Simontornya had been captured and a bridgehead established over the Sio Canal, one of the initial objectives for I SS Panzer Corps. German units were already feeling the effects of shortages of fuel and ammunition, though, to say nothing of their crippling losses in men and tanks. Although the Germans had maintained a forward momentum, they were now slowing drastically as Soviet resistance intensified. By mid-March, the 6th SS Panzer Army had only around 200 tanks and self-propelled guns still operational, prompting Dietrich to ask, without success, that the offensive be halted.

Along the line of advance allocated to the *Leibstandarte* Division, it was once again Joachim Peiper who achieved the greatest progress. Due to the dreadful ground conditions, successful progress could only be made along the few good roads in the area and, of course, the Soviets had concentrated their defences along these routes. Peiper threw caution to the wind and remained on the roads, nonetheless, fighting his way through all the Soviet attempts to halt him. Within four days of the offensive beginning, he had advanced some 72km (45 miles) and was within 40km (25 miles) of Budapest itself.

> **By mid-March, the 6th SS Panzer Army had only around 200 tanks and self-propelled guns operational**

THE RUSSIANS HIT BACK

Despite Peiper's success, the bulk of the German force was still floundering way behind schedule when, on 18 March, the Soviets launched their main counter-offensive and smashed into the lead German and Hungarian units. Although the Germans withstood this initial assault, their Hungarian allies simply disintegrated. By 19 March the Hungarians had vanished. A great gap now existed in the German lines, into which the Soviets pushed masses of men and tanks.

General Wöhler immediately called off the offensive and started to pull his divisions back to plug the gap left by the Hungarians. It was an exceedingly irate Peiper who grudgingly halted and retreated to defend the main Budapest–Vienna highway. The Soviets who followed him were sure that the Germans were fleeing in disarray, but they reckoned without Peiper. The armoured divisions which pursued him lost over 120 of their Josef Stalin II tanks to the Panthers of his battle group. Nevertheless, it was a Parthian shot.

By now the German line was in danger of complete disintegration. The Waffen-SS divisions were being bled white. Dietrich desperately reshuffled his divisions to cover crisis spots, but as soon as one was moved, the area it had vacated was overrun. Meanwhile, IV SS Panzer Corps, consisting of the *Totenkopf* and *Wiking* Divisions, was struggling desperately to hold positions to the northwest of Budapest, effectively the German base line for these operations.

At Stuhlweissenburg, the *Wiking* Division had been surrounded, only to be ordered to hold at all costs. Its commander, SS-Oberführer Karl Ullrich, decided that he was not prepared to carry out this order and sacrifice the lives of thousands of his men in a vain attempt to hold the town. He ordered an immediate evacuation, aided by SS-Brigadeführer Sylvester Stadler and his *Hohenstaufen* Division. Both men risked death for disobeying a direct order from Hitler.

During this phase of the fighting the commander of the Sixth Army, General Hermann Balck, known for his dislike of the Waffen-SS, decided to pay a visit to the *Hohenstaufen* Division. During his journey he spotted what he took to be Waffen-SS soldiers fleeing westwards. On his arrival at Stadler's headquarters, he berated the Waffen-SS as cowards and a furious quarrel erupted between the two. Stadler insisted that if the soldiers Balck had seen were Waffen-SS, they were certainly not from his division.

On his return to his own headquarters, Balck, by now grudgingly accepting that it was not men from the *Hohenstaufen* that he had seen, simply blamed the *Leibstandarte* instead, without any supporting evidence whatsoever. The situation soon spiralled. The conversation was reported back to Hitler by the army group commander, General Wöhler, saying that if the *Leibstandarte* Division would not hold its ground, what could Hitler expect of other units. The result was entirely predictable. Hitler flew into a paroxysm of rage, which resulted in an amazing message being sent to Dietrich as commander of the 6th SS Panzer Army: 'The Führer believes that the troops have not fought as the situation demanded and orders that the SS Divisions *Leibstandarte*, *Das Reich*, *Totenkopf* and *Hohenstaufen* be stripped of their armbands.'

In fact, most of the Waffen-SS troops involved in the offensive had already removed their distinguishing armbands (or rather cuffbands) in accord with the

Above: Preparations for 'Spring Awakening'. Men and materiel are moved towards the front. It took 290 trains to move the 6th SS Panzer Army from the West to Hungary – and to certain defeat.

numerous security precautions invoked prior to the offensive. Nevertheless, the insult was acutely felt by these soldiers, who valued their status as the Führer's élite and wore their insignia with great pride.

Dietrich was all the more disappointed because he heard through the grapevine that, during Hitler's diatribe against the cowardice of the Waffen-SS, Reichsführer-SS Heinrich Himmler had said not a single word in defence of his own troops. Although furious and saddened at the insult, Dietrich could not bring himself to blame Hitler, to whom he still owed great personal loyalty. Dietrich felt that the whole situation had arisen because Hitler had been misinformed of the true circumstances, and contented himself with sending an emissary to Hitler to explain the true facts.

The hard-bitten soldiers of the Waffen-SS were less willing to be forgiving. It is reported that Peiper suggested to his men that they all gather their combat decorations together in an old chamber pot, tie their *Götz von Berlichingen* insignia round it, and send it to Hitler! This return insult would have been specially symbolic. The original *Götz von Berlichingen*, a medieval German knight, had been famed for telling the Bishop of Bamberg to 'Lick my arse!' Whether or not this anecdote is true, it does accurately reflect the feelings of many Waffen-SS soldiers by this stage of the war.

With Operation 'Spring Awakening' in total disarray, only a full-scale retreat would now save the few remaining divisions in the southern sector of the Eastern Front. By 25 March, the Soviets had ripped apart the German front, opening up a gap some 96km (60 miles) wide in the German defences.

With the last significant German offensive of the war over, the Red Army continued its inexorable march westwards in a two-pronged attack aimed at Pápa and Gyor. The retreating Germans were forced to abandon hundreds of vehicles, which had become bogged down in mud or had simply run out of fuel. However, the Soviet eagerness to overrun the retreating Germans often led to a lack of caution. Even though the Germans were in full retreat, their flight was far from being a panic, and determined rearguard actions were fought to cover the withdrawal, costing the Soviets many hundreds of tanks.

Only a full-scale retreat would now save the few remaining divisions in the southern sector

THE END OF THE WAFFEN-SS DIVISIONS

By 2 April, the Red Army had swept past the Neusiedler Lake on the Austro-Hungarian border and, by 4 April, the last German troops had been pushed out of Hungary and into Austria. The *Hohenstaufen* and *Leibstandarte* Divisions had been so badly battered in Hungary that they no longer existed as cohesive units, but fought on in small battle groups in numerous rearguard actions during the withdrawal towards Vienna. The *Hitlerjugend*, too, had been severely weakened, and withdrew into the mountainous region to the southwest of the Austrian capital, in and around the Wienerwald, but was forced out of these positions within a few days. Of the *Totenkopf* Division, only shattered remnants remained also. The *Das Reich* Division was described in a German report as being only of 'average' strength, but it did put up a stubborn resistance to the south of the Austrian capital before withdrawing into the city, where it became involved in

further bitter fighting around the Florisdorfer Bridge. By this time this once mighty panzer division had only two or three tanks left intact. Elements of the 16th SS Panzergrenadier Division *Reichsführer-SS* had also been involved in the closing stages of the offensive around the Platensee. It, too, became fragmented, some elements surrendering around the River Drau, while others withdrew into Austria and were able to surrender to the Western Allies.

By this point of the war it had become clear that the fighting could last at most a few more weeks, and the prime consideration of most German soldiers was to surrender to the Anglo-American forces. Few relished the idea of surrendering themselves to the mercy of the Soviets, Waffen-SS men in particular, especially in view of the atrocities they had committed in the East over the previous four years. The remnants of the *Hitlerjugend* accordingly trekked some 100km (62 miles) westwards to surrender to the Americans at Linz on 8 May. The few pitiful, but still proud, remnants of the *Hohenstaufen* Division surrendered, along with the *Leibstandarte*'s survivors, at Steyr in Austria. Although the last members of the *Totenkopf* were also able to surrender to the Americans, their relief at doing so was short-lived, as they were promptly handed over to the Soviets. Very few of these *Totenkopf* soldiers survived Soviet captivity.

Above: German troops on the attack during Operation 'Spring Awakening'. The poor ground conditions and Russian resistance slowed progress to a crawl, which was compounded by German shortages in fuel, ammunition and spares.

For the *Das Reich* Division, however, there was still one operation to perform before its war came to an end. The Czech capital, Prague, was under imminent threat of being overrun by the Red Army at the end of April 1945. SS-Obersturmbannführer Otto Weidinger, the commander of the *Der Führer* Regiment, a highly competent soldier who carried the Knights Cross with Swords and Oak Leaves, was tasked with taking a Waffen-SS battle group into the city to cover the evacuation of the German-speaking civilian population, plus considerable numbers of German wounded whose fate the High Command assumed would be grim if they were to fall into Soviet hands.

Otto Weidinger was tasked with taking a Waffen-SS battle group into the city to cover the evacuation

THE FINAL MOVES

Weidinger fought his way into the city, encountering several Czech roadblocks on the way. Czech emissaries demanded the surrender of his unit, but Weidinger made it clear that his battle group would deal harshly with any attempts to interfere with its progress. The Czechs decided not to escalate the matter, and Weidinger was allowed to continue. In the city Weidinger was dismayed to discover, in addition to the German civilians who were to be evacuated, large numbers of female signals auxiliaries, as well as a full train-load of German wounded who had been abandoned to their fate in a railway siding. Weidinger set about organising a convoy to evacuate his charges. By the time it was ready to depart it numbered over 1000 vehicles!

Ignoring the attempts of diehard SS officers in the city, who wanted his unit to aid a last-ditch attack on the Soviets, Weidinger and his convoy set off westwards. Once again they found their route blocked, but were able to negotiate a free passage in return for the surrender of their weapons, which of course they spiked before handing over. Weidinger's mercy mission ended at Rokiczany, where he surrendered to the Americans. It is ironic that the last official action by a Waffen-SS unit in this sector of the Eastern Front was in fact a mercy mission, which resulted in the saving of the lives of thousands of civilians, noncombatants and wounded personnel, as opposed to the wholesale slaughter that accompanied some Waffen-SS operations.

If the objectives for the Ardennes offensive had been over-optimistic to say the least, those for Operation 'Spring Awakening' were ludicrous. Although much effort had been put into reforming and re-equipping the Waffen-SS panzer divisions after their withdrawal from the Ardennes, they were still little more than a shadow of their former selves, with drafts of poor-quality replacements being brought in from the Luftwaffe and Kriegsmarine to make up numbers.

The divisions of the 6th SS Panzer Army had been faced by a Red Army of immense power, with large quantities of men and materiel. If the cold weather had held, and had the ground conditions remained suitable for the use of the German heavy armour, Dietrich's army might have succeeded. As it was, insistence that the original timetables and objectives be rigidly adhered to condemned the offensive to inevitable failure. Once the last few battle-worthy panzer divisions in Hitler's armoury had been expended, there was nothing left to stop the Soviets pouring over the Austrian border and into the Reich.

Left: German troops in retreat following the failure of 'Spring Awakening'. Reports had reached Hitler of Waffen-SS soldiers deserting in the face of the enemy, which prompted him to order SS soldiers throughout the 6th SS Panzer Army to remove their cuffbands. Himmler also established flying courts-martials, with powers to execute deserters and other wrongdoers on the spot. In the men's eyes this was scant reward for six years' bloody service.

For the Third Reich, and the Waffen-SS, the war was over. For Himmler's legions, they could look back on nearly six years of blood-soaked action, in which they had performed superbly on the battlefield. However, they had also slaughtered countless thousands, hundreds of thousands, both on and off the battlefield. They enjoyed fighting, they enjoyed killing. They were the twentieth century's most able soldiers, and also its most ruthless.

ORDER OF BATTLE OF THE WAFFEN-SS

1st SS Panzer Division *Leibstandarte SS Adolf Hitler*

2nd SS Panzer Division *Das Reich*

3rd SS Panzer Division *Totenkopf*

4th SS Panzergrenadier Division *SS-Polizei*

5th SS Panzer Division *Wiking*

6th SS Gebirgs Division *Nord*

7th SS Freiwilligen-Gebirgs Division *Prinz Eugen*

8th SS Kavallerie Division *Florian Geyer*

9th SS Panzer Division *Hohenstaufen*

10th SS Panzer Division *Frundsberg*

11th SS Freiwilligen-Panzergrenadier Division *Nordland*

12th SS Panzer Division *Hitlerjugend*

13th Waffen-Gebirgs Division der SS (kroatische Nr 1) *Handschar*

14th Waffen-Grenadier Division der SS (ukrainische Nr 1)

15th Waffen-Grenadier Division der SS (lettische Nr 1)

16th SS Panzergrenadier Division *Reichsführer-SS*

17th SS Panzergrenadier Division *Götz von Berlichingen*

18th SS Freiwilligen-Panzergrenadier Division *Horst Wessel*

19th Waffen-Grenadier Division der SS (lettisches Nr 2)

20th Waffen-Grenadier Division der SS (estnische Nr 1)

21st Waffen-Gebirgs Division der SS (albanische Nr 1) *Skanderbeg*

22nd Freiwilligen-Kavallerie Division der SS *Maria Theresia*

23rd Waffen-Gebirgs Division der SS *Kama*

24th SS Gebirgs Division *Karstjäger*

25th Waffen-Grenadier Division der SS (ungarische Nr 1) *Hunyadi*

26th Waffen-Grenadier Division der SS (ungarische Nr 2) *Hungaria*

27th SS Freiwilligen-Panzergrenadier Division (flämische Nr 1) *Langemarck*

28th SS Freiwilligen-Panzergrenadier Division *Wallonien*

29th Waffen-Grenadier Division der SS (russische Nr 1)

29th Waffen-Grenadier Division der SS (italienische Nr 1)

30th Waffen-Grenadier Division der SS (weissruthenische Nr 1)

31st SS Freiwilligen Grenadier Division

32nd SS Freiwilligen Grenadier Division *30 Januar*

33rd Waffen-Kavallerie Division der SS (ungarische Nr 3)

33rd Waffen-Grenadier Division der SS (französische Nr 1) *Charlemagne*

34th Waffen-Grenadier Division der SS *Landstorm Nederland*

35th SS Polizei Grenadier Division

36th Waffen-Grenadier Division der SS

37th SS Freiwilligen-Kavallerie Division *Lützow*

38th SS Grenadier Division *Nibelungen*

Angolia, John R, *Cloth Insignia of the SS*, published by Bender Publishing, San Jose, Calif. (1983)

Bender, Roger J & Taylor, Hugh P, *Uniforms, Organisation and History of the Waffen-SS*, volumes 1-5, published by Bender Publishing, San Jose, Calif. (1969-83)

Browning, Christopher R, *Ordinary Men*, published by HarperCollins Publishing, New York (1992)

Buss, Phillip H & Mollo A, *Hitler's Germanic Legions*, published by McDonald & James, London (1978)

Cross, Robin, *Citadel, The Battle of Kursk*, published by Michael O'Mara Books (1993)

Davis, Brian L, *Waffen-SS*, published by Blandford, Poole (1985)

Höhne, Heinz, *The Order of the Death's Head*, published by Verlag Der Spiegel, Hamburg (1966)

Littlejohn, David, *Foreign Legions of the Third Reich*, vols 1-4, published by Bender Publishing, San Jose, Calif. (1979-87)

Lucas, James, *Das Reich*, published by Arms & Armour Press, London (1991)

Lucas, James, *Hitler's Mountain Troops*, published by Arms & Armour Press, London (1992)

Lumsden, Robin, *The Black Corps*, published by Ian Allan, Shepperton (1992)

Mollo, Andrew, *Uniforms of the SS*, vols 1-7, published by the Historical Research Unit (1969-76)

Padfield, Peter, *Himmler: Reichsführer-SS*, published by Macmillan, London (1990)

Quarrie, Bruce, *Weapons of the Waffen-SS*, published by PSL, Cambridge (1988)

Quarrie, Bruce, *Lightning Death*, published by PSL, Cambridge (1991)

Read, Anthony & Fisher, David, *The Fall of Berlin*, published by Pimlico, London (1993)

Reitlinger, Gerald, *The SS: Alibi of a Nation*, published by Heinemann, London (1956)

Stein, George H, *The Waffen-SS: Hitler's Elite Guard at War 1939-45*, published by Cornell, New York (1966)

Taylor, Simon, *Germany 1918-1933*, published by Duckworth, London (1983)

Additionally, the following histories of the Waffen-SS combat units, published by Munin-Verlag of Osnabrück, contain information on the units and the personnel who served with them:

Lehman, Rudolf, *Leibstandarte*

Meyer, Hubert, *Die Kriegsgeschichte der 12 SS Panzer Division*

Proschek, Rolf, *Verweht sind die Spuren*

Schulze-Kossens, Richard & Ertel, Karl-Heinz, *Europaische Freiwilligen*

Stöber, Hans, *Die Sturmflut und das Ende*

Truppenkameradschaft der 4 SS-Polizei Division, *Die guten Glaubens waren*

Ullrich, Karl, *Wie ein Fels im Meer*

Weidinger, Otto, *Division Das Reich*

INDEX